WORLD PASS

Expanding English Fluency

Susan Stempleski
Nancy Douglas
James R. Morgan
Kristin L. Johannsen

HEINLE
CENGAGE Learning·

Australia · Brazil · Japan · Korea · Mexico · Singapore · Spain · United Kingdom · United States

HEINLE
CENGAGE Learning

Advanced World Pass: Expanding English Fluency
Susan Stempleski, Nancy Douglas, James R. Morgan, and Kristin L. Johannsen

Publisher: Christopher Wenger

Acquisitions Editor: Mary Sutton-Paul

Director of Product Marketing: Amy Mabley

Director of Product Development: Anita Raducanu

Senior Development Editor: Jean Pender

Development Editor: Rebecca Klevberg

Associate Editor: Christine Galvin-Combet

Editorial Assistant: Bridget McLaughlin

Production Editor: Tan Jin Hock

Sr. Print Buyer: Mary Beth Hennebury

International Marketing Manager: Ian Martin

Contributing Development Editor: Barbara Wood

Compositor: Christopher Hanzie, Ronn Lee, TYA Inc.

Photo Researcher: Christopher Hanzie, Ronn Lee

Illustrator: Raketshop Design Studio (Philippines)

Cover/Text Designer: Christopher Hanzie, TYA Inc.

Cover Image: TYA Inc. PhotoDisc, Inc.

For product information and technology assistance, contact us at
Cengage Learning Customer & Sales Support, 1-800-354-9706
For permission to use material from this text or product,
submit all requests online at **www.cengage.com/permissions**
Further permissions questions can be emailed to
permissionrequest@cengage.com

Library of Congress Control Number: 2005926696

ISBN-13: 978-0-8384-0670-0

ISBN-10: 0-8384-0670-X

Heinle
20 Channel Center Street
Boston, MA 02210
USA

Cengage Learning is a leading provider of customized learning solutions with office locations around the globe, including Singapore, the United Kingdom, Australia, Mexico, Brazil, and Japan. Locate your local office at **www.cengage.com/global**

Cengage Learning products are represented in Canada by Nelson Education, Ltd.

Visit Heinle online at **elt.heinle.com**

Visit our corporate website at **www.cengage.com**

Text Credits

Page 21: "'I left home to find home,' interview with Chimamanda Ngozi Adichie," by Carl Wilkinson. Copyright © Guardian Newspapers Limited 2005. Reprinted with permission.; page 71: "On the Tap-Tap," by Kent Annan. Copyright © 2005, Orion Magazine, January/February 2005. Reprinted with permission.; page 85: "Born to be Wild," by Emilie Le Beau. Copyrighted 6/15/2004, Chicago Tribune Company. All rights reserved. Used with permission.; page 97: "Jan. 24 called worst day of the year," by Jennifer Carlile. Copyright © 2005 MSNBC Interactive. Reprinted with permission of MSNBC.com.; page 123: "In *All my Life for Sale*, a man learns it's not the stuff, it's the stories," by Winda Benedetti. Reprinted with permission of Seattle Post-Intelligencer © 2002.; page 135: "Tales of Toronto," by Anna Bowness. Reprinted with permission of Broken Pencil Magazine © 2004.; page 147: Adapted from "The Gathering World Storm and the Urgency of Our Awakening," by Duane Elgin. Used with permission of the author.

Photo Credits

Unless otherwise stated, all photos are from PhotoDisc, Inc. Digital Imagery © copyright 2006 PhotoDisc, Inc. and TYA Inc. Photos from other sources:
page 4: Vincent Kessler/Reuters/Landov; page 5: Morton Beebe/CORBIS; page 6: Laura Cavanaugh/UPI/Landov; page 10: Niviere/EPA/Landov; page 16: (bottom) Royalty-Free/CORBIS; page 20: Nnamdi Chiamogu; page 34: (top) Jacques Langevin/CORBIS SYGMA, (bottom) Jerry Cooke/CORBIS; page 39: (top left) Paul Chinn/San Francisco Chronicle/CORBIS, (top right) Royalty-Free/CORBIS, (bottom) Royalty-Free/CORBIS; page 45: (top left) The Image Bank/Yellow Dog Productions/Getty Images, (top center) Royalty-Free/Andrew Ward/Life File/Photodisc, (top right) Henry Romero/Reuters/Landov, (bottom left) Royalty-Free/Phil Boorman/Photodisc, (bottom center) Reuters/Landov, (bottom right) Ronen Zvulun/Reuters/Landov; page 52: (left) Peter Steiner/CORBIS, (center) Dave G. Houser/CORBIS, (right) Macduff Everton/CORBIS; page 64: (top) Richard Naude/Alamy; page 69: (center) Royalty-Free/Jack Hollingsworth/Photodisc, (right) Dave Turnley/CORBIS; page 72: (top) Reuters/CORBIS, (bottom) Louise Gubb/CORBIS SABA; page 77: (bottom) HIRB; page 80: Heinle ELT; page 83: Heinle ELT; page 94: Royalty-Free/photos.com; page 97: Royalty-Free/AbleStock/Index Stock; page 119: Royalty-Free/John Luke/Index Stock; page 128: (top) Geray Sweeney/CORBIS, (bottom) Charles & Josette Lenars/CORBIS; page 129: (left) Fernando Rivero, (center) Tobias Bernhard/zefa/CORBIS, (right) Ken Straiton/CORBIS; page 130: Royalty-Free/Photos.com Select/Index Stock; page 131: CORBIS; page 135: (top) Jose Fuste Raga/CORBIS, (bottom) Dave G. Houser/CORBIS; page 142: Mark M. Lawrence/CORBIS; page 144: Randy Faris/CORBIS; page 153: (top row) Royalty-Free/Photos.com, (bottom) Royalty-Free/Index Stock

Every effort has been made to trace all sources of illustrations/photos/information in this book, but if any have been inadvertently overlooked, the publisher will be pleased to make the necessary arrangements at the first opportunity.

Printed in China by China Translation & Printing Services Limited
9 10 11 12 13 14 13 12 11 10

Acknowledgments

We would firstly like to thank the educators who provided invaluable feedback throughout the development of the *World Pass* series:

Byung-kyoo Ahn, Chonnam National University; Elisabeth Blom, Casa Thomas Jefferson; Grazyna Anna Bonomi; Vera Burlamaqui Bradford, Instituto Brasil-Estados Unidos; Araceli Cabanillas Carrasco, Universidad Autónoma de Sinaloa; Silvania Capua Carvalho, State University of Feira de Santana; Tânia Branco Cavaignac, Casa Branca Idiomas; Kyung-whan Cha, Chung-Ang University; Chwun-li Chen, Shih Chien University; María Teresa Fátima Encinas, Universidad Iberoamericana-Puebla and Universidad Autónoma de Puebla; Sandra Gaviria, Universidad EAFIT; Marina González, Instituto de Lenguas Modernas; Frank Graziani, Tokai University; Chi-ying Fione Huang, Ming Chuan University; Shu-fen Huang (Jessie), Chung Hua University; Tsai, Shwu Hui (Ellen), Chung Kuo Institute of Technology and Commerce; Connie R. Johnson, Universidad de las Américas-Puebla; Diana Jones, Instituto Angloamericano; Annette Kaye, Kyoritsu Women's University; Lee, Kil-ryoung, Yeungnam University; David Kluge, Kinjo Gakuin University; Nancy H. Lake; Hyunoo Lee, Inha University; Amy Peijung Lee, Hsuan Chuang College; Hsiu-Yun Liao, Chinese Culture University; Yuh-Huey Gladys Lin, Chung Hua University; Eleanor Occeña, Universitaria de Idiomas, Universidad Autónoma del Estado de Hidalgo; Laura Pérez Palacio, Tecnológico de Monterrey; Doraci Perez Mak, União Cultural Brasil-Estados Unidos; Mae-Ran Park, Pukyong National University; Joo-Kyung Park, Honam University; Bill Pellowe, Kinki University; Margareth Perucci, Sociedade Brasileira de Cultura Inglesa; Nevitt Reagan, Kansai Gaidai University; Lesley D. Riley, Kanazawa Institute of Technology; Ramiro Luna Rivera, Tecnológico de Monterrey, Prepa; Marie Adele Ryan, Associação Alumni; Michael Shawback, Ritsumeikan University; Kathryn Singh, ITESM; Grant Trew, Nova Group; Michael Wu, Chung Hua University, Carmen Pulido Alcaraz, Instituto Cultural Mexico-Norteamericano, Guadalajara; Maria Isabel de Souza Lima Baracat, Centro de Comunicação Inglesa, Garça; João Alfredo Bergmann, Instituto Cultural Brasileiro Norte-Americano, Porto Alegre; Elisabeth Blom, Casa Thomas Jefferson, Brasília; Flávia Carneiro - Associação Brasil América; Salvador Enriquez Casteñeda, Instituto Cultural Mexico-Norteamericano, Guadalajara; Ronaldo Couto, SBS, São Paulo; Maria Amélia Carvalho Fonseca, Centro Cultural Brasil-Estados Unidos, Belém; Henry W. Grant, Centro Cultural Brasil-Estados Unidos, Campinas; Leticia Adelina Ruiz Guerrero, ITESO, Guadalajara; Brian Lawrence Kilkenny, PrepaTec, Guadalajara; Lunalva de Fátima Lacerda, Cooplem, Brasília; Raquel Lambert, CCBEU - Centro Cultural Brasil Estados Unidos de Franca; Alberto Hernandez Medina, M. Ed., Tecnológico de Monterrey, Guadalajara; Michelle Merritt-Ascencio, University of Guadalajara; Evania A. Netto, ICBEU - São José dos Campos; Janette Carvalhinho de Oliveira, Universidade Federal do Espírito Santo, Vitória; Ane Cibele Palma, CCBEU/Interamericano, Curitiba; Danielle Rêgo, ICBEU - MA; Marie Adele Ryan, Associação Alumni, São Paulo; Hector Sanchez, PROULEX, Guadalajara; Dixie Santana, Universidad Panamericana, Guadalajara; Rodrigo Santana, CCBEU/Goiânia; Debora Schisler, SEVEN English & Español, São Paulo; Sávio Siqueira, ACBEU Salvador; Eric Tejeda, PROULEX, Guadalajara; Carlos Eduardo Tristão, DISAL; Joaquin Romero Vázquez, Tec de Monterrey, Guadalajara; Liliana Villalobos ME, Universidad Marista de Guadalajara, Universidad de Guadalajara

---

A great many people participated in the making of the *World Pass* series. In particular I would like to thank the authors, Nancy Douglas and James Morgan, for all their hard work, creativity, and good humor. I also extend special thanks to development editor Ellen Kisslinger. Thanks are also due publisher Chris Wenger, acquisitions editor Mary Sutton-Paul, and all the other wonderful people at Heinle ELT who have worked so hard on this project. I am also very grateful to the many reviewers around the world, whose insightful comments on early drafts of the *World Pass* materials were much appreciated.

Susan Stempleski

We'd like to extend a very special thank you to Chris Wenger at Heinle ELT for spearheading the project and providing leadership, support, and guidance throughout the development of the series. Jean Pender and Ellen Kisslinger edited our materials with speed, precision, and a sense of humor. Susan Stempleski's extensive experience was reflected in her invaluable feedback that helped to shape the material in this book.

Thanks also go to those on the editorial, production, and support teams who helped to make this book happen: Anita Raducanu, Sally Giangrande, Jin-Hock Tan, Bridget McLaughlin, Christine Galvin-Combet, Rebecca Klevberg, Mary Sutton-Paul, and their colleagues in Asia and Latin America.

I would also like to thank my parents Alexander and Patricia, for their love and encouragement and to my husband Jorge and daughter Jasmine—thank you for your patience and faith in me. I couldn't have done this without you!
Nancy Douglas

I would also like to thank my mother, France P. Morgan, for her unflagging support and my father, Lee Morgan Jr., for instilling the love of language and learning in me.
James R. Morgan

I would like to thank my husband, Kevin Millham, for his support and saintly patience.
Kristin L. Johannsen

To the Student

Welcome to *World Pass*! The main goal of this two-level, upper-intermediate/advanced level series is to help you increase your fluency in English. By fluency, I mean the ability to say what you want in more than one way, and to communicate your ideas clearly, confidently, and easily. To help students increase their fluency, *World Pass* focuses on dynamic vocabulary building, essential grammar, and stimulating listening, speaking, and writing activities that emphasize the language people need for real world communication. Features of *World Pass* that emphasize the development of oral and written fluency include the following:

- **Vocabulary Focus sections.** A *Vocabulary Focus* section opens each of the 12 main units and presents topic-related vocabulary along with opportunities to practice using the new words and expressions in a variety of ways. The section includes a "Vocabulary Builder" activity that helps you expand your vocabulary through the use of a particular vocabulary-building tool (e.g., words families, root words, or compound nouns). Many of the *Vocabulary Focus* sections conclude with an "Ask & Answer" task that can be used as a basis for discussion by pairs, groups, or whole classes of students, and provides opportunities to actively use new vocabulary to express personal ideas, opinions, and experiences.

- **Listening sections.** To become a fluent speaker, you need to be a fluent listener. These sections provide opportunities for you to improve your listening comprehension through active practice with a variety of materials, such as interviews, news reports, and discussions. For added conversational fluency practice, each *Listening* section ends with an "Ask & Answer" discussion task.

- **Language Focus sections.** These sections focus on essential grammar points and provide opportunity for fluency practice through a wide variety of activity types, from more controlled exercises to more personalized, free-response type activities and open-ended communication tasks such as role plays or interviews.

- **Speaking sections.** Each of these sections presents a specific speaking skill or strategy and outlines a communicative activity that helps you to develop your fluency by providing opportunities for you to use new language and vocabulary items in a natural way.

- **Writing sections.** Each of these sections in *World Pass* provide instruction and practice with different kinds of writing such as, business and personal letters, summarizing information, and persuasive writing.

- **Communication sections.** The *Communication* sections that conclude each main unit consolidate and review the language material presented in the unit. Communication tasks vary widely and contribute to the development of fluency by focusing on meaningful speaking practice in activities such as games, presentations, interviews, and discussions.

- **Expansion Pages.** Each unit of *World Pass* is followed by *Expansion Pages*. The *Expansion Pages* are designed for students who want to learn additional vocabulary on their own and to have additional practice with the words and expressions presented in the units. Because the *Expansion Pages* are meant for self-study, they consist of exercises that you can do independently and then check your own answers.

SOME LANGUAGE LEARNING TIPS

Becoming a fluent speaker of English can be challenging, but it can also be a highly rewarding experience. Here are a few tips to help you make the most of the experience.

To increase your vocabulary:
- **Keep a vocabulary log.** Keep a list of new vocabulary items in the back pages of a notebook. From time to time, count up the number of words you have learned. You will be surprised at how quickly the number increases.
- **Use new words in sentences.** To fix news words in your mind, put them into sentences of your own. Do the maximum, not the minimum, with new vocabulary.
- **Make flashcards.** Create vocabulary flashcards that allow you to categorize, label, personalize, and apply new words. Put the words and their definitions on individual cards. Include a sample sentence that shows how the word is used in context.

To improve your speaking skills:
- **Read aloud.** Reading examples and texts out loud is a way of gaining confidence in speaking and letting the patterns of English "sound in your head." Even speaking out loud to yourself can be good practice.
- **Record yourself speaking.** Try recording yourself whenever you can. When you listen to the recording afterwards, don't worry if you sound hesitant or have made mistakes. If you do this several times, you will find that each version is better than the last.

To improve your reading skills:
- **Read passages more than once.** Reading the same reading passage several times will help you increase your reading speed and improve your fluency.
- **Summarize what you read.** When you summarize, you tell the main facts or ideas without giving all the details. Summarizing is a good way to be sure you really understand what you have read.

To improve your writing skills:
- **Increase the amount of writing you do.** For example, you might keep a personal diary in English, write small memos to yourself, or write a summary of a reading passage. The more you write, the more fluent and error-free your writing will become.
- **Analyze different types of writing.** Look at examples of different types of writing you may want to do: essays, formal letters, e-mail messages. Notice the form of the writing and think about what you could imitate to increase your fluency in writing.

To improve your listening comprehension:
- **Listen to recorded material several times.** You aren't expected to understand everything the first time your hear it. If you listen several times, you will probably understand something new each time.
- **Predict what you will hear.** Try to guess what you will hear before you listen. This will help you to focus while you listen and understand more of what you hear.

As you complete each unit of *World Pass*, ask yourself the questions on the **Learning Tips Checklist** below to keep track of the tips you are using and to remind yourself to try using others. To become a truly fluent speaker of English, you will need to practice the different language skills in a variety of ways. Find out what ways work best for you and use them to your advantage.

Sincerely,
Susan Stempleski

Learning Tips Checklist
Which language learning tips did you use as you worked through the unit? Note the ones you used and think about which were most helpful. As you work through the next unit, continue using the helpful ones and try using ones you haven't yet implemented.

Did you . . .

- ❏ record new words in a vocabulary log?
- ❏ try using new words in sentences?
- ❏ make and use vocabulary flashcards?
- ❏ read aloud as often as you could?
- ❏ record and listen to yourself speaking?
- ❏ read reading passages more than once?
- ❏ summarize what you read?
- ❏ write a lot and frequently?
- ❏ analyze and imitate different types of writing?
- ❏ listen to recorded material several times?
- ❏ predict what you would hear before you listened?

Lesson A	Vocabulary Focus	Listening	Language Focus	Speaking
Unit 1 Big Screen, Small Screen				
Lesson A 2 **Feature films**	An online movie club *blockbusters, B-movies, mainstream* . . .	A low-budget indie film: Listening for gist and using abbreviations and symbols for taking notes	*Such* and *so*	And the winner is: Managing a discussion
Unit 2 The World Awaits You				
Lesson A 14 **On the road**	Dazzling destinations *bustling, atmosphere, landscape* . . .	A photographer's dream: Listening to interviews and inferring point of view; matching speakers with topics	Past modals	Would you mind: Using polite language
Unit 3 School and Beyond				
Lesson A 26 **School life**	My first year at college *apprehensive, sign up, expectations* . . .	School lunches: Listening for details and attitudes	*Hope* and *wish*	That's an interesting question: Practicing interviewing phrases and skills
Review: Units 1–3 38				
Unit 4 Contemporary Issues				
Lesson A 40 **In the city**	I can get it for free *compensated, unauthorized, unethical* . . .	Our cities are growing: Listening for the main point and key words	Past and present unreal conditionals	Without a doubt: Expressing an opinion
Unit 5 In Other Words				
Lesson A 52 **Total immersion**	What languages are you studying? *proficient, immersed, master* . . .	A TV show about language: Listening for topic and specific information	Reduced adverb clauses	As you can see: Talking about charts and data
Unit 6 Ordinary People, Extraordinary Lives				
Lesson A 64 **Follow your dream!**	A well-kept secret *aspirations, sidetracked, channeling* . . .	Running ultramarathons: Listening to a personal interview for gist, details, and key words	Reported speech	Today, I'd like to tell you about: Making a presentation to a group using presentation phrases
Review: Units 4–6 76				

Lesson A	Vocabulary Focus	Listening	Language Focus	Speaking
Unit 7 Who Are You?				
Lesson A 78 **Memory and the mind**	It completely slipped my mind. *inundated, associations, lapses . . .*	Musical mind: Listening to a news report for gist and details	Overview of the passive form	Let me explain what I mean: Expanding on a topic
Unit 8 Happy Days				
Lesson A 90 **What makes you happy?**	A love-hate relationship *simultaneously, win over, think on your feet . . .*	Who is happy: Listening to a radio interview for main points and supporting ideas	Phrasal verbs	What do you mean by: Keeping a conversation going
Unit 9 Looking Good!				
Lesson A 102 **Fashion sense**	What does your look say about you? *go together, distinctive, coordinate . . .*	Concerned about appearances: Listening for general information, matching job tasks to job descriptions and taking notes	Subject and object relative clauses	Now I'll explain: Planning, organizing, and giving a survey presentation
Review: Units 7–9 114				
Unit 10 To Buy or Not to Buy . . .				
Lesson A 116 **What's your shopping culture?**	Status symbols *flashy, class, extravagant . . .*	Shopping habits: Listening and matching questions with answers and listening for details	A review of definite and indefinite articles	On the other hand: Describing pictures and comparing and contrasting similarities and differences
Unit 11 The Impact of Art				
Lesson A 128 **What does it say to you?**	A Master of Mandalas *oval-shaped, collaborative, dismantle . . .*	Conversations in an art gallery: Listening to conversations for speaker opinions and key words	Using fronted structures for emphasis	I find that hard to believe: Arguments and counterarguments
Unit 12 Our Changing World				
Lesson A 140 **Looking to the future**	What does the future hold? *coexist, facilitate, breakthroughs . . .*	A new spin on familiar products: Listening to descriptions of inventions for specific details and general information	Talking about the future	This has the advantage of: Describing benefits and supporting points and giving support to main points

1 VOCABULARY FOCUS

An online movie club

WARM UP What kinds of movies do you enjoy and what do you find appealing about them?

A **Pair work. Look at the box of informal words used to describe movies. Which ones do you know? With a partner, try to guess what kinds of movies the unfamiliar words refer to.**

chick flick	tearjerker	blockbuster
B-movie	mainstream	indie

B **Some people have joined an online movie club. Read their postings.**

WHAT KINDS OF MOVIES DO YOU LIKE?

Alejandro, Madrid

I'm a sucker for any kind of action movie. I love the big blockbusters with lots of explosions and other things going on. Unfortunately, my girlfriend prefers a good tearjerker—she says it's healthy to cry sometimes. We usually strike a compromise: one week she picks a movie, the next week I get to choose.

Real English
be a sucker for (something) = (informal) have trouble resisting something

I have small children, so I usually see those wholesome films that are "suitable for the entire family." I love my family, but my real interest lies with B-movies. My favorite is Fantastic Creature from Beyond. Most people haven't heard of it, but it's terrific! (I'd tell you about it, but I don't want to give away the ending!)

Carolyn, Vancouver

Real English
chick flick = (slang) movie targeted at a female audience

indie = independent film

Nan, Singapore

Basically, I don't like big-budget mainstream movies. They're so predictable! I prefer the smaller, indie films. Foreign films are great, too, especially when they're shot on some exotic location. There's only one drawback: I don't like to read those subtitles on the screen! Too distracting!

David, Sydney

I enjoy horror or suspense films. On the one hand, I can't stand the tension—it's too nerve-wracking. On the other hand, they're very exciting. Don't tell anyone, but I'd have to say romantic comedies are at the top of my list. I know that they're chick flicks, but they're a kind of guilty pleasure for me.

C Match the expressions on the left with their definitions on the right.

1. blockbuster _d_
2. tearjerker _i_
3. strike a compromise _b_
4. wholesome _j_
5. B-movies _l_
6. give away _f_
7. mainstream _h_
8. shot on location _e_
9. drawback _a_
10. distracting _g_
11. nerve-wracking _c_
12. guilty pleasure _k_

a. disadvantage
b. reach an agreement
c. making you feel tense
d. a very successful book or movie
e. not filmed in a studio
f. reveal
g. making it difficult to focus on something
h. popular, appealing to most people
i. a sentimental movie or story that can make people cry
j. considered to have no bad influence
k. something you feel embarrassed about enjoying
l. low-budget films with poor scripts and little-known actors

▶▶▶ Vocabulary Builder ▲

Match the words to form compound nouns that are used when talking about movies. In what kind of movie would you expect to find each of these things?

a. stunts
b. chases
c. illness
d. effects
e. romance
f. forces

1. car _b_
2. failed _e_
3. daring _a_
4. superhuman _f_
5. life-threatening _c_
6. special _d_

2 LISTENING

A low-budget indie film

What's the name of an indie film you've seen? Did you like it? Why or why not?

A Pair work. When you listen and take notes, it's helpful to use abbreviations and symbols. With a partner, look at the ones in the box. What do you think they mean?

L.A.   P.A.   info   <   >   1ST   w/o   hmtwn   cmdy

B Listen. You will hear an interview with Jesse, a film director. Listen and complete the notes below. Try to use the symbols and abbreviations in A to make your note-taking faster. (CD Tracks 01 & 02)

Jesse	His movie
Age: _23_	Title: _False information_
Where from: _L.A._	Shot where: _L.A._
1st job in filmmaking: _Production Assistance_	Cost: _<500,000 300,000_
	The movie has made: _12,000,000_
	Kind of film: _comedy, indie, funny_

C Listen again. How did Jesse make his film? Circle your answers. There may be more than one answer for some items. (CD Track 03)

1. Money was raised for the film when people read about it / met Jesse / saw Jesse's short film.
2. Jesse's cast and crew stayed in people's homes / hotels / his hometown hotel.
3. Jesse didn't pay the actors / the cameraman / to shoot on location.
4. Jesse used celebrities / friends / his father in the movie.
5. Jesse based his movie on a book / his life / a dream he had.

D Pair work. Use your notes to retell what you know about Jesse and his movie.

▶ **Ask & Answer**

Imagine that you are making a low-budget movie. What would the movie be about? Where would you shoot it? You can't pay the actors. Who would you use in your movie?

3 LANGUAGE FOCUS

Such and *so*

A Read this exerpt from a movie review. Underline six more examples using *such* or *so*. How does this reviewer feel about the movie?

👎👎👎👍 **movie** review

There was <u>so much hype</u> around this movie before it opened. Unfortunately, it didn't live up to expectations. First of all, the special effects were <u>so distracting</u> that it was hard to focus on the story. And the story was not believable at all. The dialog seemed <u>so forced</u> that this drama sounded more like a comedy. If that wasn't bad enough, then there was the plot: it unfolds in <u>such a confusing series of flashbacks</u> that you can't keep the story straight. I still don't understand it! The worst part, though, is the ending. The movie ends <u>so predictably</u> that you'll wish you had left the theater earlier.

This movie is not a complete disaster, however. The opening scenes are fascinating. The opening is shot in <u>such an interesting</u> way that you'll forget you're watching a movie. And Ella Baker, playing the role of the mother, is phenomenal. She embodies her character with <u>such confidence</u>. Unfortunately, she has <u>so little screen</u> time that we hardly see her.

One recent moviegoer, when asked about this movie, said it for all of us: "I was <u>so disappointed!</u>"

B Look at the phrases you underlined in **A**. Then write the sentences in which they are used in the chart below.

> **Real English**
> Use *so* and *such* for emphasis.

***so* + adjective (+ *that* clause)**
1. The special effects were so distracting that it was hard to focus on the story.
2. *The dialog seemed so forced that this drama sounded more like a comedy*
3. *I was so disappointed*

***so* + adverb (+ *that* clause)**
4. *The movie ends so predictably that you'll wish you had left the theater earlier*

***so* + determiner* + noun (+ *that* clause)**
5. There was so much hype around this movie before it opened.
6. *She has so little screen time that we hardly see her.*

***such* + (*a/an* + adjective) + noun (+ *that* clause)**
7. The plot unfolds in such a confusing series of flashbacks that you can't keep the story straight.
8. *The opening is shot in such an interesting way that you'll forget you're watching a movie*
9. *She embodies her character with such confidence*

* determiner = *much/little; many/few*

C Complete these sentences with *so* or *such*.

1. I was __so__ excited to hear that a movie starring Gael García Bernal was opening in my town.
2. I bought __such__ a beautiful outfit for the premiere. You should have seen it!
3. Unfortunately, there were __so__ many people at the premiere that I couldn't get in.
4. I was disappointed that I couldn't see Gael García Bernal at the premiere. He's __such__ a talented actor.
5. Acting is __such__ a difficult profession.
6. First, there's __so__ much competition for acting jobs.
7. Second, there are __so__ few jobs that pay well.
8. Most work pays __so__ poorly that actors have to take a second job to support themselves.

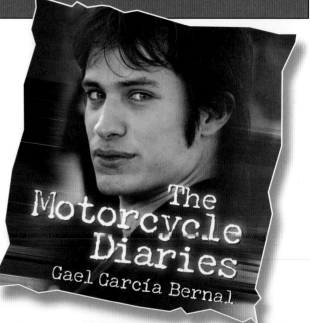

The Motorcycle Diaries
Gael García Bernal

The Castro Theater in San Francisco was built in 1922. It has a gorgeous interior and features live organ music before the movies are shown.

D Read about the Castro Theater in San Francisco. Then combine the sentences with *so* or *such*.

1. The organ music is <u>popular</u>. People clap and sing along with it. (so)

   The organ music is so popular that people clap and
   sing along with it.

2. It's hard to imagine that the theater is over 80 years old. It's <u>a well-preserved theater</u>. (such)

   _____

3. Sometimes the audience will <u>boo loudly</u> at the movie. You can't hear the movie. (so)

   _____

4. The atmosphere in the Castro is <u>fun</u>. You should see a movie there. (such)

   _____

5. The Castro Theater is <u>beautiful</u>. It was designated as a national landmark in 1977. (so)

   _____

6. <u>Few</u> old movie theaters are left. It's important to preserve old movie theaters. (so)

   _____

E Pair work. Choose one of these two situations and create a role play with your partner.

Situation 1:
You rented a movie from your local video store. The sound quality of the video was terrible. It was muffled in places and there was a lot of static. Also, you couldn't read some of the subtitles. Return the video and ask for your money back. Explain your reasons.

Situation 2:
You paid for an expensive $25 ticket to see a major blockbuster on an IMAX screen. Inside the theater, there were crowds of noisy kids sitting all around you. It was dirty—the floor was sticky—and there were too many advertisements before the movie even started. Speak to the theater manager and ask for a refund. Explain your reasons.

Grammar X-TRA *-ed* and *-ing* adjectives

I was **amazed** to hear we won the award.
   (I felt amazed.)
The **satisfied** audience left the theater
   with smiles on their faces.
   (The audience felt satisfied.)

That movie is **amazing**.
   (That movie causes amazement.)
It was a **satisfying** show.
   (The show caused a feeling of
   satisfaction.)

Pair work. Tell your partner about a movie you've seen. Include some adjectives. Talk about these topics and others of your own.

   plot   setting   actors   music   special effects

amused
amusing

disappointed
disappointing

entertained
entertaining

excited
exciting

fascinated
fascinating

interested
interesting

shocked
shocking

The plot was very confusing, but I still enjoyed the film because I was fascinated by the special effects.

4 SPEAKING

And the winner is . . .

A Pair work. In your opinion, what makes a movie enjoyable? Memorable? Disappointing? Give examples from movies you've seen. Ask questions about any movies your partner mentions that you haven't seen.

B Pair work. Look at this list of international film awards that are given out each year and answer the questions below with a partner. Check your answers on page 168.

> ### INTERNATIONAL FILM AWARDS
> The Academy Awards
> The Cannes Film Festival
> The BAFTA Film Awards
> Hong Kong Film Awards

1. What is the name of the small statue that is given to winners at the Academy Awards? _____

2. What country hosts the Cannes Film Festival? _____

3. What does BAFTA stand for? (complete) _____ Academy of Film and _____ Arts

4. In what year was the first Hong Kong Film Awards held: 2001, 1991, or 1982? _____

C Group work. **Imagine that you represent** *The International Movie Fans' Association.* **Follow the steps below.**

1. You are in charge of giving away the "Decade Awards." You must choose the five best movies of the last ten years.

2. Work together to choose the winner for each category. Use language from the box below to manage the discussion.

3. Agree on your choice for each category.

Most romantic movie: _____

Most exciting movie: _____

Most frightening movie: _____

Funniest movie: _____

Your own category: _____

Managing a discussion		
Requesting clarification:	**Taking your turn:**	**Keeping the discussion moving:**
Sorry, I'm not sure I understand.	*Can I just add something here?*	*To get back to our topic . . .*
Why do you say that?	*I have a point I'd like to make.*	*Let's hear what someone else*
Can you clarify your reason?	*Sorry to interrupt, but . . .*	*has to say.*
		We only have five minutes left.

D Class activity. Take turns explaining your group's awards to the class. Did any groups make the same decisions? Were there any surprising awards?

UNIT 1

Big Screen, Small Screen

Lesson B	TV time

1 GET READY TO READ

Reality TV

 WARM UP What are two of the most popular reality shows right now? Why do you think these shows are popular? With a partner, make a list of reasons.

A Pair work. **Read about the four reality shows below. Can you spot the reality show that's fake (not an actual reality show)? Explain your ideas to a partner. Then check your answer on page 168.**

TV Guide

Doctors' Diaries is a docu-drama that examines the events that take place in a busy hospital as well as the stories of the doctors, nurses, and medics who work there.

In each episode of **Blind Love**, a person sets up his or her pet on a blind date with another person's pet. The show follows the romantic, sometimes disastrous, outcome.

The Call tells the stories of three actors competing for roles in actual TV and film productions. Who will get that first big break?

The World's Most Daring Robberies presents the boldest bank robbers ever caught on tape and their infamous crime sprees. The program includes interviews with the FBI, bank tellers, and even the robbers themselves.

B Pair work. **What do each of these adjectives mean? Discuss your ideas with a partner. Use your dictionary to help you.**

addictive	disturbing	heartfelt
compelling	dramatic	inspiring
cutthroat	entertaining	shocking

C Pair work. **Discuss these questions with a partner.**

1. Which of the words in B would you use to describe the shows in A?
2. In your opinion, which of the reality shows in A would be most popular? Why?
3. Which one(s) would you watch? Which wouldn't you watch? Why?

I think the most entertaining show would be . . .

World Link

On average, camera crews for reality TV shows shoot 100 hours of video for every hour of the show! Without good editing, viewers would lose interest long before they found out who the winner was!

Source: *Bunim-Murray Productions*

A Read the two summaries below. Then read the article on page 9 and check (✓) the summary that best describes the article.

❑ Early critics believed that interest in reality shows wouldn't last long. Today, though, these shows are more popular than ever and can be seen all over the world. Nevertheless, people are beginning to question whether or not this kind of "reality entertainment" is suitable—especially for younger viewers.

❑ Reality shows are often advertised as a genuine look at the lives of real people. The fact is, though, that many of these shows are not as "real" as they claim to be. A variety of techniques are used—including using scripted dialog and editing scenes—to make the shows more dramatic and interesting to the public.

B Read the article again. Then complete each sentence by circling the correct answer.

1. The problem with filming real people for a reality show is that it can be very expensive / most people's lives aren't that interesting / it takes a long time to do.
2. Some reality show producers have hired professional actors / filmmakers / scriptwriters to help those being filmed say things in a more dramatic way.
3. Gideon Horowitz, who injured himself while filming *The Restaurant*, was asked to resign from the show / refilm the fall that broke his elbow / return to work 24 hours later.
4. On reality shows, footage is often edited to make people on the show look more attractive / seem to have a certain kind of personality / appear to be less nervous on screen.
5. A woman on *The Apprentice*, was loved / disliked by the public because she was always / never seen smiling and laughing on the show.

C Find these words in the reading. Then write each in the correct place in the chart below.

> *authentic* (line 33)   *staged* (line 63)   *contrived* (line 82)
> *unrehearsed* (line 36)   *scripted* (line 66)

Describes something that is real or genuine	Describes something that is fake or invented

D Pair work. Check (✓) the statements below that you think the author of the reading would probably say. What information in the reading helped you make your choices? Discuss your ideas with a partner.

1. Reality show producers will do just about anything to boost ratings. ❑
2. One good thing about these shows is that you do see people expressing genuine, heartfelt emotion. ❑
3. I used to dislike reality shows, and frankly, I still do. ❑
4. I think that reality shows ought to be banned from television. ❑

> **Inferring an author's opinion or attitude**
>
> The author may not always state his or her opinion directly. Often a reader must infer, or make guesses about it, using the information that is available in the text.

▶ **Ask & Answer**

Was any of the information in the reading surprising to you? Why or why not? If you could be on a reality show, which kind would you appear on? Why? Which kind would you avoid?

Real English

contestant = person on a
game show who competes
against others to win
something

Real English

average Joe = typical man
nerdy = socially awkward

A Dose of Reality
Colin Flemming

I was on the bus the other morning on my way to work when I was distracted by two young women chatting behind me.

". . . I know, did you see the clothes he had on?" the first one laughed.

5 Must be talking about some poor guy at school, I thought.

"And when he started singing . . . I almost died I laughed so hard!" Now I was feeling really bad for the guy.

"The thing is," says girl number two, now somewhat seriously, "if *this* guy can get on TV—especially *American Idol*, anyone can. I think 10 he's totally inspiring in a way."

"Yeah, you're right," agreed number one. "He couldn't sing, but there was something very real . . . you know, genuine and sweet, about him . . ."

Oh, now I get it. They're not laughing at someone they actually 15 know . . . they're talking about some guy who was on the reality show *American Idol*. I should've known. Based on the British show *Pop Idol*, *American Idol* is one of the top-rated programs in the U.S. For those of you who've been living in a cave for the last several years and have never heard of the show, it's basically a talent contest in which the 20 winner is given a recording deal. This career-launching reality show has become so popular that it has produced various spin-offs (e.g., *Canadian Idol* and *Australian Idol*) as well as shows with similar formats including *Fama* in Brazil, *Operación Triunfo* in Argentina and Spain, *La Academia* in Mexico, and *Factory of Stars* in Russia.

25 Early critics of reality TV (OK . . . I was one of them) believed that the popularity of shows like *Idol*, *Survivor*, *Big Brother*, and others would be short-lived. Guess what? We were wrong. Once popular primarily in the U.K. and the U.S., one can now tune in to a variety of reality shows all over the world. There are courtroom dramas and 30 makeover specials, historical re-creations, and kitchen competitions. You name it . . . and there's probably a reality show about it.

So, what makes shows like these so popular? For many, it's the idea that what they're watching is somehow authentic. Sure, there's a bit of fantasy thrown in, but unlike a sit-com or TV 35 drama, viewers believe that what they're seeing are regular people in unscripted, unrehearsed situations: young go-getters vying for a job, couples meeting and falling in love, singers competing to win a recording contract, or castaways on an island struggling to survive. Episodes are full of dramatic moments, surprising twists, heartbreaking 40 losses, and thrilling wins. And it's all real. Or is it?

The ironic truth about a lot of reality TV is that it relies more on fiction than fact to get the public to watch. Reality show producers are interested in filming the average Joe going on a date or winning that million—as long as the footage can be used to boost ratings. The 45 unfortunate reality, though, is that Joe's life doesn't always provide the compelling highs and lows that make a TV show interesting to the public.

And so, what can a reality show producer do? Some have gone as far as to bring professional scriptwriters on to the set to help 50 those being filmed to "express themselves better." While subjects aren't necessarily being encouraged to act, they are being "helped" to see that instead of saying, for example, "That was scary.", it might be more interesting to say "I was so *afraid* that my heart almost stopped!" The feelings are still the same, say the shows' producers. It's just that 55 they're a little more *heartfelt* now.

Reality show producers will also use "creative editing" to ensure that there's plenty of drama (great for ratings) in every episode. The program *The Restaurant*, for example, focused on celebrity chef Rocco DiSpirito and his high-profile establishment in New York City. 60 During filming, employee Gideon Horowitz fell and broke his elbow. Perfect, right? Not quite. When Horowitz returned to work, the show's producers, who felt that his fall hadn't been dramatic enough, asked him to refilm it. The staged fall was included in the show that aired for the public.

65 Creative editing is also used to make those being filmed more like characters in a scripted TV show ("the good girl," "the nerdy guy," "the party animal"). And the public loves it. On the first season of *The Apprentice*—a show in which billionaire businessman Donald Trump interviewed different job applicants to head one of his companies— 70 the show's producers edited large amounts of footage to make one of the job applicants appear to be a nasty, scheming woman. According to Ms. Omarosa Manigault-Stallworth, all instances of her smiling or talking in a friendly way with other contestants were edited out of the final footage shown on TV. For a time, Stallworth was hailed as "the 75 most hated woman on television"—an image that she claims was created by the show's producers and editors. In the end, Stallworth didn't get the job, but *The Apprentice* was a huge hit—thanks in great part to Stallworth's "character" on the show.

What does this all mean? Am I saying that reality TV is bad or 80 that you shouldn't watch it? Not at all. Just keep in mind the next time you tune in that many of the scenes that make you laugh, cry, cheer, or shout, were probably contrived by the show's producers to get that exact reaction. Just like on your favorite scripted TV show.

A Read the DVD review below. Fill in the best topic sentence for each paragraph.

Paragraph 1
- *The Last Samurai* features actors from Japan and the U.S.
- *The Last Samurai* is a good movie, but not a great one.
- *The Last Samurai* is one of the best movies I've ever seen.

Paragraph 2
- The movie's plot is loosely based on Japanese history.
- This is definitely one of Tom Cruise's best movies.
- The samurai were warriors in traditional Japan.

Paragraph 3
- This was one of the most popular movies of the year.
- *The Last Samurai* has wonderful scenery and costumes.
- There's a lot to enjoy in *The Last Samurai*.

---

myDVDstore

myDVDstore

CUSTOMER REVIEWS: *The Last Samurai*

PhilB says: ★ ★ ★ ★

_____.
It's a drama that mixes entertainment with a message about honor and loyalty. As entertainment, it's terrific, but the message doesn't really come through.

_____.
The Last Samurai is about an American soldier named Nathan Algren (Tom Cruise) who goes to Japan in 1876 to help the Emperor's army catch a samurai warlord named Katsumoto (played by Ken Watanabe), who is challenging the government's authority. Algren is captured by Katsumoto, and comes to understand the samurai way of life that Katsumoto is fighting to preserve. I won't give away the ending, but I thought the final battle scene was totally unrealistic.

_____.
It's filled with great camera work, nice action scenes, and plenty of drama. The acting (particularly Watanabe's) is superlative. The big problem is the simplistic story. Why would a samurai army need help from an American? Overall, I gave this 2003 movie four out of five stars. This is a fun DVD for a Saturday night when there's nothing good on TV—just don't think too hard about what it all means.

Write your own review! Click <u>here</u>

B Write a review of a movie or TV program that you especially liked—or disliked. Give it a star rating of one to five stars. Include a topic sentence for each paragraph.

Paragraph 1: Introduce the movie or program.
Paragraph 2: Describe the movie or program.
Paragraph 3: Explain the reasons for your rating and say who might enjoy this DVD.

C Pair work. Exchange reviews with a partner. Did your partner's review make you want to buy, or not buy, this DVD? Why? Make suggestions for improving or clarifying the review.

4 COMMUNICATION

Activity 1: Is TV controlling your life?

A Pair work. Interview a partner using the questionnaire below. Ask your partner to explain his or her answers.

How often do you . . .	often	sometimes	never
1. watch television while doing other things (e.g., eating, doing homework, talking on the phone)?			
2. come home and immediately turn on the television?			
3. schedule your day or week around shows you want to watch on TV?			
4. hum or sing along to commercials that are on TV?			
5. talk to friends about certain TV shows and the people on them?			
6. record TV shows so that you can watch them later?			
7. fall asleep with the TV on?			

B Pair work. Calculate your partner's score. Then read the description below to your partner.

> **often** = 3 points   **sometimes** = 2 points   **never** = 1 point

19–21 points	Wow . . . you watch so much TV that it's hard to believe you don't have it on now. My friend, TV is controlling your life. Time to break free and find a new hobby!
11–18 points	Congratulations! Though some of you may watch more TV than you probably should—especially if you scored 16 to 18 points—your life is definitely not ruled by what's on and when.
7–10 points	No doubt about it . . . you're the one in control, not the television. The only drawback may be that you won't be able to chat with your friends about TV shows.

Activity 2: Watch this show!

A Pair work. You and your partner are going to create a new reality TV show. Discuss the questions below. Assume that the show will be on once a week for an hour.

1. What kind of reality show is it going to be (e.g., talent contest, docu-drama, makeover special, dating competition, historical re-creation)?
2. Who is the show's target audience (children, teenagers, young adults, adults)?
3. What exactly will happen on the show?
4. Why do you think people will watch your new show? Use three adjectives (e.g., compelling, heartfelt, shocking) to describe the show and explain your answer.

B Group work. Using the information in A, create a two-minute sales pitch for your show and present it to the class. Your classmates will listen, take notes, and ask you questions.

C Pair work. After everyone has presented their shows, look over your notes and discuss the questions below with a partner.

1. In your opinion, which of your classmates' reality shows would most likely be picked up by a TV network? Why?
2. Which one(s) would you watch?

 Check out the CNN® video.   **Practice your English online at** elt.heinle.com/worldpass

Unit 1: Big Screen, Small Screen

A Complete the sentences with movie terms from the box. Use your dictionary as necessary.

> dubbed   subtitled   on location   soundtrack   credits
>
> studios   screenplays   flashback   stunts

1. At the end of the movie, you can read the names of the actors and of all the people who worked on the film in the _____.
2. When a movie is _____, actors speak the dialog in a language different from the original.
3. For many popular movies, you can buy a CD of the music from the _____.
4. In a _____ movie, you read the dialog translated into another language at the bottom of the screen.
5. It's sometimes very expensive to shoot a movie _____ in the actual place where the story takes place.
6. During a _____ in a movie, the action goes back to an earlier time in the story.
7. Special actors do dangerous _____ such as crashing cars or jumping out of burning buildings.
8. Many movies are made in _____, which have areas that look like different parts of the world.
9. The _____ for some famous movies are based on popular novels.

B Match the questions and answers about movies.

1. What kind of movie is it? ____
2. What's it about? ____
3. When was it made? ____
4. Where is it from? ____
5. Who's in it? ____
6. Who's it by? ____
7. Where is it showing? ____
8. How is it? ____

a. A new director that I've never heard of.
b. Tom Cruise and Julia Roberts.
c. A few years ago, I think.
d. Kind of slow at first, but the end is really scary!
e. At CineClub, downtown.
f. China. It's subtitled in English.
g. A detective story.
h. Two guys who are in love with the same woman.

> ### I didn't know that!
> *Humor* comes from the Latin word for "liquid." Centuries ago, philosophers believed that people's personalities were controlled by the liquids in their bodies. If these liquids were out of balance, the personality would be unbalanced too. Originally, a *humorous* person was strange or odd. Over time, the meaning changed to someone who could make other people laugh.

C Here are some more common abbreviations and symbols that can be used in taking notes while listening. Determine the meaning of each and write it on the line.

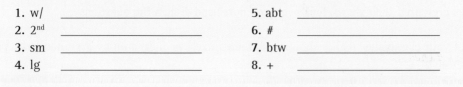

1. w/ _____
2. 2nd _____
3. sm _____
4. lg _____
5. abt _____
6. # _____
7. btw _____
8. + _____

D Review the words from the reading "A Dose of Reality" on page 9. Then write them next to their meanings.

distracted (line 2)   spin-off (line 21)   episode (line 39)   producer (line 48)

genuine (line 12)   vying (line 36)   footage (line 44)   nasty (line 71)

1. real, not artificial or false _____
2. a TV series based on another earlier series _____
3. one part in a continuing TV story _____
4. have your attention taken away by something _____
5. competing with someone to get something _____
6. the person who finances and plans a TV program _____
7. film of a particular scene or event _____
8. unkind and unpleasant _____

E Complete the paragraph with the correct forms of the TV words in the box.

antenna   remote   show   host

cable   satellite   network   channel

My boyfriend says I'm a complete couch potato, and the fact is, I'm fascinated by TV. I can sit for hours with the **(1)** _____ in my hand, just switching from one program to another. In my country, there are only two TV **(2)** _____, and they're really boring. One of them, TVN, is run by the government, and the other is independent. Last year my parents finally got **(3)** _____ TV, so now we can watch 40 different **(4)** _____. I would really like to get **(5)** _____ TV, but we would need a special **(6)** _____ outside and that's a problem. We live in an apartment and there's no good place to put it outside. There's one **(7)** _____ that I just have to see every day. It's called *Everybody's Talking* and there are always a lot of interesting guests. The show's **(8)** _____ is a comedian named Johnny Sung, and he's SO funny!

In Other Words

The audience (a collective noun) is the group of people at a theater: *The audience applauded at the end of the movie.*
Spectators watch a sports event: *All of the spectators were wearing blue and white, their team's colors.*
Viewers are people who watch a TV program: *An announcement before the program warned viewers that it contained scenes that were not appropriate for children.*

A review is a written evaluation of a movie, TV program, book, etc.: *The new movie with Tom Hanks got great reviews in all the newspapers.*
A critic is a person who writes reviews: *My sister is a movie critic for* Today *magazine.*
A critique is a detailed written explanation of problems and their causes: *Dr. Lee is writing a critique of the health care system in our country.*

Watch out!

see and watch
You can *watch* TV, or you can *see* something on TV, but you don't "see TV."
   We watched TV until midnight last night.
   I saw an interview with the president on TV.
   I saw ~~television~~ after dinner.

The World Awaits You

Lesson A | On the road

1 VOCABULARY FOCUS
Dazzling destinations

WARM UP Take one minute and write down the places in the world you would most like to visit. Compare your list with a partner. Discuss the places you chose.

A Pair work. Read this blurb about a new travel book. Discuss with a partner. Would you buy the book? Why or why not?

DAZZLING DESTINATIONS

Are you restless—you can't sit still and don't know why? Maybe it's time to take a trip!

Do you prefer visiting places that are relatively well-known or ones that are off the beaten track? Do you want to sleep in a four-star hotel or bed down under the stars? Are you comfortable in a crowd or do you relish having a destination all to yourself? Are you looking for stunning mountain scenery, white sandy beaches, or bustling urban centers?

No matter what your tastes may be, we've got it covered in this latest edition of **Dazzling Destinations**. We've surveyed the world's best travel writers and come up with these twenty must-see places and activities for your reading pleasure. And, with over two hundred glossy photographs that are guaranteed to grab your attention, you won't be able to put this book down!

Our award-winning staff of writers and photographers have had firsthand experiences visiting all of these destinations. The information is up-to-date and tells you which sites to take in and which ones to avoid.

In this book, you'll find many places which have become household names, such as the Great Wall of China or Carnaval in Rio. We also feature less familiar destinations, such as the Pushkar Camel Fair in India. And it's not all serious travel tips: you'll also learn all about the Coney Island hot dog eating contest! This book is a traveler's dream—the next best thing to actually being there.

"The photos in this book are so good that you can soak up the atmosphere of each place without leaving your own armchair!"
Sylvia Feinstein, *World Traveler News*

"There are a lot of wonderful sites in the world and these photos show the beauty of the landscape so perfectly. This book is hypnotic—I couldn't put it down!"
M. Perretti, *travelxyz.com*

ISBN 0-X3B4-XXXX-X

New Edition   Made in U.S.A.

B Pair work. **Ask and answer these questions with a partner. Use a dictionary for words you don't know.**

1. Are you a restless person or are you easily satisfied?
2. How would you answer the questions in the first paragraph of the blurb on page 14?
3. In your opinion, what travel destination would be guaranteed to be fun?
4. Have you had firsthand experience traveling somewhere exciting? What things did you take in when you were there?
5. What travel destinations are household names in your country?
6. What two or three words would you use to describe the atmosphere of your city?
7. What kind of photos do you prefer in a travel book: local handicrafts, people, or landscapes?
8. The book in A is described as *hypnotic*. What do you think that word means?

Real English
up for (something) = willing or capable of doing something

C Pair work. **These people are looking for their own "dazzling destinations."**
What destination would you suggest for each person? Compare your ideas with a partner.

Vera

"It should be physically challenging or even dangerous. I'm a real thrill-seeker."

Sean

"I'm not single anymore, so it should be a place that's appropriate for the entire family . . . but interesting for us adults too."

Monique

"I'm up for going anywhere that has a lot of eating or dancing—the two things I love to do most!"

>> Vocabulary Builder ▲

These words all end in *-less*. Write them in the chart. Then complete the sentences. Not all words are used.

~~ageless~~   countless   meaningless   priceless
~~childless~~   effortless   powerless   timeless

-less = lacking something	*-less* = exceeding a category
childless	ageless

1. We're _____ to do anything about the situation. We should give up.
2. She may be almost 60 years old, but there's a kind of _____ beauty about her.
3. The time I spent with my grandmother before she died was _____.
4. The government is worried about the increasing number of _____ couples.
5. He's such an accomplished mountain climber. He makes it look _____.

2 LISTENING
A photographer's dream

> Have you ever taken a memorable travel photo?
> What was special about it? Describe it to your partner.

A Pair work. Each of these three photographs appeared in the book *Dazzling Destinations*. Where do you think each photo was taken? Discuss with a partner.

B You will hear three photographers talking about their work. Listen and match each photographer to the photo that he or she took. Write the number in the box. (CD Tracks 04 & 05)

1. Leslie 2. Olga 3. Diego

C Listen again. Circle the statements that each person would say. There may be more than one answer. (CD Track 06)

1. **Leslie**
   a. I'm patient.
   b. I visit each place once.
   c. I like contrast in colors.

2. **Olga**
   a. It took me a long time to figure out the kind of photos I wanted to take.
   b. I'm not into the latest photography techniques.
   c. The development process is easy.

3. **Diego**
   a. I photograph birds mainly.
   b. I think people and animals have a lot in common.
   c. There was a lot to see in Antarctica.

> ▶ **Ask & *Answer***
> What places do you think are a photographer's dream? Why?

3 LANGUAGE FOCUS
Past modals

A Pair work. Hilary is meeting Sam at the airport. Read their conversation and notice the phrases in blue. Then, with a partner, circle the correct answers in the sentences on page 17.

Hilary: Hi, Sam. Have you been waiting long?
Sam: About an hour and a half. My flight got in early.
Hilary: Oh no. You should've phoned me! I would've come to the airport earlier.
Sam: I tried calling you at home, but there wasn't any answer.
Hilary: I must've left already. You could've tried my cell phone.
Sam: That's true, but I left your number at home. I should've written it down!
Hilary: Yeah, it would've been easier. I was waiting at the wrong place and when I didn't see you, I thought "he couldn't have arrived yet. His plane isn't due until 2:00." Anyway, how are you?
Sam: Good. Listen, I could've booked a hotel before I arrived, but I thought I'd wait and ask for your advice. Can you recommend a place to stay?
Hilary: Don't be silly, Sam! You're staying with us. Now, do you need help with your luggage?

1. When Hilary says "You should've phoned me," she is giving Sam a strong / polite suggestion.
2. When Hilary says "I would've come to the airport earlier," she is showing her willingness / unwillingness to do something.
3. When Hilary says "I must've left already," she is giving advice / a conclusion.
4. When Hilary says "You could've tried my cell phone," she is giving a strong / polite suggestion.
5. When Sam says "I should've written it down," he is giving advice / expressing regret.
6. When Hilary says "He couldn't have arrived yet," she is expressing possibility / impossibility (or disbelief).
7. When Sam says "I could've booked a hotel," he is expressing possibility / impossibility.

B Read this story about Blaine's first trip to New York fifteen years ago. On a separate piece of paper, answer the questions below using the modal phrases from A.

> My first day in New York was a disaster. I took a taxi from the airport into the city and it was very expensive. I didn't have a hotel reservation, so I went to the youth hostel looking for a room. They were booked up. It took me three hours and many phone calls before I could find a place to stay. I was hungry, so that evening I put my wallet in my back pocket and went out to dinner. I got lost because I didn't have a subway map and I was by myself. When I finally got to the restaurant, I was famished and I ordered a lot of food. When I went to pay, I realized my wallet was missing! I couldn't believe it!

pick poket

1. What could Blaine have done when he got lost?
2. What do you think happened to his wallet?   *Someone could have stolen it*
3. How do you think he felt when he realized his wallet was missing?   *upset, panic*
4. Is there any advice you would have given Blaine at the time?
5. What would you have done differently if you had taken the trip to New York?

C Pair work. Which sentence logically follows the first one? Circle your answer. Then explain your answers to a partner.

1. She shouldn't have called him.
   a. I know. What a mistake!
   b. Maybe she can do it tomorrow.
   past possibilty
2. Jim couldn't have gone to Hawaii last week.
   a. He was in the office every day.
   b. He might have been in the office.
3. How was the concert last night?
   a. It was great. I could go, but I didn't.
   b. I don't know. I could have gone, but I didn't.

4. Where's Tom?
   a. His computer is turned off. He must have left already.
   b. His computer is turned off. He must not have left already.
5. What would you have done in that situation?
   a. I don't know, but I would've done what you did.
   b. I don't know, but I wouldn't have done what you did.

phone is about to die.

D Read the sentences. Circle the letter that shows the one incorrect part of each sentence and correct it.

1. You shouldn't have leave the car headlights on. Now the battery is dead.   *left*
      A   B   C   D
2. If I were you, I would've tell him the truth about your travel plans.   *told*
      A   B   C   the truth
                    D
3. I could've went to a bustling city, but then I wouldn't have met any of the local people.   *gone*
   A   B   C   D   *whatever*
4. I think the projector must not have been work well because they never showed the in-flight movie.   *have*
                    A   B   C   D
5. I'm not sure, but he could board the flight in Miami. We'll have to check with the airline.   *boarded*
                        A   B   C   D

E Read this letter to the editor of a travel magazine. What advice would you give to "Jet Lagged in Jakarta"?

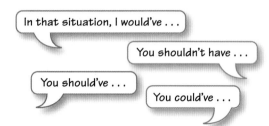

In that situation, I would've . . .

You shouldn't have . . .

You should've . . .

You could've . . .

Dear Editor,
I recently took a trip to Jakarta. I booked the cheapest flight I could find. It was an overnight flight and they didn't serve any meals. I was so hungry! By the time we landed, I had a terrible headache. I got to my hotel by 2:00 P.M. and took a two-hour nap. That night, I couldn't sleep at all. I didn't enjoy my trip because I had terrible jet lag. Can you give me some advice?
— "Jet Lagged in Jakarta"

Grammar X-TRA   Showing regret in the past with *wish*

- I *wish* I **hadn't** lost my passport. It was such a hassle to get a new one.
- We didn't arrive on time. I *wish* we **had**.

Pair work. Tell your partner about a time you took a trip and something went wrong. Your partner will suggest things that you could've or should've done differently.

A: I flooded the bathtub in our hotel room last summer.
B: Really? You should've watched the water more closely.
A: Yeah, I wish I'd done that.

4 SPEAKING

Would you mind . . .

A Group work. Read this phone conversation. Look at the underlined expressions where the speakers are using overly casual or inappropriate language. Discuss what they could say to sound more polite.

How may I direct your call

Operator:	Thank you for calling the Sun Coast Hotel. (1) <u>Who do you want to talk to?</u>
Jennie:	(2) <u>Reservations.</u>
Operator:	(3) <u>OK.</u> (4) <u>Hold on a minute.</u>
Clerk:	Good afternoon, (5) <u>I'm Cassandra.</u> (6) <u>What do you want?</u>
Jennie:	Hello? (7) <u>How much is a double room?</u>
Clerk:	The rate is $125 for a standard double.
Jennie:	Oh . . . (8) <u>That's too expensive.</u>
Clerk:	Well, we also offer a special weekend rate of $70 for Saturday and Sunday nights.
Jennie:	That sounds perfect. Do you have a double room available for March 16th and 17th?

Clerk:	Just a moment . . . yes, we do.
Jennie:	Also, (9) <u>is your hotel on the beach?</u>
Clerk:	Yes, it is. We have our own private beach for guests.
Jennie:	Perfect! Then I'd like to make a reservation.
Clerk:	May I have your name, please?
Jennie:	Jennie Tranh.
Clerk:	(10) <u>How do you spell that?</u>
Jennie:	That's T-R-A-N-H.
Clerk:	And could I have your credit card number, please?
Jennie:	Sure—it's . . .

B Group work. Now look at the polite language in the box. Match each expression to its underlined counterpart in A. Then practice the polite version of the conversation.

a. I'm afraid that's a little out of my price range. (8)
b. How may I direct your call? (1)
c. How may I help you? (6)
d. Certainly. (3)
e. I was wondering whether your hotel is located on the beach or not. (9)
f. This is Cassandra. (5)
g. Would you mind spelling that for me? (10)
h. One moment, please. (4)
i. Could you please tell me the cost of a double room? (7)
j. I'd like to speak with someone in Reservations, please. (2)

C Pair work. Choose one of the hotels in the photos. With a partner, work together to role-play a phone conversation to make a reservation.

Skytop Hotel

River Guest House

Mountain View Lodge

The World Awaits You

Lesson B | There and back

1 GET READY TO READ

"Not all those who wander are lost."

WARM UP What are some reasons why people travel?
Think of a trip you have taken. Why did you go?

A Pair work. Read these quotes and then discuss the questions below with a partner.

> Not all those who wander are lost.
> ~J. R. R. Tolkien

> A man travels the world over in search of what he needs, and returns home to find it.
> ~ George Moore

> Not I - not anyone else, can travel that road for you. You must travel it for yourself.
> ~ Walt Whitman

World Link

Residents of popular tourist destinations must sometimes feel as if visitors are crawling around everywhere. It's no wonder the Anangu Aboriginal people of Australia sometimes call tourists "minga," a word which also means "ants."

Source: *traveloasis.com*

> Wherever you go, the sky is the same color.
> ~Persian saying

> The real voyage of discovery consists not in seeking new landscapes, but in having new eyes.
> ~Marcel Proust

1. What do you think each quote means?
2. Which quote do you like or agree with most? Why? Are there any quotes that you disagree with? Why?
3. Can you think of any other sayings related to travel and journeys?

B Pair work. You're going to read an interview with a woman from Nigeria. How much do you know about this country? Take the quiz below and then compare ideas with a partner. Check your answers on page 168.

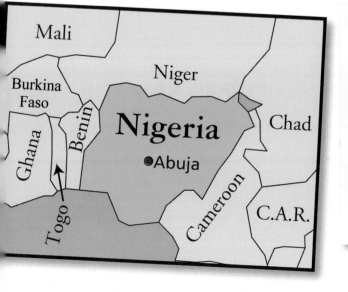

The Nigeria Quiz

1. Nigeria has the largest / smallest population of any African country.
2. The official language of Nigeria is Yoruba / English / French.
3. Skiing / Cricket / Soccer is the country's most popular sport.
4. Nigeria's largest export is clothing / oil / exotic fruit.
5. Many Nigerian dishes tend to be hot and spicy / plain and watery.
6. Which of the following people was born in Nigeria? the musician Sade / actress Halle Berry / Secretary-General of the United Nations, Kofi Annan

2 READING

I left home to find home

Chimamanda Ngozi Adichie was born in Nigeria in 1977. Her short stories and novels have won or been nominated for several important literary awards including the Booker Prize and the Orange Prize for fiction.

A Pair work. You are going to read an interview with author Chimamanda Ngozi Adichie. First look at her photo and read the information about her. Then read the title of the interview on page 21. Discuss with your partner what you think the reading is going to be about.

B Pair work. Now read the interview and write the questions below on the correct lines in the text. Then compare your answers with a partner.

Will you travel more now?

~~Do you remain rooted in Nigeria or are you keen to travel?~~

Has travel given you a strong sense of being Nigerian?

When did you make your first trip outside Nigeria?

What do you love about Nigeria?

Have you traveled within Africa?

C Read the interview again. Then using your own words, answer the questions below on a separate piece of paper.

1. How old was Ms. Adichie the first time she traveled abroad? Where did she go and how long did she stay there?
2. Why was she a little disappointed by her first trip abroad?
3. How old was Ms. Adichie when she moved to the U.S. to live? How long did she live there and how did she feel about it?
4. How did living in the U.S. change Ms. Adichie? What did she learn by living there?
5. What are the things that Ms. Adichie loves most about her country?
6. Where did Ms. Adichie go in 2002? Did she enjoy the trip? Why or why not?
7. Where would Ms. Adichie like to go next?

D Find the words or phrases in the reading. Then circle the word or phrase each is most similar to.

1. *wanderlust* (line 7)   feeling of boredom   desire to travel
2. *can-do* (line 13)   doubt and concern   optimism and strength
3. *rooted* (line 18)   settled, connected to a place   unattached, free
4. *surreal* (line 27)   familiar   weird, bizarre
5. *sorted out* (line 31)   understood, solved   hid or concealed

E Fill in the blanks below with the correct word or phrase from the reading.

1. In line 11, *there* refers to _____.
2. In line 16, *they* refers to _____.
3. In line 21, *It* refers to _____.
4. In line 23, *there* refers to _____.
5. In line 26, *it* (twice) refers to _____.

> ▶ **Ask & Answer**
>
> Is there anything that you especially love about your country and its people? What do you think you could learn about yourself and your country by being abroad?

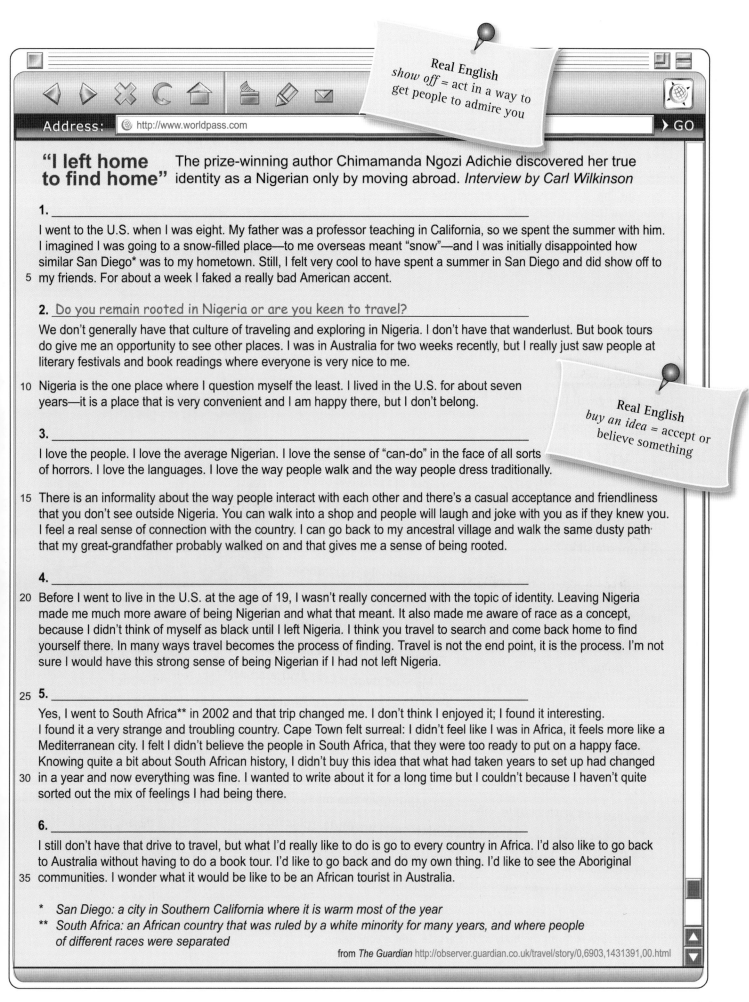

Real English
show off = act in a way to get people to admire you

"I left home to find home"

The prize-winning author Chimamanda Ngozi Adichie discovered her true identity as a Nigerian only by moving abroad. *Interview by Carl Wilkinson*

1. _____

I went to the U.S. when I was eight. My father was a professor teaching in California, so we spent the summer with him. I imagined I was going to a snow-filled place—to me overseas meant "snow"—and I was initially disappointed how similar San Diego* was to my hometown. Still, I felt very cool to have spent a summer in San Diego and did show off to
5 my friends. For about a week I faked a really bad American accent.

2. Do you remain rooted in Nigeria or are you keen to travel? _____

We don't generally have that culture of traveling and exploring in Nigeria. I don't have that wanderlust. But book tours do give me an opportunity to see other places. I was in Australia for two weeks recently, but I really just saw people at literary festivals and book readings where everyone is very nice to me.

10 Nigeria is the one place where I question myself the least. I lived in the U.S. for about seven years—it is a place that is very convenient and I am happy there, but I don't belong.

Real English
buy an idea = accept or believe something

3. _____

I love the people. I love the average Nigerian. I love the sense of "can-do" in the face of all sorts of horrors. I love the languages. I love the way people walk and the way people dress traditionally.

15 There is an informality about the way people interact with each other and there's a casual acceptance and friendliness that you don't see outside Nigeria. You can walk into a shop and people will laugh and joke with you as if they knew you. I feel a real sense of connection with the country. I can go back to my ancestral village and walk the same dusty path that my great-grandfather probably walked on and that gives me a sense of being rooted.

4. _____

20 Before I went to live in the U.S. at the age of 19, I wasn't really concerned with the topic of identity. Leaving Nigeria made me much more aware of being Nigerian and what that meant. It also made me aware of race as a concept, because I didn't think of myself as black until I left Nigeria. I think you travel to search and come back home to find yourself there. In many ways travel becomes the process of finding. Travel is not the end point, it is the process. I'm not sure I would have this strong sense of being Nigerian if I had not left Nigeria.

25 **5.** _____

Yes, I went to South Africa** in 2002 and that trip changed me. I don't think I enjoyed it; I found it interesting. I found it a very strange and troubling country. Cape Town felt surreal: I didn't feel like I was in Africa, it feels more like a Mediterranean city. I felt I didn't believe the people in South Africa, that they were too ready to put on a happy face. Knowing quite a bit about South African history, I didn't buy this idea that what had taken years to set up had changed
30 in a year and now everything was fine. I wanted to write about it for a long time but I couldn't because I haven't quite sorted out the mix of feelings I had being there.

6. _____

I still don't have that drive to travel, but what I'd really like to do is go to every country in Africa. I'd also like to go back to Australia without having to do a book tour. I'd like to go back and do my own thing. I'd like to see the Aboriginal
35 communities. I wonder what it would be like to be an African tourist in Australia.

*   *San Diego: a city in Southern California where it is warm most of the year*
** *South Africa: an African country that was ruled by a white minority for many years, and where people of different races were separated*

from *The Guardian* http://observer.guardian.co.uk/travel/story/0,6903,1431391,00.html

A Read this article submitted by a student in response to the newspaper ad. The editor has marked it with correction symbols that indicate the type of mistake made. Correct the errors.

Sp	spelling	VT	verb tense
WF	word form	WW	wrong word
P	punctuation	WO	word order
X	word(s) missing	??	I don't understand this

What was your best travel experience—or your worst? The International Institute's student newsletter wants your articles! Write about 200 words and include a photo if you can. The best articles will appear in next month's special Travel Issue.

Last year, my friend and I went on a backpacking trip in the Sierra Nevada Mountains in California. We planned to hike the John Muir Trail **P** which runs 150 miles through the mountians. **Sp** We knew that the scenery will **VT** be fantastic, but we never expected to meet a fascinating character.

We have **VT** saved up our money for months to buy equipment. I bought a new sleping **Sp** bag, tent, and lots of camping gadgets. But we brought too much with us, and our packs were heavy and uncomfortable.

On our third day on the trail, we met an elderly man who was walking along. His name was Bernie. He told us that his backpack was from his army days as a young man—fifty year **WF** ago! We had **X** fancy tent. He slept under a tree. We cooked on a portable camping stove. He heated his food over a fire. And if a bear came too close, he said, he just through **WW** rocks at it. At 78 years old, he was finishing his twice **??** hike of the trail.

No matter how beautiful the place you visit, it's your firsthand encounters with people that you'll remember the most. I learned something important from Bernie: to have a wonderful trip, atttitude **Sp** is more much **WO** important than money. (212 words)

> ### Writing an article
>
> An article for a newsletter or magazine should inform and entertain the reader. It should include an introduction to attract the reader's interest, one or more paragraphs to form the body of the article, and a conclusion that pulls the article together.

B Write a similar article about your own best (or worst) travel experience. Include an introduction, one or more paragraphs to form the body of the article, and a conclusion.

C Pair work. Exchange papers. Mark any mistakes you see on your partner's paper with correction symbols from the box above. Give your partner other suggestions for improving the article.

4 COMMUNICATION

Activity 1: Lost at sea

A Pair work. Read the true story below. Then with a partner, take turns describing what happened to Maralyn and Maurice Bailey using your own words.

THE BAILEYS' TRAVELS

In the early 1970s, a young British couple named Maralyn and Maurice Bailey decided to move to New Zealand. Rather than flying to their destination, the couple chose instead to start their new lives by sailing from England to New Zealand aboard their yacht Auralyn. Though Maralyn had never learned to swim and Maurice's knowledge about long-distance sailing came primarily from books, the couple was certain their trip would be a success, and set off enthusiastically in June of 1972.

Several months into the voyage, just after the couple had passed through the Panama Canal, the Auralyn came into contact with a whaling ship. A few hours later, the Auralyn was struck by an injured whale. The blow from the animal created a large hole in the yacht. With the boat sinking fast, Maralyn and Maurice inflated two rubber life rafts and roped them together. Amidst much chaos and confusion, the couple managed to get off the sinking yacht and onto the life rafts with some food, water, and a few other items.

For the first week or so, Maralyn and Maurice drank rainwater and ate the food they'd brought from their boat. Within a couple of weeks, though, the food was gone. To survive, the couple caught fish and ate them raw.

Weeks passed . . . and then months. The couple drifted on the Pacific Ocean, uncertain of where they were. By day 117, the couple's raft had become very worn. Their skin was badly sunburned and both were so exhausted that they could hardly move. And then, as the couple drifted in and out of sleep on the afternoon of day 117, Maurice thought that he saw a small black dot in the distance . . .

B Pair work. Discuss the questions with your partner.

1. If you were in the Baileys' situation, is there anything you would've done differently? Give reasons.
2. When the yacht was first struck by the whale, how do you think the Baileys must've felt? How about after a week on the rubber raft? After two months?
3. How do you think this story ends? What do you think might have happened to Maralyn and Maurice? Find out what really happened on page 168.

> **Real English**
> commune with nature =
> be close to nature

Activity 2: The top three

A Pair work. Discuss the questions below and come up with three answers for each one.

In your opinion, what are the top three . . .
- ways to avoid jet lag?
- most romantic cities in the world?
- local hangouts in your city?
- souvenirs you can give from your city?
- ways to occupy your time on a long car or bus trip?
- places to commune with nature?

B Group work. Join another pair and compare ideas. As a group, come up with one final list of three for each category. Share your ideas with the class.

 Check out the CNN® video. **Practice your English online at** elt.heinle.com/worldpass

Expansion Pages

A Complete these sentences about airplane flights with an appropriate verb from the box.

> caught   missed   delayed   canceled
> got in   diverted   called

1. I had very bad luck getting here. I _____ my flight because traffic was so heavy on the way to the airport, and I had to wait hours for another flight.
2. The flight was _____ due to bad weather. We sat waiting in the departure lounge until the storm passed.
3. After the business meetings finished, Mr. Pak _____ the last flight back to Los Angeles and arrived home there at 11 P.M.
4. The airline agent _____ the flight to Bogotá and asked all the passengers to proceed to the gate.
5. When I found out that my flight was _____, I had to make a new reservation immediately to get home as soon as possible.
6. I'm really tired today. I came back from my vacation last night and my flight _____ at midnight!
7. Because of heavy snow at the Chicago airport, the flight was _____ to another airport, and the passengers had to go to Chicago by bus.

B Match the sentence parts to make questions that a guest would ask in a hotel.

1. Could I have a wake-up call ___
2. Could you please call a taxi ___
3. Is breakfast ___
4. Could you please send ___
5. Could you put this meal ___
6. Can I reserve ___
7. What time does ___
8. Is the hotel full ___
9. Do you have ___
10. Do you allow ___

a. included in the price?
b. all next week?
c. on my room bill, please?
d. any nonsmoking rooms?
e. the restaurant open?
f. at 7 A.M. tomorrow?
g. to take me to the airport?
h. pets in the hotel?
i. a room for next Friday?
j. someone to fix the shower?

There's an old saying . . . *A journey of a thousand miles begins with a single step.*
Even the biggest and most overwhelming project starts out with small, simple actions. We say this to encourage someone who is facing a difficult task.
   "I want to change careers, but it seems so hard."
   "Well, *a journey of a thousand miles begins with a single step.* Maybe you could start reading the job ads in the newspaper."

---

abroad
Abroad is an adverb, not a noun. It never has a preposition before it.
   I hope to travel abroad after I graduate from the university.
   My brother lived abroad for many years.
   I hope to travel ~~to abroad~~ after I graduate from the university.
   My brother lived ~~in abroad~~ for many years.

C Study the phrases in the box and complete the sentences with the correct form of the expression.

> **Word combinations with *passport***
>
> apply for a passport   an expired passport
> renew a passport   show your passport
> stamp a passport   check a passport
> a valid passport

1. The officer _____ my passport with red ink and wrote some numbers in it.
2. Please _____ passport and ticket to the agent before boarding the ferry.
3. I'm taking my children with me on a trip to Mexico, so I need to _____ passports for them.
4. To enter the country, all travelers need to have _____ passport and a visa.
5. They wouldn't let me get on the plane because I had _____ passport. I forgot to look at the date!
6. In this country, we need to _____ our passports every ten years.
7. The police have the right to _____ your passport at any time, so you should always carry it with you when you leave your hotel.

D English has many idioms that contain comparisons. Complete each sentence with a word from the box, using your dictionary as necessary.

> an ox   a feather   a beet   night   nails
> a bat   a mouse   a bee   a bone   snow

1. Jeff is as blind as _____ without his glasses. He can't see anything.
2. My roommate is as strong as _____. He lifts weights in the gym every day.
3. My new laptop weighs less than one kilo. It's as light as _____.
4. When I get embarrassed, my face always turns as red as _____.
5. The curtains were closed, and inside the room it was as black as _____.
6. My little sister was as quiet as _____ all evening. She didn't say a single word.
7. It hadn't rained in a month, and the soil was as dry as _____.
8. The newly painted walls of the house were as white as _____.
9. Even though she's 80 years old, my grandmother is still as busy as _____.
10. My boss doesn't care about other people's feelings. She's as hard as _____.

> ### In Other Words
>
> A traveler is anyone who takes a trip, for any purpose: *The day before the holiday, the airport was crowded with travelers.*
> A tourist is someone who is traveling for pleasure: *Tourists in my city like to visit the National Museum and the city market.*
> A passenger is someone who is traveling by plane, train, bus, etc.: *The bus driver asked the passengers to be seated.*
> A motorist is someone who is driving a car: *Police warned motorists to drive carefully during the snowstorm.*
>
> Drive can be a transitive verb: *I drive my car to work every morning.* It can also be intransitive: *Every morning, thousands of cars, buses, and trucks drive on the Metro Expressway into the city.*
> Sail is used for boats and ships: *The Titanic was sailing to New York when it hit an iceberg and sank.*
> Travel is used for trains (as well as cars/trucks/buses): *The new high-speed train travels at over 200 km per hour.*

School and Beyond

Lesson A | School life

1 VOCABULARY FOCUS

My first year at college

 What's the scariest thing about going away to college?
What's the most exciting thing about it?

> **Real English**
> ace (something) = (informal) do really well
> it seems like a blur = it happened so fast I don't remember the details

A Pair work. These three students are going away to college next week. How do they feel about leaving home? What are their concerns? Who do you think will be happiest at school?

Jamal

Andrea

Sarah

"We're driving up to school tomorrow and I can't wait to get away from home. It's only four hours from my house, but I'll be on my own for the first time. You probably won't want to come over for dinner—I'm a terrible cook, but my mom has said I can come home for meals on weekends if I need to. I don't know about that, but I may need her help with my laundry . . . at least at first."

"I'm apprehensive about leaving home. Since this will be my first extended period away, I know my parents are worried too. This will be a good opportunity for me to learn to be independent. One thing's for sure: I'm definitely going to sign up for as many afternoon classes as I can. I'm not an early riser!"

"This is embarrassing to admit, but I couldn't think of anything better to do, so I applied to this school. I don't have any expectations, really. I am worried about missing my friends and my boyfriend, though. I spent three weeks at a summer camp last year and I was homesick the whole time. I just hope I can make some new friends."

B Now read about how Jamal, Andrea, and Sarah feel at the end of their first term. How do they feel now?

Jamal: School has been harder than I thought. Between my part-time job, my studies, and everything else, I'm feeling overwhelmed. On top of it all, I'm getting a C minus in my macroeconomics class, which unfortunately is compulsory. I've been thinking about dropping out of school entirely and moving back home. I don't want to make a rash decision, so I'm going to think it over.

Andrea: The first term has gone so quickly—it all seems like a blur. My only mishap was during the first week of school—the battery in my wheelchair ran out on the way to class! Other than that, I've coped with university life pretty well. I aced all my final exams and I've really bonded with my three roommates. We're planning on getting an apartment together off campus next year. I can't wait!

Sarah: This week I'm suffering from sleep deprivation because I've been up all night studying for final exams. It's also been a challenge trying to make a budget and stick to it. That's the worst part, though. The rest of my life is awesome. I have a hectic schedule, but I live in the center of the city—so, who can complain? Best of all, I have a new boyfriend!

C Group work. Work in groups of three. Each student should take the role of Jamal, Andrea, or Sarah. Interview each other about your college experience. Try to use the new vocabulary from A and B.

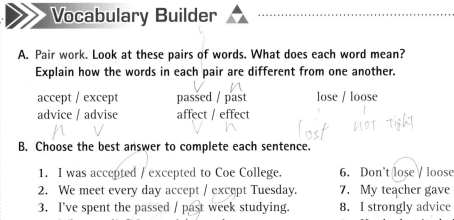

Vocabulary Builder ▲

A. Pair work. Look at these pairs of words. What does each word mean? Explain how the words in each pair are different from one another.

accept / except   passed / past   lose / loose
advice / advise   affect / effect

lost   *not tight*

B. Choose the best answer to complete each sentence.

1. I was accepted / excepted to Coe College.
2. We meet every day accept / except Tuesday.
3. I've spent the passed / past week studying.
4. What a relief! I passed / past the test.
5. My tooth is lose / loose.

6. Don't lose / loose your student ID card.
7. My teacher gave me some good advice / advise.
8. I strongly advice / advise you to take that class.
9. Her bad attitude is affecting / effecting her grades.
10. Failing that class had a terrible affect / effect on him.

> **Ask & Answer**
>
> Look back at Jamal's, Andrea's, and Sarah's comments in B. What advice would you give each of them at this point? Why?

2 LISTENING
School lunches

A   Listen to each person talking about school lunches. Complete the chart. (CD Tracks 07 & 08)

Name	Where from?	Where now?	Name	Where from?	Where now?
1. Jae Soo	*Korea*	*America*	3. Ivan	*Ukraine*	*Switzerland*
2. Annette	*London ⟷ Norway*		4. Vanessa	*puerto rico*	*Puerto rico*

B   Listen again. How does each person feel about these things? Circle *positive* or *negative*. (CD Track 09)

1. Jae Soo	a. his school lunches where he grew up Details: *good. misses Mom's cooking*	positive negative
	b. school lunches where he is now *hot steamed rice* Details: *hamburger, soda, fries, mistery meat* *16 years old*	positive negative
2. Annette	a. her school lunches growing up *fruit* Details: *mother pack no cafe, sanwich, yongourt, milk*	positive negative
	b. her daughter's school lunches now *terrible* Details: *soda bad habit atrocious* *crisps no in nutrition*	positive negative
3. Ivan *Borsch*	a. his school lunches where he grew up *three course* Details: *beet soup vegetable pancake cookie biscuits*	positive negative
	b. school lunches where he lives now Details: *excercize share with family* *go home for lunch*	positive negative
4. Vanessa	a. her school lunches growing up *rich checker* Details: *preety same beans meat. salad*	positive negative
	b. her children's school lunches now Details: *guermale fast food junk food*	positive negative

C   Listen again. Make notes in B about what words told you that people did or didn't like their lunches. Write the details.
(CD Track 10)

> **Ask & Answer**
>
> What did you eat most often for lunch when you were in school? What did you least enjoy eating? Did you ever share your lunch with others?

3 LANGUAGE FOCUS

Hope **and** *wish*

Using *hope* **and** *wish***

Use *hope* for desires or expectations that are real, probable, or possible but the outcome is uncertain. Use *wish* for desires or expectations that are unreal, unlikely, or improbable.

A   Pair work. **Study this cartoon. Notice the use of** *hope* **and** *wish***.

Later

I wish I'd studied harder.

I always get bad grades. I wish I could do better.

HW

B   The chart below explains the different uses of *hope* **and** *wish***. Complete the chart with the sentences from A.**

Uses of *hope* and *wish*	Examples
Use *hope* + simple present to describe a present or future desire or expectation. Use *hope* + *will* for future expectations only.	I hope I can pass the test on next week.
Use *wish* + *would* + base form to express annoyance or dissatisfaction with a situation in the present or future.	*I wish it would stop raining.*
Use *wish* + simple past / past continuous to express desire for a change in a present situation. *I wish = It would be nice if . . .*	*I wish (that) I had a lot of money.* *I wish (that) it weren't raining right now.*
Use *wish* + *could* / *would* + base form to express desire for a different situation in the future.	I wish that I couldn't fall down from the stairs.
Use *wish* + past perfect to express regret about a past situation.	I wish I had visited there.

C   Lana is not able to study for her exams because of the disruptions in her apartment. What do you think she would think or say about the situation? **Look at the picture and make sentences with** *I wish . . . would . . .*

1.   I wish that bird . . . would be eaten by the cat
2.   I wish that roommate would have a claim from neighbourhood
3.   I wish that cat would be more calm.
4.   I wish that car would break immideatly
5.   I wish that my consentration would be improved

D Rewrite these sentences using *I wish* and the words in parentheses.

1. My sister's failing chemistry. (study) _____
2. I want to travel to Rome. (visit) _____
3. My tuition is expensive. (cheaper) _____
4. I didn't meet anyone at school last year. (make friends) _____
5. I can't speak Italian. (speak) _____
6. I have a headache. (have aspirin) _____

E Complete these sentences with the correct form of *hope* or *wish*.

1. I have a big exam tomorrow. I __hope__ I pass.
2. Jake didn't apply for a scholarship. Now he __wishes__ he had.
3. I __hope__ you have a good time at the party.
4. She went to Yale, but she __wishes__ she'd gone to Harvard.
5. That baby has been crying for an hour. I __wish__ it would be quiet!
6. There's a woman with a baby behind us. I __hope__ it doesn't cry during the movie.
7. I __hope__ I will see you at least once over the summer break.
8. I __wish__ I hadn't lost my keys. Now I can't get into my apartment. I __hope__ I find them soon.
9. We got into an argument and I said something rude to her. Now I __wish__ I hadn't. I __wish__ I could take it all back.

World Link

Most American school lunch programs offer food that is far from gourmet. But at one New York City school, a chef trained in France serves dishes like potato-leek soup, fresh green salad, and baked fish—all for the same cost as the "mystery meat" and canned vegetables the school used to serve!

Source: *cbsnews.com*

F Pair work. Role-play the situation below. Switch roles and do the role play again.

Student A: Imagine that you are finishing your first term at college. Things are not going so well. You're bored with your classes and your grades are not good. Talk to your partner about your situation. Use *hope* and *wish* with words or phrases from the box.

Student B: Listen to your partner's problem and give him or her some advice. Use the words or phrases in the box or your own ideas.

| stick it out | take a year off | cope | transfer to another school | change your major |
| apprehensive | drop out | hectic | quit school and find a job | |

Grammar X-TRA *Make, allow,* and *let*

Read the sentences in the box. Then answer the questions below.

> They **made** us wear our uniforms during soccer practice.
> They **allowed** us to wear our uniforms during soccer practice.
> They **let** us wear our uniforms during soccer practice.

1. What do the sentences mean? How are they similar or different in meaning?
2. Using the same verbs, try to rewrite the sentences in the passive. Which one cannot be rewritten?

Pair work. Tell your partner about the rules from a school you went to in the past. What were they like? Did you or anyone else ever break any of those rules?

4 SPEAKING

That's an interesting question.

A Pair work. What are some situations in which people are interviewed in English? Have you, or someone you know, ever been interviewed in English? What happened?

B Pair work. Read these general tips about what to do before, during, and after an interview. Add your own ideas to the list. Compare your ideas with a partner.

Before an interview	During an interview	After an interview
• Get plenty of sleep the night before. • Make a list of some questions that you want to ask about the position or opportunity. • _prepare own introduction_ • _To research the person who I'm gonna interview. Also company._	• Avoid answering questions with a simple *yes* or *no* answer. • Don't rush to speak before gathering your thoughts. *beginning* • *private* _Don't ask personal question at the_ • _Should ask a salary in polite way._	• Clarify what you should do next. • Shake hands with the interviewer and thank him or her. • _give a present._ • _____

C Pair work. Read the announcement below. With your partner, prepare a list of interview questions for a candidate applying for The One World Foundation Scholarship. Include questions covering personal information, education, and language-learning experience. Add other questions of your own.

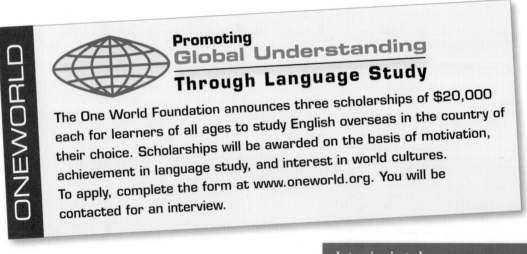

ONEWORLD

Promoting Global Understanding Through Language Study

The One World Foundation announces three scholarships of $20,000 each for learners of all ages to study English overseas in the country of their choice. Scholarships will be awarded on the basis of motivation, achievement in language study, and interest in world cultures. To apply, complete the form at www.oneworld.org. You will be contacted for an interview.

D Pair work. Take turns role-playing an interviewer for The One World Foundation and a candidate applying for the scholarship. The candidate should try to include some of the expressions in the box.

E Class work. With the class, discuss how your interview went. Did you have any problems? What strategies did you use to overcome those problems?

Interviewing phrases

Getting time to think
That's an interesting question.
Let me think about that a moment.
Just so that I understand, what you're asking is . . .

Rephrasing your answer
What I meant was . . .
What I'm trying to say is . . .
Let me put it another way.

Asking for clarification of a question
What do you mean by . . . ?
When you asked . . . , did you mean . . . ?
Are you asking about . . . ?

UNIT 3

School and Beyond

Lesson B | New school, old school

1 GET READY TO READ

School days

 How would you rate the quality of public education in your country? What could be done to improve it?

A Pair work. **Look at the illustrations below. How are these two classrooms different? Which would you rather be in? Why?**

B Pair work. **Think about your experiences in high school. Which of the statements below describe what your education was like? Check (✓) your answers. Then compare and discuss your answers with a partner.**

	Usually	Sometimes	Hardly ever
1. Teachers were strict.			
2. We had a lot of tests.			
3. We went on field trips to learn more about a subject.			
4. Classes featured drills and memorization of facts.			
5. Most classes had no more than twenty students.			
6. Classes were engaging; I looked forward to going.			
7. Students worked on projects in groups.			
8. Students got practical, hands-on experience outside the classroom.			
9. Classes in art and sports were offered.			
10. Other: _____			

▶ **Ask & Answer**

Was your high school experience mostly positive or negative? Do you think your education prepared you for your future? Why or why not?

A   Pair work. Read the online discussion between Yoon-Hee and Gordon on page 33, and underline the ideas you agree with. Then compare your answers with a partner.

B   Read the online discussion again. Which writer would agree with the following statements? Circle the correct answer.

1. There should be less emphasis in schools on drilling and taking tests.   Yoon-Hee   Gordon   both

2. Schools need to promote critical thinking and develop skills that students can use in the real world.   Yoon-Hee   Gordon   both

3. Giving students the chance to get more hands-on experience is a nice idea, but in the real world it's too difficult to do.   Yoon-Hee   Gordon   both

4. Students need to spend more time memorizing certain things in school.   Yoon-Hee   Gordon   both

5. Courses such as music, art, and cooking should be added to a school's standard curriculum.   Yoon-Hee   Gordon   both

6. The main reason we go to school is to learn science, math, reading, and writing.   Yoon-Hee   Gordon   both

C   Complete the sentences below with the correct word or phrase.

1. Many families in Korea spend a lot of money to send their children to _____ so that they can _____.

2. _____ believed that knowing how to _____, _____, and plant a garden were as important as studying _____ and science.

3. Many schools today have a minimum of _____ students in every classroom.

4. In a recent *National Geographic* article, only _____ % of people aged _____- _____ were able to find _____ on a map.

5. According to Gordon, too many of today's high school graduates are unable to _____ or _____.

D   Find the words in the reading. Then circle the word or phrase each is most similar to.

1. In line 1, *foster* is most similar in meaning to promote / discourage.
2. In line 12, *apply* is most similar in meaning to abandon / utilize.
3. In line 20, *cultivate* is most similar in meaning to develop / neglect.
4. In line 26, *goofing off* is most similar in meaning to studying seriously / playing around.
5. In line 31, *coherent* is most similar in meaning to logical / confusing.
6. In line 35, *a solid foundation* is most similar in meaning to a good knowledge / passing grades.

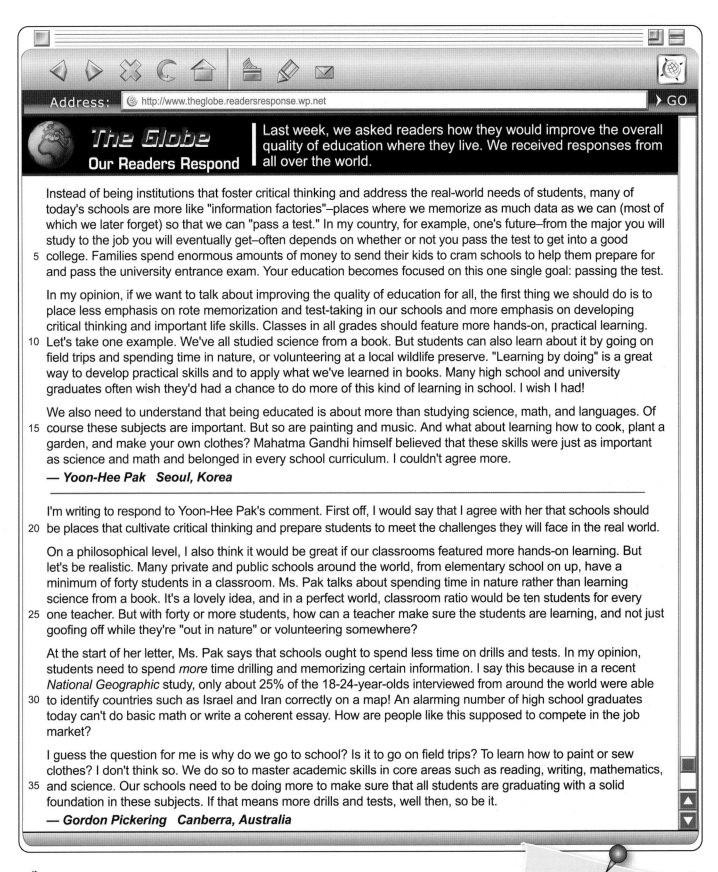

The Globe
Our Readers Respond

Last week, we asked readers how they would improve the overall quality of education where they live. We received responses from all over the world.

Instead of being institutions that foster critical thinking and address the real-world needs of students, many of today's schools are more like "information factories"–places where we memorize as much data as we can (most of which we later forget) so that we can "pass a test." In my country, for example, one's future–from the major you will study to the job you will eventually get–often depends on whether or not you pass the test to get into a good
5 college. Families spend enormous amounts of money to send their kids to cram schools to help them prepare for and pass the university entrance exam. Your education becomes focused on this one single goal: passing the test.

In my opinion, if we want to talk about improving the quality of education for all, the first thing we should do is to place less emphasis on rote memorization and test-taking in our schools and more emphasis on developing critical thinking and important life skills. Classes in all grades should feature more hands-on, practical learning.
10 Let's take one example. We've all studied science from a book. But students can also learn about it by going on field trips and spending time in nature, or volunteering at a local wildlife preserve. "Learning by doing" is a great way to develop practical skills and to apply what we've learned in books. Many high school and university graduates often wish they'd had a chance to do more of this kind of learning in school. I wish I had!

We also need to understand that being educated is about more than studying science, math, and languages. Of
15 course these subjects are important. But so are painting and music. And what about learning how to cook, plant a garden, and make your own clothes? Mahatma Gandhi himself believed that these skills were just as important as science and math and belonged in every school curriculum. I couldn't agree more.

— *Yoon-Hee Pak   Seoul, Korea*

I'm writing to respond to Yoon-Hee Pak's comment. First off, I would say that I agree with her that schools should
20 be places that cultivate critical thinking and prepare students to meet the challenges they will face in the real world.

On a philosophical level, I also think it would be great if our classrooms featured more hands-on learning. But let's be realistic. Many private and public schools around the world, from elementary school on up, have a minimum of forty students in a classroom. Ms. Pak talks about spending time in nature rather than learning science from a book. It's a lovely idea, and in a perfect world, classroom ratio would be ten students for every
25 one teacher. But with forty or more students, how can a teacher make sure the students are learning, and not just goofing off while they're "out in nature" or volunteering somewhere?

At the start of her letter, Ms. Pak says that schools ought to spend less time on drills and tests. In my opinion, students need to spend *more* time drilling and memorizing certain information. I say this because in a recent *National Geographic* study, only about 25% of the 18-24-year-olds interviewed from around the world were able
30 to identify countries such as Israel and Iran correctly on a map! An alarming number of high school graduates today can't do basic math or write a coherent essay. How are people like this supposed to compete in the job market?

I guess the question for me is why do we go to school? Is it to go on field trips? To learn how to paint or sew clothes? I don't think so. We do so to master academic skills in core areas such as reading, writing, mathematics,
35 and science. Our schools need to be doing more to make sure that all students are graduating with a solid foundation in these subjects. If that means more drills and tests, well then, so be it.

— *Gordon Pickering   Canberra, Australia*

▶ **Ask & Answer**

Whose point of view—Yoon-Hee's or Gordon's—do you agree with? Why?
If you were going to send a response to *The Globe* about improving the
overall quality of education where you live, what would you suggest?

Real English
so be it =
it should be that way

3 WRITING
Writing an opinion essay

A Do coed classes work better for boys and girls or should they be taught in separate classes? On a separate piece of paper make a list of the advantages and disadvantages of coed classes.

B Read this student's essay about coed schools and answer these questions.

1. What is the thesis statement of the essay?
2. What topic is discussed in paragraph 2? What examples are given?
3. What topic is discussed in paragraph 3? What examples are given?
4. What is the writer's opinion about coed schools?

Using a thesis statement

A thesis statement tells the reader the focus of your essay and what it's going to be about.

Essay
What are some of the advantages and disadvantages of coeducational schools? In your opinion, which are more important —the advantages or the disadvantages? Write about 250 words.

Until twenty years ago, coeducational schools were not common in my country. The modernization of our educational system means that now more boys and girls are going to school together. Attending a coed school has both advantages and disadvantages.

Coeducational schools have several important benefits. For one thing, students at these schools are better prepared for life after graduation. In the working world, we interact every day with both men and women, as supervisors, colleagues, and customers. Furthermore, diversity inside a school is very positive, not just as a preparation for work. There is much to be learned from contact with members of the opposite sex, because they may act and think differently from ourselves. And most importantly, coeducational schools are fair for everyone. All students, male and female, have access to the same teachers, courses, and opportunities.

Of course, there are also disadvantages of boys and girls studying together. Teachers and parents say that students are distracted by the presence of the opposite sex in the classroom. This can make it more difficult to concentrate on studying. A more serious problem with coed schools is that they can build stereotypes. Boys may not want to study art or music when girls are there, and girls may feel pressure to keep quiet in science classes.

In my opinion, though, the benefits far outweigh the disadvantages. Coeducational schools better prepare young people for the future, and at the same time, allow them to have a more enjoyable social life.

C Should students in secondary and high school wear uniforms? On a separate piece of paper make a list of the advantages and disadvantages of school uniforms.

D Use your list to write an essay of about 250 words answering the questions below.

What are some of the advantages and disadvantages of school uniforms?
In your opinion, should students be able to choose what to wear to school?

E Pair work. Exchange papers with a partner and make suggestions on how to improve your partner's essay.

4 COMMUNICATION

Activity 1: One-day workshop

A Pair work. Read the brochure to the right. What kind of workshop is being offered? Would you pay to attend? Why or why not?

B Pair work. You and your partner are going to design a one-day workshop. Choose a workshop type from the box below or create your own. Then discuss these questions.

1. By the end of the workshop, what should attendees be able to do?
2. What hours will the workshop be held? What are people going to do during different times? Design the course schedule. List specifics.
3. Who is going to be leading the workshop? Will you have guest speakers?
4. Do attendees need to have any experience or to bring anything to the workshop?
5. How many people in total can join the workshop?
6. What is the cost to attend?

Do you wish that you could take photos like a pro?

Join a Saturday workshop and cultivate your inner vision!

This one-day workshop emphasises hands-on learning. The morning hours are dedicated to exploring different subjects (human, natural settings, architecture, and others) and presenting various techniques, such as choice of camera, using natural light, and working with props. Attendees spend the afternoon in the field applying what they've learned.

Every Saturday from 9:00-6:00

Cost: $300
Experience: None required
Maximum class size: 10
Instructor(s): Award-winning photographers Elizabeth Yee, Anthony Parker, Satoru Watanabe, Juana Sandoval

---

Possible workshops

How to . . .
- find the perfect job
- date and find true love
- start your own online business
- think like a millionaire and make more money
- dance like a pro

- make the perfect meal
- master the art of calligraphy
- make and market your own movies
- look like a model
- speak [*name of language*] fluently

C Pair work. Using the information you discussed in B, design a simple brochure describing your workshop.

D Group work. Share your brochure and workshop schedule with at least four other pairs in your class. Answer their questions. Take notes about their workshops.

E Pair work. Choose one of the workshops to attend. Explain your choice to a partner.

Activity 2: Seven wishes and three hopes

Pair work. Complete the following seven wishes and three hopes with your own ideas. Then compare them with a partner.

I wish I had . . .　　*I wish I wasn't/weren't . . .*　　*I wish I could . . .*　　*I wish I was/were . . .*　　*I hope my teacher . . .*
I wish I hadn't . . .　　*I wish I knew . . .*　　　　　　　　*I wish I didn't . . .*　　*I hope the world . . .*　　*I hope my family . . .*

CNN Check out the CNN® video.　　**Practice your English online at** elt.heinle.com/worldpass

Unit 3: School and Beyond

A Match the university courses with the topics they include.

1. agriculture ___
2. political science ___
3. anthropology ___
4. psychology ___
5. engineering ___
6. accounting ___
7. zoology ___
8. environmental studies ___
9. economics ___
10. physics ___

a. the science of heat, energy, and light
b. how the governments of different countries operate
c. what causes prices to increase
d. designing and building machines, roads, bridges, etc.
e. the causes and effects of pollution
f. recording the income and expenses of a business
g. different types of animals and their bodies
h. similarities and differences in cultures
i. how to raise farm animals and plants
j. the human mind and how it works

B How did you do on the exam? Write the answers in the correct box, then circle the informal answers.

> Don't ask!   I aced it.   I passed. I failed.
> I flunked.   I did well.   I bombed.   I did very poorly.

🙂	☹️

> **I didn't know that!**
> The word *educate* comes from a Latin verb that means "lead out." It was believed that teachers led students out of their own world and into the world of knowledge.

C Where will these people study? Fill in the name of the institution, using your dictionary as necessary.

> technical college medical school   seminary   art academy
> dental school   university   military academy   law school

1. Alex wants to become a minister in his church. _____
2. Larissa would like to work as a lawyer for immigrants. _____
3. Omar hopes to become a doctor and work with children. _____
4. Brenda wants to study painting and drawing. _____
5. José is planning to study European history and politics. _____
6. Rosela wants to learn how to repair computers. _____
7. Young-Mi wants to help people keep their teeth healthy. _____
8. Dan intends to become an officer in his country's army. _____

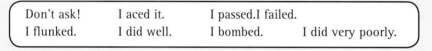

Incorrect: *Would you like to join us in a cup of coffee?*   **Correct:** *Would you like to join us for a cup of coffee?*

D Match these phrases with their meanings.

> **Word combinations with *education***
>
> 1. get an education ___   a. college and university
> 2. pay for an education ___   b. high school
> 3. primary education ___   c. go to school and complete your studies
> 4. secondary education ___   d. classes for older students
> 5. higher education ___   e. classes in sports and exercise
> 6. the standard of education ___   f. elementary school
> 7. adult education ___   g. the usual level of studies
> 8. physical education ___   h. give money for school tuition

E Use a form of one of the phrases from **D** to complete the sentences.

1. Many students in my country hope to go to foreign universities, because access to _____ here is very limited.
2. I want to work in _____ after I graduate, because I love to work with young children.
3. I never enjoyed my _____ classes in school, because I'm not very good at sports.
4. _____ in this country is coeducational. Boys and girls attend high school together.
5. My brother got a job to help _____. Tuition, books, and fees are very expensive here.
6. My mother really enjoys taking _____ courses at the community center. She's taken painting, French, and computer classes.
7. The _____ in my country is very high. Nearly everyone graduates from high school, and many students go on to university.
8. If girls in developing countries can _____, they are better prepared to get a job and help support their families.

> ### In Other Words
>
> A class is a period of teaching: *I have English class three times a week.*
> A lesson is a period of teaching a skill: *I've been taking tennis/cooking lessons on Saturdays.*
> In British English, lesson is used with a meaning similar to class: *Our math lesson is at 10:00 every day.*
> A course is a series of classes in a particular subject: *I'm taking a course in women's history.*
> A major is the main subject you study at a college or university: *Last year I changed my major from biology to environmental science.*
>
> Teacher is the most general term: *Ms. Diaz is my science/Spanish/drawing teacher.*
> A professor is a college or university teacher: *Dr. Yun is a professor of history at National University.*
> An instructor teaches a practical or physical skill: *My driving instructor is very patient with me!*
> A tutor gives private lessons: *The tutor comes to our house to give my son English lessons after school.*

> **Watch out!**
>
> faculty
> **Faculty** is a collective noun that refers to all the teachers in a particular academic program:
> > *Dr. Jones is a member of the faculty of the College of Agriculture.*
> It does not mean the academic program itself:
> > *I am a student in the ~~faculty~~ of medicine.*
> > *I am a student in the College of Medicine.*

Review: Units 1–3

1 LANGUAGE CHECK

There is a mistake in one of the underlined parts of each sentence. Rewrite the incorrect word or phrase correctly. Some sentences have no mistakes. Write OK next to them.

1. I really <u>wish</u> I <u>haven't spent</u> all my money on <u>those</u> shoes yesterday. _____ hadn't spent _____
2. We were <u>such disappointed</u> to hear <u>about</u> the <u>closing</u> of the old theater. _____
3. When you <u>didn't answer</u> the phone, I <u>knew</u> you <u>should have</u> gone out. _____
4. I <u>could have bought</u> the movie tickets last week, but I decided <u>to wait</u>. _____
5. We <u>should have remember to stop</u> the mail delivery before our vacation. _____
6. It's <u>such an</u> important book that everyone <u>should read</u> it. _____
7. I <u>hope I'd get</u> time off from work so that I <u>can</u> take a vacation. _____
8. I was completely <u>amazing to see</u> that I <u>had gotten</u> 100% on my quiz. _____
9. My best friend <u>got</u> married, but now she <u>wishes</u> she <u>is still</u> single. _____
10. <u>Don't</u> you <u>wish</u> you <u>had practiced</u> more before your driving test? _____
11. Johan <u>hopes</u> he <u>had spent</u> more time with his kids when they <u>were</u> little. _____
12. I <u>wish</u> I <u>didn't had to get</u> <u>up</u> so early every morning to go to class. _____
13. My parents <u>let us do</u> our homework every night before we <u>could</u> watch TV. _____
14. The soup was <u>so</u> spicy <u>as I couldn't</u> eat <u>much</u> of it. _____
15. We <u>shouldn't have taken</u> the kids <u>to see</u> such a <u>shocked</u> movie. _____

2 VOCABULARY CHECK

Read this summary and change and/or add to the word in parentheses to form an appropriate new word or phrase that fits in the context.

Last night, I watched a TV interview with Dexter Marshall, the director of the new movie *Dead and Gone*. He said he was (1. bore) _____ bored with _____ making Hollywood-style blockbuster movies, so he decided to shoot an old-fashioned detective movie in black and white. It's a very (2. disturb) _____ story, about the murder of an old man. It was (3. relative) _____ easy for him to find people to work on the movie. In fact, a lot of the actors are household names, and the cast really (4. bond) _____ each other while making the movie. One (5. draw) _____ of this project being in black and white was that it was necessary to have special costumes made for the black-and-white film.

Marshall had a lot of trouble finding a company that was interested in the movie. He said it was (6. nerve) _____ trying to get a studio to give him money. They said moviegoers had a lot of (7. expect) _____ about what a movie should be like, and this was too different. It took them months to (8. strike a) _____ about how to produce the movie, even though Marshall had (9. first) _____ experience from making black-and-white movies before he (10. drop) _____ of film school.

In the interview, he didn't (11. give) _____ the ending of the movie though—he said it would be out next month, and we should see for ourselves. It was really a (12. fascinate) _____ interview. I never realized how much happens behind the scenes of a big movie.

Situation 2

Situation 1

You are taking a vacation with your family next month, and you want to rent a car while you are there. Call a car rental company to make a reservation.

You and your partner are officers of the National Association of TV Fans. Every year, the association gives the Comedy Awards for the three funniest shows on TV. Work together to choose this year's winners.

Situation 3

You want to get a part-time job as an English tutor for children. You go to a job interview with the program's director.

A Pair work. Look at the pictures and imagine what the people in each situation might say. Then briefly review the language notes from Units 1–3 on pages 154–155.

B Pair work. Role-play situations 1, 2, and 3 with a partner. Notice how well you and your partner do the role play. Ask your partner's opinion about your performance.

C Now rate your speaking. Use + for good, ✓ for OK, and – for things you need to improve. Then add two goals for the improvement of your speaking.

How did you do?	1	2	3
I was able to express my ideas.			
I spoke easily and fluently, without hesitation.			
I spoke at a good rate of speed—not too fast or too slow.			
I used new vocabulary from the units.			
I used at least three expressions from the units.			
I practiced the grammar from the units.			
Goals for improvement:			
1. _____			
2. _____			

Contemporary Issues

Lesson A | In the city

1 VOCABULARY FOCUS

I can get it for free.

 WARM UP

What kind of music do you like to listen to? Has the way you listen to or purchase music changed in the past five years? How?

A Pair work. **Read this article about a controversy and answer the questions with a partner.**

1. What is the problem?
2. What are the two opposing viewpoints?

strict about something

Recently, companies in the recording industry have begun cracking down on people who download music for free on the Internet. It made the news recently when two dozen college students were taken to court for downloading copyrighted music and movies. Their case is still pending and the outcome is uncertain. It remains to be seen whether this case will have an effect on how and where consumers get their music in the future.

produce, making

Is downloading a crime? Critics argue that for years, the music industry has churned out mainstream fare that is mediocre and too expensive. Due to downloading, companies are panicking because they are losing their

独占

monopoly on music production. These large corporations are greedy, say critics, and are simply afraid of losing control.

cheat, not worth

Others argue that the artists and those who produce the products must be compensated fairly for their work. When you download music for free, you rip off the people who make the music by robbing them of their income. Supporters of this argument remind us that unauthorized copying of music is not only unethical—it's also illegal! Not all of the companies making music products are huge corporations, after all. Small companies, which often feature emerging artists, are also hurt.

(popular
新興

B **Find an expression in blue in A that means:**

1. poor in quality *mediocre* 一良くも悪くもな
2. waiting to be decided *pending* 未解決
3. beginning to be known or noticed *emerging*
4. not officially approved *unauthorized*
5. strictly enforcing laws *cracking down*
6. cheat *rip off*
7. wanting more money, control, or power *greedy* 貪欲

8. had legal action taken against *taken to court*
9. produced quickly without attention to quality *churned out*
10. complete control by a business or group of businesses *monopoly*
11. not morally right *unethical*
12. feeling fear and anxiety *panicking*
13. given payment *compensated*
14. people who buy things *consumers*

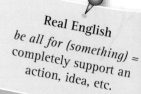
Real English
be all for (something) = completely support an action, idea, etc.

C Group work. **In the same article in A, there was a poll. Read the polling options below and vote for the one you agree with most. Then share your answers as a group.**

Reader's Poll: What do you think about downloading music from the Internet for free? Check the opinion you agree with.

☐ I'm against it. Downloading music from the Internet rips off the people who make the music.

☐ I think we need to compromise. Downloading music is good for emerging artists and consumers.

☐ I don't know. Downloading lets us listen to different kinds of music, but maybe we should pay something.

☐ I'm all for it. The Internet is about the free sharing of ideas.

>>> Vocabulary Builder ▲

Pair work. **Read these expressions that contain the words** *eye* **and** *see*.
Then work with a partner to use them to complete the story below.

> **remains to be seen** = is not certain (what will happen)
> **saw eye to eye** = agreed; had the same opinion
> **turned a blind eye** = pretended not to notice (bad behavior)
> **wait and see** = be patient
>
> **have seen the light** = understood something
> **opened my eyes** = made me aware of
> **see what I can do** = try to help

Two weeks ago I received a letter from a large record company. I was being taken to court for breaking the law.
My crime? Downloading free music from the Internet!

I couldn't believe it. I'm only a college student. I've never been in trouble before. But I guess this has been a
problem for a while. At first, the music industry (1) _turned a blind eye_ to the problem. Now they are doing
something about it.

I met my lawyer last week. "Will I have to pay a big fine?" I asked. "I don't know," he said. "That
(2) _remains to be seen_." He assured me, "I'll do my best–I'll (3) _see what I can do_." Fortunately, we all
(4) _saw eye to eye_ on one thing: no one wants to see me put in jail for this! That's a relief.

Even though I'm anxious, there's nothing I can do about it now. I'll just have to (5) _wait and see_.
This experience has really (6) _opened my eyes_ to the seriousness of downloading music illegally. Before I
received the letter, I was unaware of it. I can also say that I finally (7) _have seen the light_ when it comes to free
downloading: I'm going to stop doing it!

2 LISTENING

Our cities are growing.

A Pair work. **Read and discuss these two predictions with a partner.**
Do you think these trends are positive or negative? Why?

- According to U.N.-Habitat, 60% of the world's population will be living in cities by 2030.
- The urban population will grow from 2.86 billion to nearly five billion.

B Listen. **Two experts are being interviewed about unchecked urban growth. Which of the four statements represents
the *main* point Fiona is trying to make? Which statement best represents Hector's opinion?** (CD Tracks 11 & 12)

1. Fiona __   a. Good planning can solve urban problems.   c. It's more violent in our cities.
2. Hector __   b. We must limit the growth of our cities.   d. A more organized transportation system is the key.

C Listen again. **Complete each statement the speaker makes.** (CD Track 13)

1. Fiona
   a. In this city, for example, there's a serious _____.
   b. This unchecked urban sprawl destroys _____ for the city.

2. Hector
   a. There's widespread _____ and lack of _____.
   b. Since 1989, the citizens there have worked together to raise the _____.
   c. We can build and coordinate _____ that don't pollute the
      environment as much.

▶ **Ask & *Answer***

What issues are facing urban areas in your country? If you were an
urban planner, what improvements would you suggest for your city?

Past and present unreal conditionals

A   Study the grammar charts. Then answer the questions below.

Present unreal conditional		
if clause	main clause	meaning
If I had a car, If I were presenting in English, If I could graduate early,	I'd be happy to drive. I might be nervous. I'd do it.	*I don't have a car.* *I will probably be presenting in Spanish.* *Graduating early is unlikely.*

Past unreal conditional		
if clause	main clause	meaning
If I had passed the test, If I had been presenting in English,	I would've been happy. I might have been nervous.	*I failed the test.* *I presented in Spanish.*

1. Which verb forms can be used in the *if* clauses? Which modal forms can be used in the main clauses?
2. Which conditional do we use to talk about present or future situations that are improbable? Which one do we use to talk about situations in the past that could have happened but didn't?

B   Nick is unhappy living alone in the city. Read his letter to a friend. Underline the examples of the present unreal conditional. Circle the examples of the past unreal conditional.

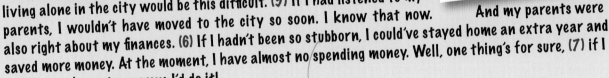

Dear Ben,

   Today marks one month in the city. It's been very difficult. First of all, I don't know anyone. (1) If I had some friends here, I might be happier. My new job has been disappointing, too. (2) If the work were more interesting, the job would be bearable. But I can't stand it! I don't like this part of the city either. (3) If I were living in a more exciting neighborhood, it might be interesting. Basically, everything around here closes around 7 P.M. so there's nothing to do but stay home and watch TV.

   (4) If you had asked me before, I never would've predicted that living alone in the city would be this difficult. (5) If I had listened to my parents, I wouldn't have moved to the city so soon. I know that now. And my parents were also right about my finances. (6) If I hadn't been so stubborn, I could've stayed home an extra year and saved more money. At the moment, I have almost no spending money. Well, one thing's for sure, (7) if I could move home tomorrow, I'd do it!

Nick

P.S. Come and visit me. I'm lonely!

C   Pair work. Look again at the numbered sentences in the letter and write *T* for true or *F* for false for the statements below. Explain your answers to a partner.

1. _T_ Nick wishes he had some friends.
2. _T_ He wishes his job were more interesting.
3. _T_ He wishes his neighborhood were more interesting.
4. _F_ He isn't surprised that living in the city is hard.

5. _T_ He wishes he hadn't taken his parents' advice
6. _T_ He thinks he was stubborn.
7. _F_ He likes his independence in the city.

D Pair work. With a partner, correct these conditional sentences so that they make sense.

1. Class was canceled. If someone told me yesterday, I wouldn't have shown up at school today.
2. If I hadn't argued with my boss, I still had a job.
3. If I would be doing better in class, I'd be getting an A.
4. If the city wouldn't be so expensive, we weren't moving to the country.

E Read about this creative solution to a problem in London. Then rewrite the sentences that follow.

London News—At certain subway stations in the city, there has been a problem with gang members hanging around and causing trouble. Officials have cracked down on the problem, using a creative solution. They pipe classical music loudly throughout the station, and it seems to drive away the troublemakers. Passengers feel safer and the city doesn't waste money on taking people to court.

1. Kids are bored, so they hang out in gangs.
   If kids weren't bored, they wouldn't hang out in gangs.

2. They skip school, so they don't get a proper education.
   _____

3. They cause trouble, so the subway passengers are scared of them.
   _____

4. A few months ago officials piped classical music into the stations, so the problem was solved.
   _____

5. The kids didn't like that kind of music, so they left the stations.
   _____

6. It has been so successful that it has been copied in Australia and Canada as well.
   _____

F Pair work. Talk to your partner about these issues in your city. Use conditionals where appropriate.

> If they hadn't cracked down on unauthorized street parking, the traffic problems would be worse.

traffic	urban sprawl	graffiti	noise
crime	transportation	trash pickup	gangs

Grammar X-TRA ▸ Low possibility

If it **happens** to rain that day, we'll cancel the picnic.
If it **should (happen to)** rain that day, we **might** cancel the picnic.
If I **were to** move to France, I'd study French before I left.

These structures are used for future conditional sentences indicating situations that probably won't happen or have a low possibility of happening.

Your friend Wally is a chronic worrier. He's going on a trip. Read his worries and answer him using a future conditional.

1. What if I miss the bus to the airport?
2. What if my flight is delayed?
3. What if I lose my passport?
4. What if I get homesick?

> If you happen to miss the bus to the airport, I'll give you a ride.

4 SPEAKING
Without a doubt

A Pair work. *One-Minute Message* is a TV program that lets viewers speak their minds on current issues for only one minute or less. Read the interview and then discuss the questions below with a partner.

Host: Today, our topic is the proposed city law that would ban smoking in all public buildings, and our guests have a lot to say on the subject. What do you think, Andrew?

Andrew: I'm convinced that the anti-smoking law is a terrible idea. The government keeps taking away more and more of our freedom. Just wait—in a few years, they'll have a law against eating pizza or french fries because they're unhealthy, or a law against watching too much TV! Next they'll start telling us what color our houses can be, or our cars. Politicians shouldn't be allowed to interfere with our personal lives like that. The government has a lot of stupid ideas, and this is another one of them.

Host: Thanks! That's all there's time for. And our next guest is Tomas. What's your opinion?

Tomas: Without a doubt, we need this law, because it will provide cleaner air for everybody. When people smoke indoors, everybody suffers, including nonsmokers. There's a lot of research that shows that breathing other people's smoke is harmful, especially to children. Smokers say they have a right to enjoy a cigarette, and that's fine, as long as other people aren't affected. But it isn't right for smokers to pollute the air in public spaces and harm other people's health.

Host: Time's up! Thank you very much. And one more point of view, Cassie.

Cassie: I think it would be better just to ban smoking in a few places—for instance, hospitals, because they're full of sick people. But when people go to a club or restaurant, they should be able to smoke if they feel like it. Of course, smoking shouldn't be allowed in taxis, or buses. Not only that, but I really hate it when people smoke on the train, because it gives me a headache. I don't smoke, so if they passed the law, it wouldn't really be a problem for me.

1. Who do you think gave the best message?
2. What made this message effective?
3. How could the other speakers explain their opinions more effectively?

B What do you think? Mark your opinions on these issues, and make notes of your reasons.

1. Should people be allowed to purchase guns and keep them in their homes?
   - ☐ Yes   ☐ No   ☐ Only if . . .
   Reasons: _____

2. Should city governments take steps to control urban growth?
   - ☐ Yes   ☐ No   ☐ Only if . . .
   Reasons: _____

3. Should scientists assist women over 40 who want to have children?
   - ☐ Yes   ☐ No   ☐ Only if . . .
   Reasons: _____

C Group work. In groups of four, role-play the *One-Minute Message* show using the issues in B. One student is the host who asks a question and times the speakers while they give their opinions. Change roles and practice again until you've covered all of the topics. Try to use some of the expressions in the box.

D Now think of an issue that is important to you and give a one-minute message about it to the whole class.

Expressing an opinion	
Stating your opinion	**Giving additional reasons**
I strongly believe . . .	*Not only that, but . . .*
I'm convinced that . . .	*Not to mention the fact that . . .*
Without a doubt, . . .	*And besides, . . .*
Illustrating your point	
For instance . . .	
Take, for example, . . .	
To give you an idea . . .	

UNIT 4

Contemporary Issues

Lesson B | Conflict resolution

1 GET READY TO READ

What's going on here?

Think of a conflict you've been involved in recently.
What was it about? How did you resolve it?

A Pair work. The words and expressions in the box are all related to conflict. Which ones do you know?
Look up the ones you don't know in a dictionary. Then discuss the meaning of each with a partner.

hurt a person with you fists   _mostly face_   _beginning of the fight_   _war situation soldiers_   _say "something wrong" in front of_   _big fight physical_

beat (someone) up	clash	combat	confront	get into a brawl
harass	intimidate	lose your temper	pick on	threaten

spoken offensive threatening   _shoves feeling scary_   _can't be patient any more_   _bullying deliberately annoy someone_   _威胁_

B Pair work. Look at the photos and describe what is happening in each.
Use the words and phrases from A as well as ideas of your own.

C Pair work. Discuss these questions.

1. How do you think each conflict in the photos started?
2. What could be done to defuse or resolve each problem?
3. Do you think each situation could have been prevented? If so, how?

Lesson B • Conflict resolution   **45**

Bullying—what can you do about it?

A   Pair work. What do you think *bullying* means? Agree on a definition for the word with your partner and write it on the line below. Then read the first two paragraphs of the article on page 47. How does the definition of bullying compare with yours?

_____

B   Now read about the three people on page 47 and complete the first two columns of the chart.

	How was he or she being bullied?	What did he or she do about the bullying?	Helpful in dealing with bullying?
Mayumi			
Adam		fought with the bullies	
Blanca			

C   Look at your answers in the second column in B. Did these actions help each person to deal with the bullying in some productive, helpful way? Write *yes* or *no* in the last column.

D   The words and expressions in the box are all in the reading. Make sure you understand their meaning. Then complete the sentences with the correct form of each one.

> fitting in (line 16)   insecure (line 48)   opponent (line 55)   behind my back (line 65)   dreading (line 68)

1. Chee's _____ the university entrance exam. He's sure he won't pass.
2. Jill is more interested in developing her own style than with _____ with the other girls.
3. Just before the match, Lynn's _____ became ill, and so the game had to be rescheduled.
4. If you're angry with Marco, tell him why. Don't talk about him _____.
5. Even though Trey is a smart, outgoing person, he becomes very shy and _____ whenever he has to talk in front of a group.

E   Complete these sentences with the correct word or phrase from the reading.

1. In line 2, *one* refers to _____.
2. In line 10, *Others* refers to _____.
3. In line 23, *it* refers to _____.
4. In line 49, *it* refers to _____.
5. In line 64, *it* refers to _____.

The problem of bullying goes beyond childhood and adolescence. At the age of thirty, people who were bullies as children are five times more likely to have been convicted of a serious crime as non-bullies.

Source: *Maine Project Against Bullying*

▶ **Ask & *Answer***

What would you have done if you were in the situations featured in the reading?
What are other things people can do to stop or prevent bullying?

4 Special Report

Bullying— what can you do about it?

Real English
keep an eye on (someone) =
look after or take care of someone
dork = nerdy, socially awkward person
lost it = got really angry

Bullies. If you haven't been the victim of one, you may know someone who has. Bullying is the act of one person or a group of people repeatedly picking on another. A bully creates an environment of fear and intimidation in order to feel powerful and in control.

Victims of bullying often deal with different types of harassment including constant teasing, name calling, or physical abuse. Others are the subject of hurtful (usually untrue) rumors.

New Kid on the Block

Mayumi Sato, 11, recently returned to Japan with her family after six years in Germany, where her father was working. Now attending middle school in Tokyo, she initially had a difficult time fitting in. "Most of the kids in Mayumi's class had gone to the same schools and grown up together, so I'm not surprised that they saw my daughter as different at first," says Mayumi's mother, Hiroko. "But some of the kids were just mean. They teased her in class and picked on her in the schoolyard." At first, Mayumi tried to ignore it, but then she finally told her mother what was going on. "I'm glad she came to me," Hiroko says. "You know, a lot of kids would be too embarrassed to talk about something like this. But if you're being bullied, you *do* need to talk about it—to a parent, a friend, or someone you trust—so that something can be done." Hiroko spoke to one of the girl's teachers, who promised to keep an eye on Mayumi and to encourage the kids in the class to be more welcoming towards her. This approach seems to be working. "Mayumi's been doing better in school and is making friends," says Hiroko. "She's definitely happier than she was those first few weeks."

On the defense

After being picked on for months by a group of older boys at the high school he goes to, Adam Wheeland, 15, had had enough. "These three guys were always calling me *dork* in the hallways and threatening to beat me up. One day I came to school, and they'd glued my locker shut. They were standing nearby laughing, and I lost it. I got into a fight with one of them." Wheeland and the other boy were suspended from school for two days for fighting. When they returned, the trouble continued. Wheeland realized he needed to approach the situation differently. "The thing about bullies is that they're often very insecure people. These guys who've been harassing me only do it when they're together. So I try to stay in a group with my friends now. Wheeland, who is a straight-A student, has also decided he needs to do things that boost his self-confidence. He's joined the debate club and is taking a martial-arts class. "Now when I see those guys around school, I think of them as the opponent in a competition. I feel less nervous, and I think they've noticed that."

Trouble at work

Thirty-year-old Blanca Montero, an up-and-coming civil engineer at Allied Systems, was assigned recently to work on a team project with Brett—a colleague who had joined the company around the same time she had. Almost immediately, there were problems. "Whenever I disagreed with his ideas, Brett became very argumentative. It was really difficult," says Montero. "Then he started complaining about me behind my back—you know, telling others that my work was second-rate." In a month, Montero went from loving her job to dreading every day. She finally decided to confront Brett about his behavior. "I scheduled a time to speak to him. Actually, before we got together, I thought about what I was going to say so that I could stay calm during our meeting." On the day they met, Montero explained the situation to Brett. "I asked how he'd feel if I—or others on the team—attacked his ideas or spread rumors about him. Though he didn't say much during our talk, he did listen and promised to work on being more considerate." So have things changed? "I've noticed that Brett is trying to be more aware of his behavior—and not just with me, but with others on the team, too. Things aren't perfect," says Montero, "but I'm glad we spoke. If we hadn't, I suspect I would've lost my temper at some point or quit the project."

Lesson B • Conflict resolution   **47**

A Pair work. **Discuss these questions with a partner.**

1. Do you ever read online message boards? What kinds of things do people discuss there?
2. Why do people like to post on message boards? Do you ever post, or do you just *lurk* (read without answering)?

B **Read these posts on a message board and answer the questions.**

1. What solution does each writer propose?
2. What reasons do the writers give to support their ideas?

PARENTS.net

Message Board

Today's hot issue: Research has found that 23% of schoolchildren worldwide say they've been bullied at some time. What can schools and communities do about this problem?

Astrid Haugen – *Oslo, Norway*:
There's only one answer to bullying: expel the bullies from school.

Kids need to learn that this behavior is unacceptable. If even minor acts of bullying had serious consequences, parents would keep a closer eye on their children's behavior. Furthermore, kids would be more likely to tell someone that they were being bullied if they knew that there would be a quick solution to their problem.

Many bullies grow up to become violent adults. This kind of behavior must be stopped as soon as it starts.

Eiji Yamada – *Tokyo, Japan*:
I disagree—expelling bullies won't help. Children who bully others have psychological problems, and they need treatment, not punishment.

Instead, we need to educate our children about the harm that bullying causes. Kids must learn to take the problem seriously, and tell a teacher if they see a bullying incident. Also, they must feel a responsibility to help classmates who are being teased and picked on.

All of our children need to feel safe and comfortable at school if they are going to get an education.

Gena Robinson – *Auckland, New Zealand*:
I have one question: Where are the teachers when bullying is taking place? Why aren't they supervising our children?

Without a doubt, class sizes are too large, and teachers are forced to spend too much time on bureaucratic paperwork. Because of this, there are a lot of places in school where no one is watching out for kids—such as lunchrooms, hallways, and playgrounds. It's a known fact that this is where most bullying takes place.

If teachers had time to pay attention to each child, bullying problems would be easier to control.

C Write your own post to this message board on another sheet of paper. State your opinion on what to do about bullying, and give reasons to support your opinion. Add a conclusion.

D Pair work. Exchange posts with a partner and make suggestions for improvements.

A Group work. Get into a group of three people. Choose one of these roles and read about your part as well as the other two.

Person A: You live in apartment 304 and are married with a nine-month-old baby. Both you and your spouse have to get up at 7:00 A.M. to go to work and take the baby to day care. Your neighbor who lives in apartment 404 makes a lot of noise after midnight—talking and laughing with friends, playing music or watching television. This is keeping you and your family awake—particularly the baby—whose room is just below Person B's living room. The noise has been going on for months, and even though you've left your neighbor notes asking him/her to be quieter, little has changed.

Person B: You live in apartment 404. You work the night shift at a restaurant (which pays more than the day shift), and don't typically get home until after midnight. Though you try to be quiet so that you don't disturb your neighbor in 304, it takes time for you to unwind when you get home from work. You can't go directly to bed. Also, since many places are closed when you finish work, you often have no choice but to go back to your apartment with friends to hang out and talk. Recently, your neighbor in 304 has been leaving you nasty notes. You feel that your neighbor is being unreasonable—especially since he/she is quite noisy in the mornings and argues frequently with his/her spouse—particularly on weekends—when you have time off.

The Building Manager: You manage the apartment building that Persons A and B live in. Person A has come to complain to you about Person B. You've called them together to discuss the problem. Your role is to help the two sides resolve their dispute. Before you meet, make a list of solutions that you could suggest to Person A and Person B.

B Group work. Follow the directions to do the exercise below. Try to use some of the language for suggesting a compromise.

The Building Manager
- Begin by asking both sides to state their names and to explain their situations.
- Refer to the list of solutions you created. Suggest these to Person A and Person B. Work with them to reach a compromise that will satisfy both.

Person A and Person B
- Explain your situation to the Building Manager and your neighbor in your own words.
- When the Building Manager offers possible solutions, think about your position, and answer with your opinion. Offer other ideas if appropriate.

Would it be possible to work a different shift at the restaurant?

But if I did that, I wouldn't...

Suggesting a compromise

Would it be possible to . . . ?
If he/she were to . . . , would you consider (verb)-ing?
Are you willing to . . . if he/she . . . ?
If he/she should happen to . . . , would you . . . ?

C Group work. Get together with another group and discuss whether or not you were able to reach a compromise or not. If so, what was it? If not, why not?

CNN® Check out the CNN® video. **Practice your English online at** elt.heinle.com/worldpass

Unit 4: Contemporary Issues

A Study the phrases in the box and then use them to complete the sentences below.

Word combinations with *peace*			
live in peace	work for peace	a plea for peace	a threat to peace
a peace treaty	the peace process	peace talks	a symbol of peace

1. At the _____, diplomats are discussing ways to resolve the conflict and end the war.
2. For many people, the white dove is _____.
3. After he was elected president, Nelson Mandela worked to help the people of South Africa _____ together.
4. The presidents of the two countries met in Geneva to sign _____ that ended five years of war.
5. Conflicts over scarce natural resources are _____ in many parts of the world.
6. The attack was carried out by a group that is opposed to _____ and is trying to start fighting again.
7. Doctors Without Borders _____ by helping all people injured in a conflict, without taking sides.
8. A group of mothers of soldiers made _____ and called for an end to the fighting.

B Review these words from the listening passage "Our cities are growing" on page 41.
Then use them to complete the sentences.

unchecked	sustainable	forefront	revitalize	slum
proposition	engage in	widespread	advocate (n)	overall

1. We need to _____ our cities by building new businesses and better housing in the city center.
2. In the _____ areas of many large cities, people live without electricity, clean water, or safe housing.
3. The capital of my country is experiencing _____ growth because thousands of people move there from the countryside every month.
4. UNICEF accepts the _____ that all children have a right to good health and a good education.
5. Some people in Brazil _____ a process called *participatory democracy* by working together to plan their cities.
6. _____, the world's largest cities are continuing to grow rapidly.
7. Many cities suffer from _____ poverty and a lack of housing.
8. In many countries, women are in the _____ of the environmental movement, and have started many new organizations.
9. The Dalai Lama is a well-known _____ for world peace.
10. If something is _____, it can continue for a long time without harming the environment.

> **There's an old saying . . .** *The squeaky wheel gets the grease.*
> If you don't complain about a bad situation, nothing will be done about it. We use this saying to tell someone that they should speak up about a problem.
> "Our boss has made me work every Saturday for the last month. It's not fair!"
> "Well, *the squeaky wheel gets the grease.* You had better say something about it before he writes the schedule for next week."

C English has many expressions involving *ears* and *hearing*. **Match these expressions and their meanings.**

1. turn a deaf ear ___
2. I'm all ears. ___
3. I heard it through the grapevine. ___
4. be up to your ears in something ___
5. It went in one ear and out the other. ___
6. have someone's ear ___
7. grin from ear to ear ___
8. lend a sympathetic ear ___
9. I've heard that one before! ___

a. I'm very interested to hear what you're saying.
b. the person will accept your advice and ideas
c. refuse to listen
d. have far too much of something
e. have a very big smile
f. I don't believe that excuse or explanation.
g. It was a rumor.
h. listen in a kind, friendly way
i. I forgot it as soon as I heard it.

D Use a form of one of the expressions from **C** to complete these sentences.

1. Don't tell me you left your homework on the train. _____.
2. I told my boss about the problems with the new computer system, but he _____.
   He said it worked perfectly.
3. My uncle gave us 20 kg of carrots from his farm. Now we _____ in carrots!
4. I knew you were going to get a promotion. _____ last week.
5. Whenever I have a problem, I talk to my older sister. She always _____.
6. Tell me about your date with Rick! _____.
7. When I saw Debbie, she was _____ because she had just won $5,000 in the lottery.
8. He told me his phone number, but _____, and now I can't remember it.
9. Professor Park _____ of many business leaders, and gives them advice about the economy.

> ### In Other Words
>
> A conflict is a state of disagreement between people or groups: *The conflict in the Middle East has continued for over 50 years.*
> An argument is an angry spoken disagreement: *I had a big argument with my parents because they don't want me to buy a car.*
> Uninterested means not interested: *I'm completely uninterested in baseball. I think it's boring.*
> A fight can have a symbolic meaning (as in *fight for women's rights*), but it also means a physical conflict: *Two men were having a fight in the street outside the bar.*
>
> ---
>
> If something is illegal, it is against the laws of a place: *In my city, smoking in restaurants is illegal.*
> If something is unethical, it is morally wrong: *I think it's unethical for teachers to accept presents from their students in exchange for a better grade.*
> Unauthorized means without permission from the person or authority: *Jess was reprimanded by the boss for making unauthorized personal phone calls during work time.*

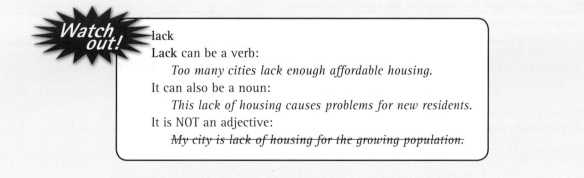

Watch out!

lack
Lack can be a verb:
  Too many cities lack enough affordable housing.
It can also be a noun:
  This lack of housing causes problems for new residents.
It is NOT an adjective:
  ~~My city is lack of housing for the growing population.~~

In Other Words

Lesson A | Total immersion

1 VOCABULARY FOCUS

What languages are you studying?

WARM UP

What are the most difficult factors about learning a foreign language?

A Pair work. Read about these people's experiences learning a foreign language. Pay attention to the words and phrases in blue. Then discuss these questions with a partner.

1. What languages is each person studying now and why?
2. How would you describe each person's approximate language level in that language now? Explain your reasons.

Greg Anderson, 19: I'm studying ASL. My professor says that while I may be able to convey basic ideas by signing, I won't be truly proficient for another two or three years. Most of the deaf people I've met have been so patient with my halting ability to sign. This summer I'm going to study at a university for the deaf and hard of hearing. I'll be immersed in deaf culture—and am hoping this will help me to improve skills.

Guy Lagace, 23: I'm French Canadian. My primary language is French and I speak passable English at work. My high school Spanish, however, was pretty rusty, so last summer I spent a month in Guatemala brushing up on the language. At the end of my stay, I could carry on basic conversations. Not bad for only a month of studying.

Akemi Sato, 24: Japanese is my mother tongue. Growing up in Japan, I studied English. At college, I felt that it was important to master at least one other foreign language. On a whim, I decided to study Chinese. Now I am working in China as a Japanese teacher. When I first got here, it was difficult for me to retain words—I was always forgetting new vocabulary.

B Pair work. With a partner, divide the words and phrases in blue from the profiles in A into the following categories:

Adjectives that describe language level or ability: __proficient__ _halting, passable, rusty_
Verbs that describe using or learning a language: _convey, carry on, brushing up on, master, retain_
Words that describe one's first language: _primary language, mother tongue_

C Group work. What is the best way to learn a foreign language? Read the opinions and rank them from 1 (strongly agree) to 5 (strongly disagree). Discuss your answers.

1. _4_ Focus exclusively on the new language from the beginning. Don't depend on dictionaries.
2. _1_ Immerse yourself in the language and culture. It's the only way to really become proficient.
3. _5_ You only need to be able to carry on a basic conversation. Concentrate on learning how to do this.
4. _3_ The key to learning any language is to retain what you've studied, so take notes and memorize.
5. _2_ To master a foreign language, spend all your time with speakers of that language.

Vocabulary Builder ▲

A. Pair work. Acronyms and initialisms are types of abbreviations. Use words from the columns to construct the acronyms and initialisms below. Explain your answers to a partner.

1st word		2nd word		3rd word		4th word
air	personal	be	soon	announced	machine	Friday
as	thank	conditioning	teller	as	number	possible
automated	to	God		it's		
		identification				

1. AC = _air conditioning_
2. ASAP = _as soon as possible_
3. ATM = _Automated teller machine_
4. PIN = _personal Identity number_
5. TBA = _To Be Announced_
6. TGIF = _Thank God It's Friday_

B. Which of the items in **A** might you hear or see:

   a. in an office?   **b.** at a bank?   **c.** in an airport?

2 LISTENING
A TV show about language

A You will hear five short excerpts from a TV series on words and language. Which episode does each excerpt come from? Listen and check the correct boxes. (CD Tracks 14 & 15)

	1	2	3	4	5
Episode 1: *Language and Personal Identity*	✓	☐	☐	✓	☐
Episode 2: *The History of the English Language*	☐	☐	✓	☐	☐
Episode 3: *Endangered and Dead Languages*	☐	✓	☐	☐	✓

B Listen several times (if necessary) and complete these profiles with the correct information. (CD Track 16)

1. Pilar was born in ___Mexico___ and grew up speaking ___Spanish___ at home, but ___English___ outside her home. Today, she works as a ___Salesrepresent___ for a ___Spanish language TV station___

2. The local island language in Guernsey is a dialect of Norman ___French___. The ___young___ don't learn the language and usually ___leave___ the island to ___work___ on the mainland.

3. Many expressions in ___English___ come from Shakespeare. Many people may be familiar with the expression *one quickly fell swoop*, but they probably don't know the ___origin___ of the word *fell* and what it means.

4. Although Doruk grew up in ___Turkey___, he now lives in ___Germany___, where he doesn't speak the ___language___ so well. He may have a German ___passport___, but he ___doesn't feel___ it's his true identity.

5. ___Latin___ is a dead language, but some people are trying to bring it back. Teachers believe that it teaches students ___analitical___ skills. They plan to use the ___internet___ to get students interested in studying.

▶ Ask & Answer
Should efforts be made to revive languages that are dying out? Why or why not?
How much of your personal identity is connected to the language you speak?

A Read the sentences and underline the adverb clauses. Write *T* for a time clause and *R* for a reason clause.

1. Before he was accepted to college, he studied a lot. __T__
2. He worked part-time while he was attending college. __T__
3. Because he was a good student, he won a scholarship to study abroad. __R__
4. He became an interpreter after he graduated from college. __T__
5. Since he worked in the UN Building, he lived in New York City. __R__
6. Because he didn't like New York, he moved to Geneva. __R__

reason

Adverb clauses

- Adverb clauses of time and reason tell when or why something happened. They modify the verb or the main clause in a sentence.
- Many adverb clauses beginning with *before, after, while, because,* and *since* can be reduced and retain the same meaning.

B Now look at the same sentences. The adverb clauses have been reduced in each case. Notice how the sentences are different from those in **A**.

1. Before ~~he was~~ being accepted to college, he studied a lot.
2. He worked part-time while ~~he was~~ attending college.
3. ~~Because he was~~ Being a good student, he won a scholarship to study abroad.
4. He became an interpreter after ~~he graduated~~ graduating from college.
5. ~~Since he worked~~ Working in the UN Building, he lived in New York City.
6. ~~Because he didn't like~~ Not liking New York, he moved to Geneva.

C Read these sentences. Underline the subject of each clause and rewrite the sentence if it can be reduced.

1. After their language died out, the villagers tried to revive it.
   can't be reduced

2. Because many expressions in English come from his plays, we should study Shakespeare.
   _____

3. While she spoke Spanish at home, she used English exclusively at work.
   _____

4. Since he moved to Germany two years ago, he's struggled to learn the language.
   _____

5. Before the students took the test, their teacher warned them it would be difficult.
   _____

6. After I mastered Korean, I decided to study Chinese.
   _____

7. Because he studied hard, John passed the test.
   _____

8. Since my mother couldn't speak French, she couldn't communicate with the local people.
   _____

9. Because their parents speak Chinese at home, many second-generation Chinese-Americans grow up speaking the language.
   _____

D Study the information in the box below.

Reduced adverb clauses with present (-*ing*) and past (-*ed*) participles		
present participle	The car drove into a tree at a high speed, shocking everyone.	This has an active meaning and focuses on the *cause* of the experience.
past participle	Shocked by the car accident, Bill called an ambulance.	This has a passive meaning and focuses on the *person* that has the experience.

E Combine these two sentences into one. Start with the word in parentheses.

1. He was frightened by a loud noise. He sat up in bed. (frightened)
   Frightened by a loud noise, he sat up in bed.

2. He ate dinner. After that, he called his mother. (after)
   After eating dinner, he called his mother.

3. He juggled two plates. At the same time, he sang a song. (while)
   While juggling two plates, he sang a song

4. I moved to Spain. I feel calmer. (since)
   Since moving to Spain, I feel calmer.

5. He pulled out a gun. The bank employees were threatened. (threatening)
   Threatening the bank employees, he pulled out a gun.

F Read this excerpt from a play called *Late One Night*. Use the correct form of each verb in parentheses.
What do you think the note says?

Narrator: It is a cold, windy night. Mary, a young woman, is at home alone, reading a book.
We hear a noise upstairs. (1. Frighten) _Frightened_ by the noise, Mary walks
upstairs to the bedroom door. She opens the door, (2. surprise) _Surprising_ the cat.

Mary: Oh, it's only the cat.

Narrator: (3. Embarrass) _Embarrassed_ that she was so scared, Mary smiles to herself. And yet,
while (4. relieve) _relieved_, she still looks a little nervous. (5. Comfort) _Comforting_ the
cat, she returns downstairs. (6. Calm) _Calming_ herself down, she makes a cup of tea.
The doorbell rings. When Mary answers the door, there is no one there. (7. Confuse) _Confused_,
she looks down to see a small box. (8. Intrigue) _Intrigued_ by the package, she picks it up and
brings it inside. 陰謀

Mary: I wonder what this is.

Narrator: She opens the box quickly, (9. disappoint) _disappointed_ to find it's empty.

Mary: Wait . . . there's a note inside . . .

G Pair work. Now write your own scary scene. You may want to use some of the verbs in the box.
Be sure to include a part in your scene for a narrator. Then perform your scene for the class.

alarm	captivate	frighten	puzzle	surprise
bewilder	confuse	relieve	overwhelm	shock

As you can see . . .

A Pair work. **Look at the charts to complete the descriptions.
Then label the features of the charts with the words in the box below.**

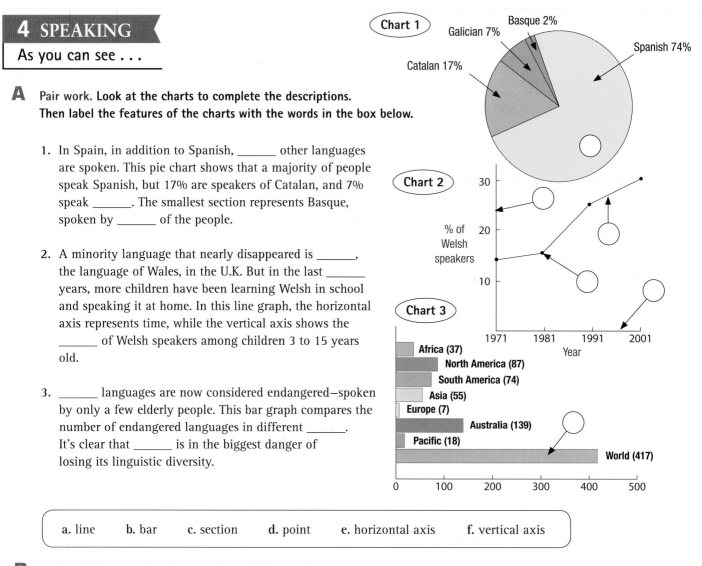

Chart 1

Basque 2%
Galician 7%
Catalan 17%
Spanish 74%

Chart 2

% of Welsh speakers

30
20
10

1971   1981   1991   2001
Year

Chart 3

Africa (37)
North America (87)
South America (74)
Asia (55)
Europe (7)
Australia (139)
Pacific (18)
World (417)

0   100   200   300   400   500

1. In Spain, in addition to Spanish, _____ other languages are spoken. This pie chart shows that a majority of people speak Spanish, but 17% are speakers of Catalan, and 7% speak _____. The smallest section represents Basque, spoken by _____ of the people.

2. A minority language that nearly disappeared is _____, the language of Wales, in the U.K. But in the last _____ years, more children have been learning Welsh in school and speaking it at home. In this line graph, the horizontal axis represents time, while the vertical axis shows the _____ of Welsh speakers among children 3 to 15 years old.

3. _____ languages are now considered endangered–spoken by only a few elderly people. This bar graph compares the number of endangered languages in different _____. It's clear that _____ is in the biggest danger of losing its linguistic diversity.

> a. line   b. bar   c. section   d. point   e. horizontal axis   f. vertical axis

B Pair work. **Look at the charts below and discuss these questions with your partner:**

1. What are some important changes that will occur?
2. What effects will these changes have on your country? The world?

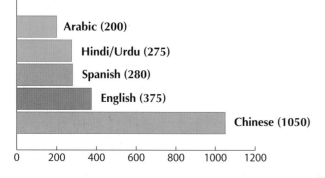

Native Speakers of Major Languages, in millions: 2000

Arabic (200)
Hindi/Urdu (275)
Spanish (280)
English (375)
Chinese (1050)

0   200   400   600   800   1000   1200

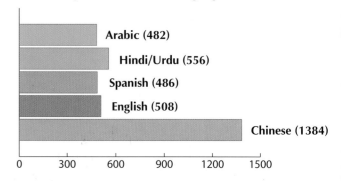

Native Speakers of Major Languages, in millions: 2050

Arabic (482)
Hindi/Urdu (556)
Spanish (486)
English (508)
Chinese (1384)

0   300   600   900   1200   1500

C Group work. **Look at the different charts on this page. In groups, discuss which information is the most interesting and why. Try to use some of the expressions for talking about charts and data.**

Talking about charts and data	
This chart explains . . .	*This ____ represents . . .*
As you can see, . . .	*This ____ stands for . . .*
The key point is that . . .	*This ____ shows . . .*
It's clear that . . .	*This ____ describes . . .*
It's important to note that . . .	*This ____ compares . . .*

In Other Words

Lesson B | Talk to me.

1 GET READY TO READ

It's in the writing.

 Do you think men and women have different speaking styles? How about writing styles?

A Pair work. **Read the two e-mail messages. One was written by a man, the other by a woman. Can you tell who wrote which? How? Check your answers on page 168.**

Hi Liam,

How wonderful to hear from you! How's your girlfriend—what was her name—Ciara? I heard that you're planning to visit Spain. Lovely! You'll stay with us, of course. We've got an extra room that overlooks a charming little garden. It's hot here in August, so your best bet is probably to come in September. I'll be on vacation then too, and we can do some sightseeing together.

Hey Liam,

Greetings from Seville! I got your e-mail saying you were planning on visiting. It'd be great if you came over and stayed for a couple of weeks! Be aware that the temperatures here in the south soar in August (last year they were up in the 40s), so that may not be the best time to visit. Late September or October are perfect, though. Let me know what your plans are.

B Pair work. **Read the information below, and then discuss these questions.**

1. What did the group of Israeli scientists create?
2. How does the tool work?
3. What belief does the findings of the Israeli scientists' reinforce? Do you agree with this belief? Why or why not?

Professor Moshe Koppel and a group of scientists at Bar Ilan University in Israel have developed a computer program that they say allows them to analyze a piece of writing and to determine with 80% accuracy whether the author is male or female.

Interestingly, the tool does this by analyzing smaller words used in a text (e.g., *the, a, what, and, I, he*). According to Koppel, when one examines this data, certain patterns emerge.

Using the program they developed, Koppel and his team analyzed over 600 texts. What they found was that women's writing included more personal pronouns and possessive adjectives (e.g., *you, he, I, me, her, our,* etc.), while men more often used words such as *a, the, these, that,* as well as numbers, and quantity words such as *a lot*. Koppel has since used this tool to analyze everything from fiction to more "gender-neutral" scientific texts—predicting with 80% accuracy the sex of the writer.

According to some, Professor Koppel's findings only reinforce what many have always believed—that women tend to focus more on people, while men prefer things and ideas.

C Pair work. **Analyze the e-mail messages in A using Professor Koppel's theory. Does it work?**

A Pair work. **Read the statements below and circle** *True* **or** *False.* **Compare your answers with a partner. Then scan the article on page 59 about men's and women's communication styles to find the answers. How many did you get right?**

1. If you talk to a woman about a problem, she's not likely to be a very sympathetic listener.   True   False
2. For many men, it is important to be in control in a conversation.   True   False
3. In conversations, women don't give others many chances to speak.   True   False
4. Women tend to talk more than men in the workplace and classroom.   True   False

> ### Understanding text organization using contrasts
>
> When an author contrasts things, he or she explores differences. Words and phrases such as *but, however, in contrast, on the other hand, though, unlike, whereas,* and *while* are used to signal a contrast.

B **Now read the article on page 59 carefully. How are men's and women's conversational styles different? Complete these sentences with the correct information from the reading.**

1. In conversation, women tend to build rapport and _____. Many men, though, focus on _____.

2. If you tell a woman about a problem, she'll be likely to _____. A man, on the other hand, _____.

3. When women listen to someone, they will often _____. However, men do this less because _____.

4. In public conversations, women will often _____. In contrast, men tend to _____.

5. In personal settings, _____ tend to _____ than _____.

C **Look at the words and phrases in bold in the reading on page 59. Match them with a synonym from the list below.**

1. *thinks* _____
2. *control* _____
3. *talk* _____
4. *indifferent, uncaring* _____
5. *create a connection* _____
6. *result* _____

D Group work. **Do you agree that men's and women's communication styles are generally different? Give examples from your own experience.**

> ▶ **Ask & Answer**
>
> Do you think the communication styles described in the reading are true for you or the people you know? Why or why not?

World Link

> One researcher has found that male/female communication differences also apply to e-mail discussion groups. Many more "aggressive" or "sarcastic" remarks are made by male participants, while women tend to contribute many more "supportive" comments.
>
> Source: *Paolo Rossetti* on *iteslj.org*

YOU JUST DON'T GET IT!

For centuries, people have known that men and women communicate differently. Author G.K. Chesterton once said, "Women prefer to talk in twos, while men prefer to talk in threes." More recently, contributions made by linguists and those in the field of gender studies have popularized the notion that *Men are from Mars, Women are from Venus*—not just in terms of how they behave, but how they **converse**. Consider the following example: Ken and Emily, both college students, recently had this conversation:

Ken: How's it goin', Em?

Emily: Not so good. I think that Jane is upset that I was accepted to the study abroad program and she wasn't. She hasn't spoken to me all week or returned my e-mail or phone calls.

K: What? That's silly.

E: I know. Still . . . it's tough, you know, because we're such good friends.

K: Maybe you ought to talk to a counselor in the program or confront Jane about it.

E: Yeah, well, the thing is that this whole situation makes me feel terrible . . .

K: I know, but I'm serious, Em. Talk to a counselor or Jane sooner rather than later.

E: But, oh . . . never mind, Ken. You just don't get it.

K: Get what?

E: I *know* that I should talk to Jane and work this thing out.

K: Right, so what's the problem?

E: The *problem* is that I feel bad about it all. I'm just looking for a little understanding . . .

K: I *do* understand, and I think I've suggested something you can do about it.

E: *(frustrated)* OK, thanks for your advice. Let's change the subject.

> **Real English**
> *Men Are from Mars, Women Are from Venus* = a book by therapist John Gray that explores the differences between men and women

What's going on in the conversation above? According to Deborah Tannen, a professor of linguistics at Georgetown University, men and women often use distinctly different strategies when talking, and the result at times is a total communication breakdown. In conversation, says Tannen, women often work to **build rapport** and make connections. Mention a problem you're having to a woman, for example, and she will likely respond sympathetically first, and then suggest a possible solution. For many men, though, conversation is more akin to what Tannen calls "report-talk" in which the focus is on gathering information and then doing something with it. Mention the same problem to a man, and he will likely give direct feedback or suggest a solution right away.

In Ken and Emily's case, Emily's frustration stems from the fact that she is expecting Ken to listen and offer sympathy, and then perhaps some advice about her situation at school. Ken, on the other hand, hears Emily's story, and in an effort to be helpful, immediately offers a solution to her problem. Emily, though, **perceives** Ken's suggestion as inconsiderate and **dismissive** of her feelings. The result? A breakdown in communication and a mutual sense on both sides that the other just "doesn't get it."

Are you paying attention?

Studies have shown that there are other ways that men's and women's communication styles can lead to misunderstanding. Women, for example, will often use words and phrases like *uh-huh*, *right*, *I know what you mean*, or will quickly relate some personal information to show that they're paying attention and are involved in the conversation. However, for men, who typically work to maintain status and control in a conversation, this is often perceived as an attempt to interrupt. Men, therefore, tend to use this strategy less. When a woman is talking and is not receiving this sort of feedback, however, she may think the other person is not listening or isn't interested in what she's saying.

Talk amongst yourselves

According to Deborah Tannen, another key element in how men's and women's conversational styles differ is in how much they talk in a given setting. In public settings, such as the workplace and classroom, studies have shown that women ask others for their ideas and give participants frequent opportunities to speak. In contrast, men tend to talk more often and for a longer period of time than women—which results in fewer participants speaking, unless they interrupt. What's the **upshot** of this? A sense, on the part of women, that men tend to **dominate** conversations, and a feeling among men that the women are often a little too quiet or don't have much to say. Interestingly, other studies have shown that in more personal settings, such as on the phone or with friends, women tend to talk more than men. The result? The widespread perception that women, in general, are the more talkative of the two sexes.

What does all this mean?

Is the point of all this to suggest that one conversational style is better than the other? Hardly, say specialists. The key, they say, is to understand that men and women have different ways of communicating. Being aware of these differences will enable us to avoid communication breakdown and to build happier, healthier relationships.

A Read this report and write a heading for each section.

Facilities for Neptunian Speakers in Metroville

Introduction

This report describes and assesses the facilities available for Neptunians in our city. In the past ten years, the number of Neptunian speakers has increased considerably, due to the large number of extraterrestrial companies that have established branch offices here.

1. _____

Metroville offers a number of news and entertainment sources for Neptunian speakers. TV3 has a Neptunian-language news broadcast daily at 11:30 P.M., and several radio stations have daily Neptunian programming. Neptunian newspapers are available, but they are generally several days old. On the whole, Neptunian speakers report that the Internet is their main source of news. Neptunian movies with subtitles are frequently shown at downtown movie theaters, and videos and DVDs dubbed in Neptunian can be rented at many stores.

2. _____

Metroville has two Neptunian-medium schools. In general, extraterrestrial children ages 5–14 attend Metroville Intergalactic School, where all classes are taught in Neptunian. There is also a smaller school, Intergalactic Academy, for children ages 6–12. At present, there is no Neptunian high school in this region of the country, so high school students must attend boarding schools in other cities.

3. _____

Very few of the emergency services telephone operators understand Neptunian. Last year, an extraterrestrial patient died in a waiting room at Metroville Hospital because he was unable to communicate his problem to the nurses there. Many doctors and nurses speak Neptunian, but they are not always available to translate.

4. _____

Metroville provides good educational and entertainment facilities for its Neptunian-speaking residents, but emergency services remain a problem. It is recommended that the government set up a special emergency telephone number for extraterrestrials, with Neptunian-speaking operators. In addition, it would be advisable to provide extraterrestrial residents with a list of doctors who speak Neptunian. Finally, the government should consider supporting an intergalactic high school.

B Find, underline, and label these things in the report in A.

    a. an expression introducing the purpose of the report
    b. two expressions for talking about overall patterns
    c. two expressions for making recommendations

C You are a member of the National Committee for Better Education, and you have been asked to provide information on the status of foreign languages in your country. Write a report with four short sections and give a heading to each one. Report the following:

> **Writing a report**
>
> A report is an objective summary of facts on a topic, written in an impersonal style. It is usually divided into sections with separate headings, and may contain a series of recommendations at the end.

    1. the importance of foreign languages in your country
    2. the current situation of foreign language teaching in schools
    3. opportunities for learning foreign languages outside of the school system
    4. recommendations for improving people's foreign language ability in your country

D Pair work. Exchange reports with your partner and make suggestions for improving each other's report.

Debate the issue

A Group work. **Get into groups of four. Read this statement and then take one of the roles below.**

> Everyone in the world should have to learn a second language.

Student A: You are IN FAVOR OF the statement above.	Student B: You are AGAINST the statement above.	Students C & D: You are the JUDGES.
• On a piece of paper, make a list of as many reasons as you can that will support your side of the argument. • Try to anticipate some of the points your opponent will make. • Study the rules for debate below.		Listen to the two sides debate the topic. Your role is not to agree with one side or another, but to moderate the debate and to ultimately decide which side argued better—based on the rules for debate below. Take notes as you listen to the two sides.

Rules for debate
- State each reason in your argument clearly.
- Use facts or other data to support your point.
- Do not go over the time limit (see B).
- Important: Don't introduce ideas randomly. When you offer a rebuttal, make sure that it's related to something your opponent has just said.
- At the end of the debate, summarize your arguments briefly.

B Group work. **Get together with your group and begin the debate.**

1. Student A begins by stating his or her first point. Time limit: 45 seconds
2. Student B responds with an opposing idea. Time limit: 45 seconds
3. Repeat steps one and two for 3–4 rounds.
4. Then each side should summarize its main points.
5. The Judges will compare notes, choose a winner, and explain their decision.

> *I think everyone should have to learn a second language because . . .*

> *Yes, but on the other hand . . .*

C Group work. **Choose one of the statements below. Then switch roles and repeat the exercises in A and B.**

- Second-language learning should begin when children are in the first grade.
- A language teacher should be a native speaker of that language.
- A government should protect endangered languages in its country.

CNN® **Check out the CNN**® **video.** **Practice your English online at** elt.heinle.com/worldpass

Unit 5: In Other Words

A Study the phrases in the box and use them to complete the sentences below.

> **Word combinations with *discussion***
>
> take part in a discussion   under discussion
> broaden the discussion   a pointless discussion
> generate a discussion   a great deal of discussion
> a heated discussion

1. This is _____! We're arguing about where to go out for dinner, but we don't have any money!
2. We need to _____ about immigration and hear more different points of view.
3. In the kitchen, two chefs were having _____ about how to cook the sauce, and all the customers in the restaurant could hear them shouting.
4. Our teacher likes to ask us questions about the news in order to _____.
5. A plan to build a swimming pool in Memorial Park is _____ by the city council.
6. I want to _____ about energy conservation at the environmental conference next week.
7. At the employee meeting, there was _____ about the new vacation schedule. We talked for two hours.

B Circle the word or expression in each line that doesn't belong.

1. native language	mother tongue	first language	sign language
2. difficult	proficient	skillful	fluent
3. retain	lose	remember	acquire
4. expression	idiom	phrase	verb
5. passable	halting	rusty	poor
6. conversation	dialog	speech	discussion

> ### I didn't know that!
> The words *grammar* and *glamour* originally came from the same root, the Greek word for *letter*. In the Middle Ages, *grammar* came to mean all forms of knowledge. People at that time thought that science was a mysterious form of magic. In Scotland, *grammar* was pronounced *glamour*, and *glamour* became a term for magic spells. Nowadays, *glamour* means a mysterious attractiveness—but most students don't see any *glamour* in *grammar*!

C Where is it spoken? Match the language with a country where it is spoken, using your dictionary as needed.

1. Swahili ___   a. Brazil
2. Farsi ___   b. Philippines
3. Urdu ___   c. Iran
4. Arabic ___   d. Egypt
5. Filipino ___   e. India
6. Portuguese ___   f. Pakistan
7. French ___   g. Kenya
8. Hindi ___   h. Canada

D Review these words and phrases from the reading "You just don't get it!" on page 59. Then use them in the correct form to complete the sentences.

> build rapport   feedback   perceive   dismissive   dominate   widespread   upshot   interrupt

1. I hate it when my boyfriend _____ me while I'm speaking. I never get to finish what I'm saying!
2. Whenever I have dinner with my parents, my mother _____ the conversation with news about all of my old friends who have already gotten married.
3. After I gave my presentation, I got good _____ from my colleagues. They said I explained everything very clearly.
4. There is a _____ belief that women talk more than men, but research shows that that isn't true.
5. The _____ of Dr. Tannen's book is that we need to understand that men and women have different ways of communicating.
6. My boss is always so _____ of my ideas. She doesn't listen, and she doesn't take them seriously.
7. Women sometimes _____ men as being inconsiderate because they give advice instead of just listening.
8. An important part of conversation is to _____ with other people.

E Spell check! These words were taken from a list of those most commonly misspelled by native speakers of English. Rewrite them correctly. Three of them have no mistakes—write OK by them.

1. allready _____
2. ilegal _____
3. address _____
4. develope _____
5. ocurred _____
6. February _____
7. proffessor _____
8. saftey _____
9. recieve _____
10. afect _____
11. def inate _____
12. twelvth _____
13. suceed _____
14. goverment _____
15. disapear _____
16. jewelery _____
17. assistent _____
18. unbeliveable _____
19. forty _____
20. neccessary _____

> ### In Other Words
>
> A **language** is a system of spoken and (usually) written communication that is used by the people of a particular country or region: *Chinese is the world's most widely spoken language.*
> A **dialect** is a variety of a language spoken in a particular area: *People used to be surprised when I first moved to Tokyo because I spoke the Osaka dialect of Japanese.*
> An **accent** is the way you pronounce words when you speak: *When I heard the woman's accent, I could tell that she came from the southern part of our country.*

> **Slang** means informal language used by a particular group of people, such as teenagers: *Americans have a lot of slang words for money, such as* dough *and* bucks.
> **Jargon** is words used by experts in a subject, which other people don't understand: *I tried to read the manual for my laptop, but it was all written in computer jargon.*
> **Terminology** is vocabulary that's used only in a particular field: *I had a broken leg, or a fractured tibia in medical terminology.*

Watch out!   slang
Slang is a noncount noun. Therefore, it cannot be used in the plural.
   My friend is teaching me American slang.
   ~~I've learned a lot of good slangs.~~
   I've learned a lot of good slang expressions.

1 VOCABULARY FOCUS

A well-kept secret

 Look at the photos and read the title of the article below. What do you think the article is going to be about?

A Pair work. **Read this article about Peter Alvarez. Then close your books and take turns telling your partner his story.**

Changing Gears

focus

(1) "I've always loved to cook," says newscaster Peter Alvarez with a twinkle in his eye. "I remember having aspirations to grow up and become a chef. Somewhere along the way, I got sidetracked, and I fell into broadcasting."

And it's been quite a storied career for Mr. Alvarez. The only child of working-class parents, he started at the bottom and worked his way to the top to become one of the most watched TV reporters on the evening news.

(2) Cooking came back into his life in an unexpected way. He bumped into an old high school friend of his on a flight to Mexico City. As it turned out, his friend was attending cooking classes and invited Peter to join her.

From that first class, Peter was hooked. Soon he was juggling his busy day job at the TV station along

with his full-time studies in pastry cooking at night. "I was channeling all my energy into the cooking and neglecting my regular job. And I was getting exhausted—it's not easy to wear three hats . . . as broadcaster, pastry student, and parent."

After a year of studies, Peter realized that he wanted to study with some of the more renowned pastry chefs in France. With his family's blessing, he took some time off and flew to France.

(3) Upon his return, he knew what he had to do—quit the TV station. His resignation initially caused quite a stir, since he had been such a fixture at Channel 4. When asked what his plans were, he smiled and said, "Don't worry. I have something in mind . . ."

That "something" was working as an apprentice to the pastry chef at the acclaimed Barbar Hotel. How does he feel about swapping his role as glamorous TV personality for that of kitchen assistant?

"I couldn't be happier," he beams. And we couldn't be happier for him, either.

B Pair work. Look back at the article in **A** and with a partner find the words and expressions that have the same meaning.

Section 1	1. distracted; diverted _sidetracked_ *(life changed direction)*	4. a bright sparkle _twinkle_
	2. having an interesting history _storied_	5. unexpectedly ended up doing _fell into_
	3. dreams; goals _aspiration_	
Section 2	1. famous, well-respected _renowned_	4. met unexpectedly _bumped in to_
	2. focusing; directing _channeling_	5. doing several things at the same time
	3. approval _blessing_	_juggling_
Section 3	1. thinking about an idea _having something_	4. permanent feature _fixture_
	2. surprised; shocked _caused a stir in mind_	5. assistant _apprentice_
	3. exchanging _swapping_	

C Group work. **Discuss these questions.**

1. What aspirations did you have as a child?
2. Why do you think people get sidetracked in their lives?
3. What is something in the news that has caused a stir recently? What exactly happened?
4. If you had all the free time you wanted, what would you channel your energy into?
5. Complete this sentence: *If I could, I would swap my _____ for _____.*

Vocabulary Builder ▲

Read these sentences and match each underlined expression with its definition in the box.

| a. already known and not interesting | c. admire | e. immediately |
| b. perform more than one job or task | d. not tell anyone | |

1. I have to <u>take my hat off to</u> her. She finished the project under budget. _____
2. He was secretly studying at the pastry school and had to <u>keep it under his hat</u>. _____
3. That gossip about Britney Spears is <u>old hat</u>. I heard it last month. _____
4. I <u>wear two hats</u>: during the day I'm a teacher and at night I'm a singer in a rock band. _____
5. Don't encourage him. He'll start telling terrible jokes <u>at the drop of a hat</u>. _____

2 LISTENING
Running ultramarathons

A Pair work. **You are going to hear an interview with Duncan, a man who competes in very long races called "ultramarathons." Look at the chart below. Can you predict any of the answers you will hear? Write your predictions on a separate piece of paper.**

Average marathon distance	_26_ miles _385_ yards OR _4l.3_ kilometers
Possible ultramarathon distance	_100_ miles OR _160_ kilometers
Examples of ultramarathon timed races	_15_ hours AND _48_ hours
Temperature during desert race	_120_ Fahrenheit OR _48_ Celsius

B Now listen to the first part of the interview and complete the chart in **A**. (CD Track 17)

C Now listen to the entire interview and circle *T* for true or *F* for false. **Write key words to support your answers.** (CD Track 18)

1. Duncan depends on luck to some degree. — (T) F — *weather*
2. He doesn't like the feeling when he's running. — T (F) — *great so alive*
3. He's eaten pizza during a race. — (T) F — *challenging call delivery*
4. He always takes breaks to sleep. — T (F) — *sleep running*
5. He started running because he was ambitious. — T (F) — *28 depressed hate job dear hot head*
6. He says you need five years' running experience. — T (F) — *2 or 3 years more than 1 marathon*

regularly 4 hours or more

▶ **Ask & Answer**

What do you think of Duncan's passion for running? What are some of the healthy and unhealthy aspects of being enthusiastic about something?

3 LANGUAGE FOCUS

Reported speech

A Study the information in the box.

We use reported speech to "report" to another person what someone else has said.
    Quoted speech: "I have something in mind," he said.
    Reported speech: He said (that) he had something in mind.
We use reporting verbs to introduce the reported statement.
    They <u>reported</u> (that) she had left her job.
    My mother <u>told</u> me not to go.
The verb in the reported statement may shift in reported speech.
    Quoted speech: "<u>I've been</u> to Europe three times," he said.
    Reported speech: He said (that) he <u>had been</u> to Europe
       three times.

Say **and** *tell*

He said (to me) (that) he had run two marathons.

Other verbs like *say*: announce, complain, mention, propose, reply, report

He told me (that) he had run two marathons.
He told me to train hard for the race.

Other verbs like *tell*: advise, ask, convince, instruct, persuade, remind

B Pair work. With a partner, read these sentences and choose the appropriate reporting verb. Then underline the changes from quoted speech to reported speech.

1. "Your papers are due on Friday."
The teacher ___b___ us that our papers were due on Friday.
a. proposed   b. told   c. announced

2. "She's guilty."
I didn't agree, but finally he _____ me that she was guilty.
a. convinced   b. admitted   c. proposed

3. "The meeting has definitely been canceled."
They _____ (that) the meeting had definitely been canceled.
a. announced   b. advised   c. told

4. "Don't forget. It's getting late and you need to get up early tomorrow."
He _____ me it was getting late and that I needed to get up early the next day.
a. said   b. reminded   c. mentioned

5. "Mary, you should take some time off and enjoy yourself."
He _____ (that) she should take some time off and enjoy herself.
a. persuaded   b. proposed   c. instructed

6. "My shoes are hurting my feet."
She _____ (that) her shoes were hurting her feet.
a. advised   b. told   c. complained

C Look at the information in the chart. What follows the reporting verb in *yes/no* and *wh-* questions? What do you notice about the word order?

Reported questions
"Where do you live?" he asked. → He asked where I lived.
"Are you happy?" she asked. → She asked if I was happy (or not).
She asked whether (or not) I was happy.
She asked whether I was happy (or not).

D A female news reporter is interviewing a man who runs ultramarathons. Read part of the interview below. Then rewrite each sentence in reported speech.

1. Q: How many marathons have you run?
2. A: I completed my fourth one yesterday.
3. Q: Who do you train with?
4. A: I train with my brother.

5. Q: Do you have a family?
6. A: Yes, I do.
7. Q: Do they approve of your running?
8. A: They don't love it, but they accept it.

1. _____
2. _____
3. _____
4. _____

5. _____
6. _____
7. _____
8. _____

E Read this letter Pat wrote about her new friend. Find the seven errors in reported speech and correct them.

Dear Mom and Dad,

Campus life has been great so far. I'm studying hard and making new friends. One of my new friends sits next to me in history class. Her name is Ethel. She says that she was 70 years old! I don't believe her.

I asked Ethel why she did wait so long to go back to college. She told to me that she had had to raise a family and work, so she couldn't go to college. I asked her where was she working before she became a student. She said that she was retired to me.

I also asked her if or not she liked college life. She said she loved it! I really admire Ethel because she's so upbeat. I asked her what your secret was. She told me that she always looks at the bright side of things.

Anyway, I'll write again soon.
Love, Pat

F Pair work. Imagine that you are a reporter. You are going to interview your partner for a special interest story. Ask your partner these questions and add three questions of your own.

1. What have you done in your life that is different?
2. What made you decide to do it?
3. Is there anything you wish you hadn't done?

4. _____
5. _____
6. _____

G Pair work. Now tell another partner about your interview. Describe the questions you asked and the responses you received.

> I asked Anita what she had done in her life that was different. She replied that she had . . .

4 SPEAKING

Today, I'd like to tell you about . . .

A Group work. **Discuss these questions.**

1. Have you ever spoken to a group in your native language? In English?
2. What are some situations in which people have to make presentations?
3. How do you feel about speaking in front of a group? Why do you feel that way?

B Group work. **Read this student's presentation. How is a presentation similar to an essay? How is it different?**

> Today, I'd like to tell you about a person who has had a very big influence on my life—my Aunt Rita. Her husband died when I was very young, and she came to live with my family. She was like a second mother to me and my brothers.
>
> One thing Aunt Rita did was to teach me to love books and reading. Every year, on my birthday, she took me to a bookstore and let me choose any book I wanted. She read stories to me every night when I was little, and helped me learn to read when I started school. She also taught me to love nature. My parents both worked very long hours, so Aunt Rita always took us to the zoo or the park, and helped us plant a flower garden. But most importantly, Aunt Rita encouraged my dreams, even when they seemed hopeless. After high school, I wanted to go overseas and study environmental science. I knew my family couldn't afford that, but Aunt Rita persuaded me to apply for a scholarship, and I was able to come here to this university.
>
> In conclusion, my Aunt Rita has had a very important influence on my life, and my future. If she hadn't encouraged me, I wouldn't be a student here today. Thank you.

C You are going to give a short presentation (about two minutes) about a person who has had an important influence on you, such as a teacher or family member. Plan your presentation by completing the outline with words and short phrases.

A person who has influenced me

Person's name: _____

Words or phrases describing the person: _____, _____, _____

Ways this person has influenced me:

1. _____

Example: _____

2. _____

Example: _____

3. _____

Example: _____

Conclusion: How would your life be different without this person? _____

D Pair work. **Practice giving your presentation to a partner. Your partner will time you and give you advice for improving your presentation.**

E Group work. **Work with a group of four. Take turns giving your presentations. While you listen to each speaker, make notes about these things on a slip of paper. When all the speakers have finished, give them your notes.**

> **voice:**
>
> **eye contact:**
>
> **best thing about the presentation:**

Presentation phrases

Introducing a presentation
Today, I'm going to talk to you about . . .
I'd like to tell you about . . .
In this presentation, I'm going to . . .

Ending a presentation
Before I finish, let me say . . .
So in conclusion, . . .
To conclude, . . .

UNIT 6

Ordinary People, Extraordinary Lives

Lesson B | The kindness of strangers

1 GET READY TO READ

A helping hand

Have you ever been in a situation in which you had to ask someone you didn't know for help? What happened?

A Pair work. **Look at the photos below and describe to your partner the people and what is happening in each one.**

Guessing meaning from context

To guess the meaning of important but unfamiliar words in a text:
- Think about how the word is related to the overall topic.
- Read the surrounding sentences. These often include information that will give clues to the meaning of the new word.
- Notice prefixes, suffixes, and familiar parts of the word, e.g., *displeased* = *dis-* + *pleased*.

B Pair work. **Study the box in A. Then look at the underlined words in each sentence below and discuss these questions with a partner.**

- Without looking at a dictionary, what do you think each underlined word means?
- What information helped you to understand the meaning of the underlined words?

1. How did I get here? I used to have a job, an apartment, nice clothes. Now look at me. I'm <u>filthy</u> from not bathing for days. My clothes are torn and <u>stained</u> with food. Who'll help me now?

2. We got off the train at the wrong stop and had no idea where we were. We were completely <u>disoriented</u>. There were no other trains for the rest of the day, and we were worried we'd be <u>stranded</u> in that strange place overnight.

3. The <u>drought</u> has hit this part of the country very hard and water is <u>scarce</u>. People are forced to survive on a <u>meager</u> diet of rice and milk. As a result, many—especially young children—are suffering from <u>malnutrition</u>. As relief organizations work out the <u>logistics</u> of bringing in clean water and giving out food, people grow more <u>desperate</u> and tensions in the region are rising.

▶ Ask & Answer

Think about the situations above. If you encountered people like this on the street or saw an ad asking for help, what would you do?

HAÏTI

Gonaïves

Port-au-Prince ★

- Located in the Caribbean
- **Capital city:** Port-au-Prince
- **Official languages:** Creole, French
- One of the poorest countries in the world
- In 2004 was struck by a powerful hurricane that left thousands dead or homeless

A Pair work. Read this background information about Haiti. Then look at the title and subtitle of the reading on page 71. What do you think the story is going to be about?

B Read the entire article. As you read, use the strategy you practiced in Get Ready to Read on page 69 to understand the meaning of unfamiliar words and phrases.

C Pair work. Look at the underlined words and phrases in the reading. Which category do they belong in? Complete the chart and then compare answers. Discuss the meaning of the expressions with a partner.

describing positioning or a lack of space	under water	describing things moving quickly	describing something very messy or smelling bad	describing something blocked
sandwiched between				

D Read the article on page 71 again and complete the sentences by circling the correct answer. Then find key words in the reading that support your answers and write them on the line below.

1. The conditions on the tap-tap were very comfortable / crowded.

   _____

2. Recently, life in Haiti has been calm / chaotic.

   _____

3. The city of Gonaïves was hit hard / escaped major damage when Hurricane Jeanne struck.

   _____

4. The young man from Gonaïves was very anxious / relieved as he talked about his situation.

   _____

5. The young man from Gonaïves was poorly / well dressed.

   _____

6. The passengers had / didn't have a lot, but they were stingy / generous.

   _____

E Pair work. Using the key words in the chart, take turns with a partner to retell the story in your own words.

Student A	Student B
tap-tap	filthy clothes
Port-au-Prince	white polo shirt
hurricane	market lady
young man from Gonaïves	ten-gourde note

▶ **Ask & Answer**

Why do you think the author wrote this story? What do you think his message is? Has someone ever helped you in a time of need? Explain what happened.

ON THE TAP-TAP   After the storm, a generous spirit shines through in Haiti

by Kent Annan, from Orion

"Leve pye ou." Lift your feet. "Fon ti avanse." Move over a bit. I was sandwiched between two middle-aged ladies up near the front of a freight truck converted for passengers, a large version of the public-transportation vehicles that Haitians call "tap-taps." Women who had been selling goods all day at the market stuffed their sacks and baskets under benches that ran along the sides. The middle aisle filled with cargo, people crammed into the center. Others hung out the back door.
5 Almost everything in Haiti seemed scarce; seats to Port-au-Prince in the late afternoon were no exception.

The tap-tap jostled to a start after a driver's assistant banged loudly on the metal siding. Talk soon turned to Gonaïves. Forty miles in the opposite direction, Haiti's fourth-largest city was submerged after Hurricane Jeanne hit it a week earlier. People were still stranded on rooftops. Aid was slow to arrive; relief organizations could not deal with the logistics, armed gangs, and mobs of desperate people.

10 It was late September, 2004. In less than a year, this small island country of eight million people had experienced political upheaval, flooding that killed three thousand, malnourishment, widespread unemployment, and, now, hurricane flooding that had killed two thousand more. From a distance, those watching the news must wonder how anybody makes it in Haiti. Living here, I sometimes wonder too, but less so because I see the little things.

After passengers expressed how terrible the situation was in Gonaïves, a young man, about 20 years old, spoke up. "I'm
15 from Gonaïves," he said. "Just got out." Conversation in the front half of the tap-tap quieted. He told of bodies, of water sweeping the living away to join the dead, of mad stampedes threatening any meager supplies of potable water or food. His Creole was rapid-fire and he seemed a little disoriented as he jumped between subjects. His eyes darted to different people as he talked.

People asked questions. Bridges were down, roads nearly impassable. Did he slog through the mud and water? Yes. He
20 left to find help, leaving his mother and siblings behind. Would he return soon? Yes, he hoped.

"There's nothing, nothing," he kept saying. "These clothes. Look. I've been wearing them since last Saturday." Haitians are almost always immaculately groomed, but the young man from Gonaïves was filthy. Little bits of straw and other debris littered his hair. His shirt and baggy jean shorts were stained and ragged.

Suddenly a middle-aged man reached into a plastic bag and gave him a white polo shirt. "Here. Take this," he said.
25 "Thank you," said the young man. The crowd immediately told him to take off his old shirt and put on the new one. When he did, a sharp, rancid smell was released. Within 30 seconds, someone gave him a white T-shirt. A pair of green shorts appeared. A comb. Someone else gave him a bar of soap.

Meanwhile, one of the market ladies had taken a crumpled 10-gourde note (about 28 cents) out of the fold of her skirt and squeezed her way through the tap-tap from person to person, saying, "Just give what you can. Five gourdes, ten gourdes,
30 fifty gourdes, anything." After completing her circuit, she handed the young man a fistful of bills and coins.

He was holding on to the roof rail with his right hand, revealing a few small holes in the armpit of his new shirt. He looked around. Then he started wiping tears from his eyes. "Mwen pa konnen . . ." I don't know . . ."You didn't even ask for anything, we just want to give. We're all Gonaïveians now," people said, and then were quiet for a little while as the tap-tap bounded on toward Port-au-Prince.

Source: *Orion*, Jan/Feb 2005
187 Main St. Great Barrington, MA 01230
www.oriononline.org

Real English
make it = survive
get out in time = escape just before something bad happens
sibling = brother or sister

3 WRITING
Writing a biography

A Read this biography and answer the questions that follow.

Jane Goodall is one of the world's most important researchers on animal behavior, and a strong environmental advocate. She has given her whole life to the conservation of the rainforest and animal species.

Goodall was born in London in 1934. She loved animals when she was a child, and dreamed of working in Africa. In 1956, she was invited to visit a friend's family in Kenya. There she met Dr. Louis Leakey, a famous anthropologist who was looking for someone to carry out research on chimpanzees. Jane got the job, and in 1960, she arrived in Tanzania. For more than 20 years, she lived with the chimpanzees and made many important scientific discoveries about their behavior.

But in the 1980s, Goodall became very concerned about the disappearance of the rainforest. She left Tanzania and founded the Jane Goodall Institute, which has programs to help the people of the rainforest and preserve the environment for rainforest animals. She now travels more than 300 days every year, giving presentations about the importance of conservation. She has also founded *Roots and Shoots*, an international network of 7,000 youth groups.

Jane Goodall's work with chimpanzees has inspired people around the world, and her youth groups are taking action on local problems worldwide. Her efforts have made the world better for both animals and people.

1. What order is used in presenting the information?
2. What is in the introduction?
3. What is in the conclusion?

B Read this information about Nelson Mandela and write a biography. You do NOT need to use all of the facts.

Nelson Mandela

marriages:	(1) Evelyn Ntoko (1944) (2) Winnie Madikizela (1958) (3) Graca Machel (1998)
autobiography:	*Long Walk to Freedom*, 1994
Nobel Peace Prize:	1993
favorite time of day:	sunset
after retirement:	raised money for children's charities
first language:	Xhosa
first job:	herding family's cattle (age 5)
education:	mission school; Union College of Fort Hare; studied law in Johannesburg
family:	parents Gadla and Nodekeni, 3 sisters
prison:	sentenced to life term for anti-government activities; released after 27 years, February 11, 1990
joined African National Congress (ANC):	1942
positions in ANC:	1947: Youth League Secretary; 1952: Deputy Head of ANC; 1991: President of ANC
goal of ANC:	to end the unjust system of apartheid in South Africa
ANC outlawed:	1960
favorite music:	classical (Handel, Tchaikovsky)
born:	Qunu, South Africa, July 18, 1918
first democratically elected president of South Africa:	1994–1999 (62% of vote)

World Link

The greatest glory in living lies not in never falling, but in rising every time we fall. – Nelson Mandela

C Pair work. Exchange papers with a partner and discuss the similarities and differences in your biographies.

A Pair work. Read the description of Person of the Year, and then about some people who have won the award. What do you think of these choices? Discuss with a partner.

Person of the Year—At the end of every year, the U.S. magazine *Time* features an issue dedicated to The Person of the Year. The award is given to individuals as well as couples, groups of people, machines, or places. The Person of the Year is chosen for the influence (positive or negative) that this person or thing has had on society and the world over the course of the year. Some of *Time's* selections have included:

Year	Person	Reason
1927	Charles Lindbergh	the first person to win the award; chosen for making the first solo transatlantic flight from North America to Paris
1938	Adolf Hitler	head of Germany's Nazi party who triggered World War II
1966	The Generation of People 25 and Under	selected for their influence on politics, pop culture, and society
1982	The Personal Computer	selected as low-cost PCs begin making their appearance in more businesses, universities, and some homes
1996	Dr. David Ho	doctor selected for the work he's done in AIDS research
1999	Jeff Bezos	founder of amazon.com chosen for his role in influencing how we shop and do business

B Read the directions and fill in your choice and reason.

You are an editor who works for a popular online magazine that readers around the world subscribe to. This year, your magazine is publishing an issue that is dedicated to The Person of the Year. The criteria you use to make your selection are as follows:

• The Person of the Year can be an individual, a couple, a group, an organization or company, or a generation of people. It can also be an object or invention—for example, some kind of video game that has had a profound influence on people.

• Your nomination should take into account how profound an influence the person, group, or object has had on society and the world in the last year. This influence can be positive *or* negative.

The Person of the Year: _____

Reason(s): _____

_____

C Group work. Get into a group of three to four people and compare and discuss your choices.
As a team, choose *one* Person of the Year to nominate. Write your nomination on the board.

D Class work. Look at the list of nominations on the board. Take a class vote to determine who The Person of the Year for your class will be.

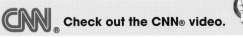

CNN® Check out the CNN® video. **Practice your English online at** elt.heinle.com/worldpass

Unit 6: Ordinary People, Extraordinary Lives

A Study the phrases in the box and match them with their meanings.

Word combinations with *life*	
1. lose your life ___	a. a complete change in your life
2. risk your life ___	b. put yourself in great danger
3. save your life ___	c. How are you? *(informal)*
4. a matter of life and death ___	d. die
5. your social life ___	e. Don't waste your time worrying! *(informal)*
6. a new life ___	f. keep you from dying
7. Life's too short! ___	g. an extremely serious situation
8. How's life? ___	h. your friendly relationships

B Complete the sentences with one of the phrases from **A**, making all necessary changes.

1. Hi, Russ. _____ I haven't seen you in ages!
2. Sachi is moving to Los Angeles because she wants to forget all her problems and start
   _____
3. Knowing how to swim is important because it can _____ in an emergency.
4. Firefighters _____ every day when they run into burning buildings to rescue people.
5. For children in poor countries, access to clean water is _____. Many of them die every year from diseases carried by water.
6. You should stop thinking about your old boyfriend all the time. _____
7. Over 200 people _____ in the hurricane last month, and thousands more were injured.
8. I was very lonely when I first moved to this city, but then I started meeting people and
   _____ improved.

There's an old saying . . . *Actions speak louder than words.*

What a person actually does is more important than what he or she says. We use this saying to tell people that they need to do what they say they will do.

"I'm really sorry for making such a mess in the kitchen, Mother."
"Well, *actions speak louder than words*. How about doing the dishes?"

C Study the underlined words. Then match the sentence parts.

1. She <u>admitted</u> ___	a. to talk to a lawyer.
2. She <u>complained</u> ___	b. that the meeting would be held at 2:00.
3. She <u>reminded</u> us ___	c. to bring our dictionaries to class tomorrow.
4. She <u>advised</u> us ___	d. that we should have a party on the last day of class.
5. She <u>mentioned</u> ___	e. that she had stolen $50,000 from her employer.
6. She <u>announced</u> ___	f. that she'd seen him, but she didn't say where.
7. She <u>proposed</u> ___	g. that her children never called her on her birthday.

Expansion Pages

D Skim the reading "On the Tap-Tap" on page 71 and review these words.
Then use them to complete the sentences below.

> disoriented immaculately submerged filthy
> impassable scarce strandedupheaval

1. I missed the last bus, and I couldn't afford a taxi, so I was _____ in the city late at night.
2. After the earthquake, the roads were _____ because of the damage.
3. My grandmother keeps her kitchen _____ clean. I don't know how she does it!
4. The accident victims seemed _____ when they climbed out of the wrecked bus.
5. In the desert, water is very _____.
6. The boat hit a rock that was _____ under the water, and two hours later it sank.
7. The little boys were _____ after playing soccer in the mud all afternoon.
8. The change in government caused a major _____ in the country.

E Read these sentences describing people's character and write the adjective that means the same thing after them.
Use your dictionary as needed.

> intelligent dishonest annoying generous unfriendly strange

1. My neighbor has a heart of gold. _____
2. His brother is a real cold fish. _____
3. Our new colleague is kind of an oddball. _____
4. Your sister is really a quick study. _____
5. Her new boyfriend is sort of a shady character. _____
6. My boss can be a real pain in the neck! _____

In Other Words

Extraordinary has a positive meaning when applied to a person: *My grandfather was an extraordinary man who taught high school for 50 years.*
Exceptional means someone or something is unusually good: *Tiger Woods is an exceptional golfer who began playing at the age of three.*
Unusual is neutral: *My youngest sister has a very unusual name.*
Strange and odd are both slightly negative: *A strange old woman lives in the house next door. She never talks to anybody. / He asked me an odd question.*

If someone is famous, they are known in many places: *Oprah Winfrey is a famous TV personality.*
If someone is eminent, they are respected by other people in their field: *Dr. Kim is an eminent heart surgeon who developed new life-saving techniques.*
If someone is renowned, they are admired by many people: *Mother Theresa was renowned for her work with the poor.*
Notorious means famous for doing something bad: *D.B. Cooper was a notorious plane hijacker in the U.S.*

 **Watch out!**

excellent
Excellent is an absolute term, and so does not have a comparative or superlative form:
  Michael Jordan was the ~~most excellent~~ basketball player in history.
  Michael Jordan was the most successful basketball player in history.

Review: Units 4-6

1 LANGUAGE CHECK

On a separate sheet of paper, rewrite the sentences using the words
or grammatical indications in parentheses and making all necessary changes.

1. It rained on Saturday, so we couldn't go to the beach. (if)
2. Because they didn't want to wake up the baby, they spoke quietly. (*reduced clause*)
3. "Are you interested in studying abroad next year?" (My teacher asked)
4. We have a lot of homework, so we can't go to the movie with you. (if)
5. "Quit smoking and lose ten kilos!" (My doctor)
6. "I had been working for an hour when my computer crashed." (Lia said)
7. I didn't set my alarm clock, so I was late for class. (if)
8. "Four languages are spoken in Spain." (Jorge told us)
9. Before he became a successful actor, Jared worked as a waiter. (*reduced clause*)
10. He got in a bad car accident while he was driving on a mountain road. (*reduced clause*)
11. "Susan, how many marathons have you run?" (He asked)
12. He became a police officer after he graduated from high school. (*reduced clause*)
13. I didn't know you were going to the party, so I didn't offer you a ride. (if)
14. The concert was boring, so we left early. (if)
15. Because she wanted to study Chinese, Melissa went to Beijing for a year. (*reduced clause*)

2 VOCABULARY CHECK

Complete the sentences with the words from the box, making all necessary changes and adding articles (*a/an*) where needed.

aspirations	retain	immersed in	master	pending	monopoly	greedy	renowned
fixture	channel (v)	mediocre	bump into	proficient	carry on	unethical	

1. I'm not very _____ with computers. I only know how to send e-mail and do simple things like that.
2. Some businesses are too _____ for profits. All they care about is money, not their customers.
3. I hadn't talked to Andrea since she changed jobs, but last week I _____ her at a party. It was great to see her.
4. When I was in high school, I had _____ of becoming a professional athlete.
5. Dr. Suarez is _____ psychologist who studies how children learn.
6. I can't believe that Mr. Harris quit his job! He's been _____ in the company for thirty years.
7. It takes a long time to _____ all the techniques of French cooking and become a chef.
8. Cheating on tests is _____. It's not fair to the students who worked hard.

9. In some countries, the government has _____ on tobacco. All tobacco is produced by one national company.
10. In order to _____ the new vocabulary words you learn and not forget them, you need to use them frequently.
11. Loretta is completely _____ her art work. She spends twelve hours a day painting in her studio.
12. I studied Spanish for six months before my trip to Central America, and by the time I got there, I was able to _____ a conversation with people I met.
13. Last year I _____ all my energy into preparing for the university entrance exam.
14. I didn't like that movie very much. I would say it was just _____.
15. A national election is _____. It will take place sometime next year.

Situation 2

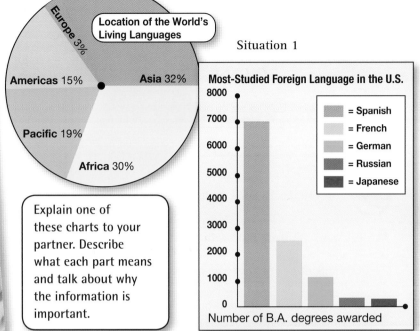

Location of the World's Living Languages

Europe 3%
Americas 15%
Asia 32%
Pacific 19%
Africa 30%

Situation 1

Explain one of these charts to your partner. Describe what each part means and talk about why the information is important.

Most-Studied Foreign Language in the U.S.

= Spanish
= French
= German
= Russian
= Japanese

Number of B.A. degrees awarded

You and your partner are talking about your families. Tell your partner about your favorite relative and why he or she is important to you. Ask questions about what your partner tells you.

A Pair work. Look at the pictures and imagine what the people in each situation might say. Briefly review the language notes from Units 4–6 on pages 155–156.

B Pair work. Role-play situations 1, 2, and 3 with a partner. Notice how well you and your partner do the role play. Ask your partner's opinion about your performance.

Situation 3

A reporter asks you, "What's the biggest problem facing your city today?" Explain your answer for one minute while your partner times you.

C Now rate your speaking. Use + for good, ✓ for OK, and – for things you need to improve. Then add two goals for improvement of your speaking.

How did you do?	1	2	3
I was able to express my ideas.			
I spoke easily and fluently, without hesitation.			
I spoke at a good rate of speed—not too fast or too slow.			
I used new vocabulary from the units.			
I used at least three expressions from the units.			
I practiced the grammar from the units.			
Goals for improvement:			
1. _____			
2. _____			

Who Are You?

Lesson A | Memory and the mind

1 VOCABULARY FOCUS

It completely slipped my mind.

 Do you have a good memory? Explain.

A Pair work. **Do these tasks with a partner. What does each task tell us about how our memory works?**

1. Think of one of your happiest memories. Are you able to recall it in detail? Describe it.
2. Tell your partner what you had for dinner every night for the past five nights.
3. Look at the list of words below for fifteen seconds. Then cover the words and write down as many as you can. How many did you recall? What helped you to remember them?

dog	seventeen	wolf	farm	anxious	organized
salary	return	break	excessive	hungry	visitor

Real English
regimen = a special plan for eating or exercising that is intended to improve your health

B Pair work. **Read the testimonials below and discuss these questions with your partner. Why did each person go to the Memory Center? How did the Center help them?**

Welcome to the Memory Center

The Memory Center   Services   [TESTIMONIALS] | FAQ   Search

水浸しにする、氾濫

"I work in a busy office and I am **inundated** with information every day. For the longest time, I always seemed to be completely disorganized. I'd show up in meetings without my notes or forget my laptop at home. Just the other day, I was supposed to have lunch with a colleague and it completely **slipped my mind**! That's when a friend told me about the Memory Center. At the Center, I learned that I could be less **absentminded** by keeping a diary and **chronicling** all the things I need to do. Instead of thinking about the people and events in my day in an **arbitrary** way, I was shown how to create **associations** between them—to think about them as if they were all part of a story. And it's really worked! Thank you, Memory Center!" ***Bea Suarez, sales representative***

reminisce
to remember with happiness
（ I だよりした）

"I found out about the Memory Center when I was struggling to prepare for my med school exam. No matter how much I studied, I still seemed to have these **lapses** where I couldn't remember anything. I'd take practice tests and **draw a blank** on entire sections. But then trainers at the Center explained that repetition and memorization of facts weren't enough. I learned to **utilize** other strategies to help me remember information. I also worked with a nutritionist to develop a proper exercise and diet regimen. The Memory Center has definitely **enhanced** my ability to retain facts. You should check them out!" ***Kendrick Leung, pre-med student***

利用する
役立てる

increase

To learn more about our flexible and affordable programs, <u>click here</u>!

C Pair work. **Read the testimonials on page 78 again, paying attention to the words in** blue. **Then in each set of words below, cross out the one that does not belong. Explain your choices to a partner.**

1. inundate	flood	overwhelm	hesitate
2. slip one's mind	be forgotten	be remembered	be overlooked
3. forgetful	absentminded	attentive	distracted
4. list	ignore	record	chronicle
5. organized	arbitrary	random	unsystematic
6. link	correlation	association	disconnection
7. gap	retention	interruption	lapse
8. remember	recollect	draw a blank	recall
9. utilize	apply	employ	reject
10. boost	reduce	enhance	promote

▶ **Ask & Answer**

If you were given a free trip to the Memory Center, what would you get help with?

Vocabulary Builder ▲

Pair work. **Look at the word pairs in bold and discuss how they are similar and how they are different. Then complete the sentences with the correct verb.**

1. **remember / reminisce**
   Clara is always (remembering / reminiscing) about her life in Paris twenty years ago.
   I still (remember / reminisce) the first time I visited New York City.

2. **concentrate / contemplate**
   I'm seriously (concentrating / contemplating) studying abroad in New Zealand next year.
   Are you (concentrating / contemplating) on your work or daydreaming about the weekend again?

3. **remind / recall**
   Can you (recall / remind) me to bring a camera to the party tomorrow?
   Do you (recall / remind) where I put my keys? I can't seem to find them.

4. **imagine / conceive**
   When I was a child, I used to (conceive / imagine) that I had an invisible friend.
   How did they manage to (conceive / imagine) of such a brilliant plan?

2 LISTENING

Musical mind

🔊 **A** **You're going to hear a news report. Listen once and complete the sentence below.** (CD Tracks 19 & 20)

The report is about a man who . . .

☐ plays music for critically ill patients.
☐ has been arrested for stealing a piano.
☐ is mistaken for a famous musician.
☐ is only able to recall how to play the piano.

🔊 **B** **Before you listen to the report again, read over the doctor's notes on page 80. Then listen and complete them. If certain information is not available, write** *N/A.* (CD Track 21)

Background

Patient was brought in by police who picked him up on a (1) _beach_ in the south of England.
Patient was wearing a (2) _suit and tie_ that was (3) _celebration_
very wet

Patient details

Patient's first and last names: (4) _No information_ N/A
Patient's age: (5) _20~early 30_ _looks late_
Physical appearance: (6) _Tall and slim blond hair_
Country of birth: (7) _Not available_ N/A
Patient was brought into the hospital without money or (8) _identification_ .

Patient behavior

Patient doesn't (9) _speak_ at all and is still very (10) _Confused_ .
memory lapse
Patient is able to (11) _play the piano_ very well and seems happy only when doing so.

Diagnosis

Patient most likely suffering from (12) _Temporary amnesia_ possibly caused by
can't remember anything
(13) _sudden shock of some kind_

C Pair work. **Listen again and check your notes. Then take turns explaining the Piano Man's story to a partner.** (CD Track 22)

▶ **Ask & Answer**

Have you ever heard of someone who could not remember his or her identity? What happened?

3 LANGUAGE FOCUS

Overview of the passive form

A Pair work. **With a partner complete the chart with the passive forms of these verbs. How is the passive formed in each case?**

	Active	Passive
simple present	teach(es), make(s), call(s)	_is/are taught_ _is/are made_ _is/are called_
simple past	taught, made, called	_____ _____ _____
present continuous	is/are teaching, is/are making, is/are calling	_is/are being taught_ _____ _____
past continuous	was/were teaching, was/were making, was/were calling	_____ _____ _____
present perfect	has/have taught, has/have made, has/have called	_has/have been taught_ _____ _____

B **Read about Franz Mesmer and mesmerism. Find and underline examples of the passive form.**

Franz Anton Mesmer was born in 1734 and was trained as a doctor. He used his hands to "pass over" his female patients to hypnotize them. These patients were supposedly cured by the special energy Mesmer had in his hands. This practice was called "mesmerism." A royal commission was set up to test his methods in 1784. His methods were proven to be false. Mesmer died at the age of 81, a poor man.

That is not the end of the story, however. Modern-day hypnotism is founded on the principles of mesmerism, and hypnotism is still being practiced today. In fact, it has been used for years to help people to break their bad habits.

C Read these sentences about amnesia. Rewrite them in the passive form.

1. The police found a young man wandering on a beach. _A young man was now found wandering on a beach._
2. People are now calling the young man "the Piano Man." _The young man is being called "the" Piano Man."_
3. A sudden shock may have caused the Piano Man's memory loss. _The piano Man's memory loss may have been caused by a sudden shock_
4. Doctors have studied amnesia for many years. _Amnesia has been studied for many years._
5. Hospital officials hope that someone will eventually recognize the Piano Man. _____
Hospital officials hope that the Piano Man will eventually be recognized by someone.

D Pair work. Complete each sentence with the correct passive form of the verb in parentheses. Look at the sentences again and circle the agent if there is one. Why do you think the agent is or isn't mentioned? Discuss with your partner.

1. Every morning the dogs _____ (walk) by a professional dog walker.
2. By the time the police got there, the businessman _____ already _____ (murder).
3. My house _____ still _____ (paint) when I moved in.
4. We _____ (inundate) with phone calls since yesterday morning.
5. The bank _____ (rob) last week. They haven't caught the culprit. The case _____ still _____ (investigate) by New York City police.
6. The capital city _____ (locate) in the southern part of the country.
7. This rare book _____ (write) around 1700.
8. A cure for that disease _____ (discover) by three Belgian scientists.
9. You _____ always _____ (require) to show a picture ID to board an airplane.
10. At the moment, the island _____ (inhabit) by only birds and insects.

> **The agent**
>
> The agent (which the *by* phrase indicates) is used when it gives important information about the doer of the action.
>
> It is omitted when: it is unknown, obvious, has been previously mentioned, or describes a state of being or location.

E Pair work. Write three sentences using the passive form about an item you know. Then read them to another pair. Can they guess the item?

It was started in Brazil.
Dancing and fighting movements are included in it.
It is now practiced by people in many countries.

Is it "capoeira"?

Grammar X-TRA   *Get* in the passive form

The *get* passive can replace the *be* passive in informal situations. It is often used in sentences where there is no agent mentioned. It can also be used in these situations:

I got married last year. (a planned event that has been carried out)
I got hit by a car on my way to school. (a sudden or unexpected event)
I get dressed every morning at 8:00. (something you do yourself)
She always gets her hair done at the same place. (using a service)

Don't use *get* with stative verbs (*see, think, feel,* etc.).

Read these sentences and circle the *get* or *be* passive form. Circle both where appropriate.

1. I (am / get) my suits dry-cleaned once a month.
2. I (was / got) shocked by the news.
3. After dating for eleven months, the couple (was / got) engaged.
4. I don't know how it happened, but somehow I (was / got) fired from my new job.
5. She (was / got) given a new bicycle for her birthday. Unfortunately, it (was / got) stolen the next day.
6. They're (being / getting) their computer repaired.
7. That movie has (been / gotten) seen by two million people.

4 SPEAKING

Let me explain what I mean . . .

A Pair work. **Discuss these questions.**

1. In elementary school, which subjects were easy for you? Which were difficult?
   Did you ever get special help at school for subjects that were difficult?
2. In some countries, children are grouped by ability into different "tracks" in their school classes.
   Is this system of tracking used in your country?
3. What are some positive and some negative points of tracking students by ability?

B **Read these opposing viewpoints about tracking students. Choose the speaker you agree with most and write notes about your reasons.**

"Tracking students by ability makes teaching easier, because all students in the class are at the same level. It's just not realistic to expect all children to master the same course work. Besides, students feel more comfortable and learn better when they're grouped with others who are like them. Furthermore, tracking enables teachers to plan the right instruction for the needs of a specific group of students. How can the same math teacher in the same class prepare some students for calculus while others are still struggling with basic arithmetic?"

Judy Johnstone, eighth grade teacher

"It's highly unfair to decide children's futures on the basis of a test they take at an early age. Tracking leads students to take on labels—both in their own minds as well as in the minds of their teachers. And for those on the lower tracks, the lower expectations lead to poor motivation in school. Once students are grouped, they generally stay at that level for their school careers, and the gap between levels becomes greater and greater over time. When we expect low achievement from a particular group of students, that's exactly what happens."

Frank DeMarini, President of Parents for Better Schools

"A much better alternative to tracking is cooperative learning, where small groups of students work together on all classroom projects. All students in a group learn the same course work together, and because they receive a grade together, they share responsibility for the success or failure of their group. The stronger students help the weaker ones, and they all support each other's efforts. For the most part, teachers act as guides and partners, not as givers of knowledge. Cooperative learning is also a good way to emphasize the development of students' social skills."

Dr. Magdalena Torres, professor of education

C Pair work. **Follow the instructions.**

1. **Student A:** Tell your partner which speaker you agree with most, and why. Use expressions from the box below.
   Try to speak for at least one minute.
   Student B: Time your partner. Ask questions only if your partner runs out of ideas.
2. Switch roles and repeat.

D Pair work. **Choose the speaker you disagree with most. This time, do NOT write notes. Take turns giving your opinion and the reasons for it while your partner times you.**

Expanding on a topic

Agreeing formally
 I am in complete agreement with . . .
 There's no doubt that . . .
 I couldn't agree more with . . .

Disagreeing formally
 I can't agree with . . .
 I can't accept that . . .
 I couldn't disagree more with . . .

Expanding on a response
 I have several reasons. First, . . .
 Take for example the case of . . .
 Let me explain what I mean by . . .
 Consider what would happen if . . .

Who Are You?

Lesson B | Personality plus

1 GET READY TO READ

Sibling rivalry

 How would you describe your family growing up? Did you get along with your siblings?

A Read what these siblings have to say about each other. Then read their mother's comments.

Sanjeev, 20

Sunita, 17

Laila, 15

It's a hassle being the oldest. My mother is always telling me I have to take on more responsibility and set a good example for the others.

What he says . . .
about Sunita: She has it easier than I did at her age. She has a lot more freedom.
about Laila: She's a good kid, but I wish she wouldn't try to tag along with me and my friends.

Right now I'm trying to keep my grades up and do well in school. I try to get along with my brother and sister and not let them get on my nerves too much.

What she says . . .
about Sanjeev: He gets all the privileges.
about Laila: She gets spoiled by my mom because she's the youngest.

I wish my parents would trust me more and stop babying me. I'm almost 16, which is old enough to do lots of things.

What she says . . .
about Sanjeev: Sometimes he's bossy—a real know-it-all. But I know he also cares about me.
about Sunita: I'm tired of being in my sister's shadow. Everyone always asks, "Are you Sunita's sister? She's *so* smart!"

Lakshmi, 40

What their mother says . . .
They're all good kids, each one is special in a different way. Sanjeev is conscientious—he really watches out for his sisters. Sunita is the diplomatic one—she can see both sides of an issue and breaks up arguments. Laila is very social—she has lots of friends.

B Group work. Get into groups of three. Choose one sibling each from A and describe him or her in your own words.

C Pair work. Think about the birth order in your family and then discuss these questions with a partner. Try to use some of the words in blue from A in your answers.

1. What kind of relationship did you have with your siblings? If you were an only child, what kind of relationship did you have with your parents?
2. How did these relationships affect the person you are today?
3. Did you have a special role to play in your family (e.g., the responsible child, the social child, etc.)?

Skimming

To skim, quickly read through the text. Don't pay attention to the details, but try to get the gist (main point) of the text. How is it organized? How are the main points presented?

A Pair work. **Skim the article on page 85, and then circle the sentence that best describes the reading. Compare your answer with a partner.**

1. Psychologists need new theories on birth order.
2. Firstborns are the most responsible.
3. Birth order can form your character.
4. The ideal number of children is two.

B Pair work. **Look at these words with a partner. Make sure you understand their meaning. Which children do you think they describe? Why? Write the words in the chart under the appropriate heading. Then read the article carefully to see if your predictions are correct.**

> agreeable   conscientious   fun-loving   responsible
> ambitious   creative   outgoing   self-disciplined
> amusing   dependable   peacekeeper   social
> comfortable around adults   diplomatic

Oldest children	Middle children	Youngest children	Only children

C **Read the article again. Then read the sentences below and circle your answers. List examples from the article that support your answers.**

1. Bridget is the oldest / the middle / the youngest / an only child.
   She wants her siblings to pay more attention to her / get along.
   Example: _____

2. Willie is the oldest / the middle / the youngest / an only child.
   Willie listens / doesn't listen to his parents.
   Example: _____
   Example: _____

3. Diana is the oldest / the middle / the youngest / an only child.
   She's reliable / unreliable.
   Example: _____
   Example: _____

4. Justin is the oldest / the middle / the youngest / an only child.
   He amuses himself / gets bored easily.
   Example: _____

D Pair work. **Based on the article, which children do you think the expressions in the box below describe? Do you know anybody who fits these descriptions? Discuss your ideas with a partner.**

> • expected to set a good example   • gets on your nerves
> • always takes on more responsibility   • can see both sides of an issue

▶ Ask & Answer

Do you agree with the ideas in the reading? Why or why not?

Born to be wild!

Does your birth order in the family influence your personality?

The birth order can influence everything from self-discipline to sense of humor
By Emilie Le Beau

Diana is organized and reliable. She turns in her homework on time and says she's good about checking in with her parents while she's out with friends.

"I keep my grades up and I'm responsible for getting things done," says Diana, 15.

It would come as no surprise to many experts that Diana is the oldest child in her family. Some psychologists believe that your place in the family can shape your personality, influencing whether you are responsible, a risk-taker, or ridiculously funny.

"Oldest children are usually responsible," says Frank J. Sulloway, research scholar and author of *Born to Rebel* (Random House), a book on the significance of birth order.

"Firstborns are more likely to serve as parents," Sulloway says. "As a result, firstborns tend to be more conscientious."

Firstborn children, he adds, are rule keepers who also are ambitious and self-disciplined.

Diana, with two younger siblings, says the responsible part is true and that her parents tend to ask her for help first. "My parents usually ask me before they ask my brother or sister," she says. "Sometimes it's a pain."

She says some of the other firstborn characteristics, like being organized, also are a good description of her. She always sets the weekend plans with friends. "I'm always the one organizing things," she says.

While oldest children are known for being dependable, middle kids usually are peacekeepers who are social and diplomatic, according to Sulloway.

Bridget is a middle kid in her family. She's the fourth child out of nine but says she wouldn't describe herself as outgoing. "I'm more quiet when I'm not at home," says Bridget, 11.

"Peacekeeper" is a better fit for Bridget, who says she breaks up fights between her sibs. "If some of my younger siblings are arguing about a toy, I try to work it out," she says. "I find something else that someone can play with and tell them to stop arguing with each other."

The little ones might argue occasionally, but last-born children tend to be the most agreeable, fun-loving, and amusing. Older children have physical strength over the younger kids, so humor is one way last-born children can get what they want.

Youngest children are also creative, outgoing, and open to new experiences, Sulloway says. Justin H. is the youngest in his family and says that is an accurate description of him.

"My mom has always said I'm creative," says Justin, 15. "If my brother isn't around, I'm always looking for stuff to do around the house for fun."

But what happens if you're an only child?

Kids without siblings often have traits similar to firstborn kids. Only children are usually ambitious and good at following parents' rules, Sulloway says.

Willie B., 11, agrees. Willie says he doesn't talk back and always wears his helmet when inline skating. He also cares for his family's four pets.

But unlike kids with siblings, only children usually are quite comfortable around adults, Sulloway says.

"I've been around adults since I was little. I'm kind of more experienced," Willie says.

And while only children are good around adults, youngest children question authority and usually are leaders in social movements, Sulloway adds.

Exceptions to the norm

Your sister was already in high school when you were born? So are you an only or a youngest?

You might be more like an only, even if you're the youngest. Age gaps can affect sibling relationships, says Sulloway.

And if you have a much older sibling but also have a younger sib, then you are probably more like an oldest child than a middle.

Kids who don't have siblings until they are more than six years old usually are like only children, Sulloway adds.

3 WRITING
Writing a short essay

A Pair work. **Each of these sentences contains one of the following three types of errors in sentence structure. With a partner identify the type of error and rewrite the sentences correctly on a separate piece of paper.**

- fragment (F) = not a complete sentence
- run-on sentence (ROS) = two sentences not separated by punctuation
- comma splice (CS) = two sentences incorrectly connected with a comma

1. I get bored very easily, I'm always looking for new experiences. _____
2. Because I have many friends and like to talk a lot. _____
3. I get in trouble for talking without thinking people sometimes get angry at things I say. _____
4. I don't like to go out on weekends, I would rather stay home and relax. _____
5. People sometimes think I'm aloof I don't talk very much. _____
6. Even though I like to go to parties and see my friends. _____

B **Take this personality test. Check (✓) the sentences that are true about you all or most of the time.**

A	B
I like to be with groups of people. ___	I like to relax alone or with a few close friends. ___
I enjoy talking with people, even strangers. ___	My friends say I'm a good listener. ___
I like a lot of variety in my life. ___	Being very active makes me feel tired. ___
Generally speaking, I have plenty of energy. ___	I think very carefully about what I say. ___
I tend to speak first and think later. ___	I have a few very close friends. ___
I have a big circle of friends. ___	I talk a lot only when the topic is truly important. ___
Being very active gives me more energy. ___	People think I'm very calm. ___
I enjoy being in public places that are filled with activity. ___	I hate feeling rushed or being interrupted. ___

C **Count the number of sentences you checked in each list: A _____ B _____.**
Then read the description of the personality type that you had the most answers for below.

Personality A—Extroverted: Extroverts are people who focus outward and get their energy from being with other people. They are quick thinkers and quick talkers–people whose nervous systems seem to run faster. They enjoy a lot of stimulation and activity.

Personality B—Introverted: Introverts are people who focus inward and get their energy from being alone. They are deep and thoughtful people who prefer to take their time and make decisions slowly. They need plenty of peace and quiet to be happy.

D Pair work. **Work with a partner who got a different personality result from yours. Discuss your similarities and differences. You are going to write a short essay comparing and contrasting the personalities of you and your partner, so take notes to use for the essay.**

E **Write a short essay comparing and contrasting the personalities of you and your partner using your notes. Try to use some of the words in the box for comparison and contrast. Include:**

- an introduction
- a paragraph about your similarities
- a paragraph about your differences
- a conclusion

Comparing and contrasting	
Making a comparison	
both	similarly
so do I / so am I	just like I do / I am
Showing a contrast	
however	in contrast
whereas	on the other hand

F Pair work. **Exchange your essay with a different partner. Then read each other's essays and discuss.**

Brain teaser

A Pair work. **With your partner, select the best answer for each item in the test as quickly as you can. Try to be the first pair to finish in your class.**

1. STOP is to POST as 1234 is to ___*C*___.
   a. 4321   **b.** 4123   **c.** 4312   **d.** 4132

2. What number comes next in the series?
   1, 1, 2, 3, 5, 8, 13, ___*b*___
   a. 20   **b.** 21   **c.** 23   **d.** 26

3. If you rearrange the letters IIMMA, you would have the name of a ___*a*___.
   a. city   **b.** animal   **c.** color   **d.** celebrity

   Joe
   Tom Jim

4. Joe is older than Tom. Jim is younger than Joe. Which statement is true?
   a. Jim is older than Tom.   **c.** Tom and Jim are the same age.
   b. Tom is older than Jim.   **d.** It's impossible to tell.

5. Tony is 2. His cousin is three times his age. When Tony is 6, how old will his cousin be?
   a. 8   **b.** 9   **c.** 10   **d.** 12

   2×3 -

6. *Nest* is to *bird* as _____.
   a. shell / turtle   **b.** dam / beaver   **c.** flower / bee   **d.** forest / bear
   don't have plan

7. *Arbitrary* is the opposite of _____.
   a. realistic   **b.** disorganized   **c.** uncertain   **d.** systematic

8. If firstborn children are conscientious and Harry is the oldest child in his family, we can assume that he is _____ child.
   a. the least reliable   **c.** the most outgoing
   b. the most dependable   **d.** the least agreeable

9. Which of the following is least like the others?
   a. jacket   **b.** shirt   **c.** watch   **d.** sweater

10. *Extrovert* is to *sociable* as *introvert* is to _____.
    a. reserved   **b.** easygoing   **c.** demanding   **d.** absentminded

B Group work. **Check your answers on page 168. Discuss any questions that you got wrong. Which pair in your class finished fastest? Which pair got the most right?**

C Pair work. **Look at the types of questions in A. With your partner, create four test questions of your own on a separate piece of paper.**

D Group work. **Exchange questions with another pair in your class. See how fast you can answer their questions. How many did you get right?**

World Link

Even though twins are the same age, they can have different birth order traits. Researchers think this may be due to family members who assign roles to the twins in order to distinguish them from each other. In this way, the first-born twin might be thought of as the leader, while the second-born is called the baby of the family.

Source: *www.drspock.com*

CNN® **Check out the CNN® video.**   **Practice your English online at** elt.heinle.com/worldpass

Unit 7: Who Are You?

A Study the phrases with *mind* and match them with their meanings.

1. make up your mind ___
2. keep in mind ___
3. have a mind of your own ___
4. read someone's mind ___
5. speak your mind ___
6. out of your mind ___
7. take your mind off something ___
8. slip your mind ___

a. guess another person's thoughts correctly
b. disappear from your memory
c. crazy
d. think or act independently
e. express your true opinion
f. make you stop worrying
g. remember
h. decide

B Complete the sentences with one of the phrases from **A**, making all necessary changes.

1. Even though my daughter is only four, she _____. She has very strong opinions about food, toys, and everything else!
2. I meant to bring my CDs to the party, but then it completely _____, so we didn't have any good music to dance to.
3. When you asked if I wanted to take a break from studying, you _____. I was so tired!
4. Playing tennis after work helps me to _____ all the problems at the office, so I can relax when I get home.
5. You agreed to go on a date with Donald? Are you _____? The only thing he ever talks about is his mother!
6. So, what do you want for dinner tonight? You have to _____ soon, because the supermarket closes in an hour.
7. When you plan a trip to Brazil, _____ that distances can be great, so you need to allow plenty of time to get around.
8. Don't be afraid to _____ when you talk to the teacher. If you're feeling bored in class, she should know about that.

C Circle the correct word to complete each sentence.

1. I always get nervous when I go on vacation because I can't ___ if I turned off my stove!
   a. remember   b. remind   c. reminisce
2. Could you turn off the TV, please? I'm trying to ___ on my homework!
   a. concentrate   b. contemplate   c. conceive
3. Before the invention of the Internet, people couldn't ___ of such universal access to information.
   a. reminisce   b. conceive   c. contemplate
4. If you're serious about a career in international business, you should ___ getting a summer job overseas.
   a. recall   b. imagine   c. contemplate
5. Every time I get together with my old friend Kayla, we always ___ about the trip we took to Hawaii.
   a. contemplate   b. reminisce   c. imagine
6. ___ that you've just won a million dollars in the lottery. What would you do with the money?
   a. Recall   b. Imagine   c. Conceive
7. When I go to the supermarket, ___ me to get some coffee—there's none left.
   a. recall   b. remind   c. remember
8. I don't ___ the name of the person I spoke to on the phone.
   a. recall   b. imagine   c. remind

I didn't know that!

The word *nice* originally came from a Latin word that meant "ignorant." Later, the meaning shifted to "foolish," then to "foolishly precise," and then to "precise in a good way," before it finally came to have the present meaning of "pleasant or friendly."

Expansion Pages

D Complete the chart by matching each personality description in the box with the opposite meaning in the chart, using your dictionary as needed. Then circle the terms that describe your personality.

> a risk-taker   quiet   a peacekeeper   organized   bossy
> conscientious   creative   fun-loving   social   diplomatic

1. irresponsible	
2. argumentative	
3. serious	
4. agreeable	
5. standoffish	
6. talkative	
7. tactless	
8. unimaginative	
9. cautious	
10. chaotic	

E Match the sentence parts to show the meanings of the underlined expressions.

1. If you <u>see both sides of an issue</u>, ____
2. If you <u>keep your grades up</u>, ____
3. When you <u>tag along with someone</u>, ____
4. If you are <u>in someone's shadow</u>, ____
5. To <u>set a good example</u>, ____
6. If you <u>get on someone's nerves</u>, ____
7. When you <u>take on responsibility</u>, ____

a. you act in an annoying way.
b. you are in charge of doing something.
c. you do something good for others to imitate.
d. you are not as well-known as he or she is.
e. you do very well in school.
f. you go everywhere with him or her.
g. you understand different points of view.

In Other Words

If you forget something, it's gone from your memory: *I felt so embarrassed when I forgot my boss's husband's name.*

If you misplace something, you can't remember where you put it: *I always misplace my sunglasses and have to buy new ones—and then I find the old pair the next day!*

If you overlook something, you don't notice something that is important: *Lia filled out the university application form, but she overlooked the last page and didn't answer those questions.*

To remember is to access any kind of information from your past: *I can remember helping my mother cook when I was little, and I still remember her recipe for potato soup.*

If you reminisce, you talk about happy memories from the past: *At the class reunion, the students reminisced about the tricks they played on their science teacher.*

When you remind someone, you help them to remember something: *Jesse reminded me to take my books back to the library.* You can also remind yourself: *I reminded myself about my New Year's resolution to lose weight, and I didn't eat dessert.*

When you memorize something, you put it into your memory exactly: *Last year, we memorized one hundred English words that are difficult to spell.*

Watch out!

eldest

Eldest is used to describe the oldest of a group of people, especially a group of siblings. It is only used in describing people, not things.

> *My father was the eldest of twelve children.*
> *That building is the ~~eldest~~ in our city. That building is the oldest in our city.*

Happy Days

Lesson A | What makes you happy?

1 VOCABULARY FOCUS

A love–hate relationship

WARM UP Have you ever heard the expression "love–hate relationship"? What do you think it means?

A Pair work. **Read this book review and answer the questions below with a partner.**

END YOUR LOVE–HATE RELATIONSHIP WITH TV & VIDEO GAMES
a book review by Jill Halston

You may have thought video gaming and TV watching were mind-numbing activities of no educational value. An author of a brand-new book wants you to see it differently.

When I first started reading Steven Johnson's book, *Everything Bad is Good for You*, I had some **misgivings** about his ideas. They seemed so hard to believe. But as I read more, I gradually **warmed up to** his theory. Despite what many of us may think about modern pop culture, Johnson claims that it can actually contribute to our overall well-being, and that activities such as video gaming and watching TV can actually make us smarter!

Sounds **absurd**, right? That's what I thought, too. But as I **kept on** reading, Johnson started to **win** me **over** to the idea. Take video games, for example. Johnson explains that they can help us improve not only our hand-eye coordination but also our general level of intelligence as well. Unlike older, more traditional games, contemporary video games require you to figure out the rules and how to win on your own. You also have to remember a lot of information at once and be able to **think on your feet** in order to win. In addition, a lot of multiplayer games enable you to meet other players and to be part of an online community that shares the same interests. How cool is that?

The same goes for modern-day TV programming, says Johnson. Old shows often had a limited number of characters, a **linear** plot, and a predictable ending. Newer shows have many characters with several plot lines occurring **simultaneously**. There's no way that you can space out while you're watching. You need to really concentrate just to **keep up** and understand what's happening. And like multiplayer games, more shows on television today are interactive—they invite home audience participation.

Still don't buy this argument? Read Johnson's book. I was a **skeptic**, too, at first. But now I'm convinced that gaming and TV aren't just another form of **mindless** entertainment. So, the next time you **lose track** of time because you're glued to your TV set, don't feel guilty about it—you may actually be doing yourself a favor by exercising your brain!

---

1. Look at the title of the article. What do you think a "love–hate relationship" means?
2. What does Steven Johnson think about video games and TV watching?
3. What does Jill Halston, the reviewer, think of Steven's ideas?

B Circle the best answer to complete each definition.

1. When you have **misgivings** about something, you feel certain / uncertain about it.
2. If you **warm up to** an idea, you gradually / suddenly like it.
3. An **absurd** comment is logical / ridiculous.
4. To **keep on** doing something means to continue / stop doing it.
5. When you **win** someone **over** to an idea, you disagree with / convince them.
6. To **think on your feet** means to respond slowly / quickly.

Real English
space out =
(informal) be in a daze

1. When you have **misgivings** about something, you feel certain / <u>uncertain</u> about it.
2. If you **warm up to** an idea, you <u>gradually</u> / suddenly like it.
3. An **absurd** comment is logical / <u>ridiculous</u>.
4. To **keep on** doing something means to <u>continue</u> / stop doing it.
5. When you **win** someone **over** to an idea, you disagree with / <u>convince</u> them.
6. To **think on your feet** means to respond slowly / <u>quickly</u>.
7. A **linear** path is a <u>direct</u> / crooked one.

C Group work. **Do you agree or disagree with these statements? Discuss with other members of your group.**

1. You can learn a lot from watching TV.
2. Overall, video games are a negative influence.
3. There is value in the fact that watching TV is relaxing.
4. Having friends online is the same as having friends in "real life."

Vocabulary Builder ▲

Place these compound adjectives in the appropriate column. Then study the two parts of the adjective. What do you think each means? Which are used to describe people? Which are used to describe things?

~~mind-numbing~~   light-hearted   absent-minded   smooth-talking
labor-saving   long-lasting   pleasure-seeking   thick-skinned

Adjective + noun + -ed	Adjective/Adverb/Noun + present participle
	mind-numbing

Real English
peers = people who are the same age or status as you

2 LISTENING

Who is happy?

A Pair work. **You are going to hear an interview with a "happiness expert." What kind of people do you think are happiest? Look at the list in B, make your guesses and discuss them with a partner.**

B Listen to the interview and complete only the main points 1–6 in the following list. (CD Tracks 23 & 24)

In general, people who are happy . . .
  1. have their basic <u>financial needs</u> met.
   • They have fewer day-to-day <u>worries</u>.
  2. are <u>married</u>.
   • They have someone to <u>rely</u> on.
   • They have someone to share their life <u>experiences</u> with.
  3. are adults.
   • They are not as <u>unhappy</u> as younger people.

  4. have some kind of <u>spiritual belief</u> system.
   • They feel it <u>supports</u> them.
   • They feel it gives <u>meaning</u> to their lives.
  5. have a lot of <u>friends</u>.
   • They feel a sense of <u>community</u>
  6. are not necessarily people with a high <u>education</u> or good <u>IQs</u>.
   • <u>Intelligence</u> and <u>education</u> aren't guarantees for happiness.

C Listen again. Complete the notes under each main point in B with the supporting points that explain why certain people tend to be happy. (CD Track 25)

▶ **Ask & Answer**

Do you think you and your peers are happier than people your parents' age? Why or why not? How about people your grandparents' age?

Note-taking tip

Organize your notes by main points. Supporting points for each main idea are listed below and indented.

Phrasal verbs

A Read these sentences and notice the <u>underlined</u> phrasal verbs with *up* or *down*. Place the phrasal verbs in the chart below.

1. Time <u>is up</u>. Please <u>put</u> your pencils <u>down</u> and close your test booklets.
2. <u>Hold</u> your hand <u>up</u> if you know the answer.
3. The department store <u>closed down</u> because there were too few customers.
4. In many religions people sometimes <u>kneel down</u> to pray.
5. I think we've <u>used up</u> the milk. Could you buy some more?
6. By the time the fire department arrived, the building had already <u>burned down</u>.

> **Understanding phrasal verbs**
>
> - Phrasal verbs are two- and three-word verbs that consist of a verb and a particle (preposition and/or adverb).
> - The particle extends and changes the meaning of the main verb.
>   I could not have *picked* a better suitcase.
>   (*picked* = chosen)
>   I *picked up* my suitcase and walked away.
>   (*picked up* = lifted)

Up means . . .		*Down* means . . .	
upward movement	completely finished	downward movement	completely finished
Hold up	is up used up	put down kneel down	close down burned down

B Read this story. Circle the best particle to complete each phrasal verb. Use your dictionary if you need to. Then answer the questions.

1. Which verbs refer to a positive or happy condition?
2. Which verbs refer to a negative or angry condition?

[handwritten: get really angry]
[handwritten: he doesn't say anything]

My sister first met Stan five years ago. They **hit** it (1) on / off right away and soon started dating. A few months later, they decided to get married.

I remember when my sister told my father. He's the kind of person who keeps his feelings **bottled** (2) up / down, but when he heard the news he **blew** (3) up / around—he was absolutely furious. He didn't want my sister to marry Stan. I guess Dad thought Stan wasn't good enough for his "little girl."

[handwritten: little bottle]

My sister tried to talk to my father calmly—to get him to **simmer** (4) back / down—but he wouldn't listen. He **stormed** (5) through / out of the house and didn't return until hours later. My sister was really hurt. Later, she told my father she was a grown woman and could make her own decisions. My father apologized and they **made** (6) over / up.

[handwritten: to make it correct]

So in the end, Stan married my sister. On that day, the happy couple were **bubbling** (7) over / through with joy. Now my father sometimes even **bursts** (8) out / in laughing when he remembers how angry he was at first—especially since Stan is like a son to him now.

[handwritten: can't stop laughing]
[handwritten: so happy]

C Study the rules in the box.

> **Transitive and intransitive phrasal verbs**
>
> - Phrasal verbs can be transitive or intransitive.
> - Transitive verbs take an object: *She demanded <u>an answer</u>.*
> - Intransitive verbs do not: *After five minutes, we moved on to the next exhibit.*
>
> - Most transitive phrasal verbs are separable. This means the noun object can come after the particle or between the verb and the particle.
>   > *Let's call in <u>an expert</u> for another opinion.*
>   > *Let's call <u>an expert</u> in for another opinion.*
>
> - If the object is a pronoun, it comes between the verb and the particle.
>   > *Let's call <u>her</u> in for another opinion.*
>
> - There are some phrasal verbs that are transitive, but inseparable. That means you cannot separate the verb and the particle.
>   > *I ran into <u>Bob</u> downtown.*   INCORRECT: *~~I ran Bob into downtown.~~*
>   > *I ran into <u>him</u> downtown.*   INCORRECT: *~~I ran him into downtown.~~*

D Read these tips for a happy marriage. Circle the object if there is one. Then put each phrasal verb in the chart below.

1. The first tip is an obvious one. Make sure you <u>show up</u> on your wedding day!
2. When you've had a disagreement, don't go to bed angry. Always <u>make up</u> before you fall asleep. If you don't <u>clear</u> matters <u>up</u>, you'll regret it the next day.
3. If your spouse doesn't like one of your old habits, consider <u>giving</u> it <u>up</u>.
4. If you're a messy person, get organized. When you're finished with something, remember to <u>put</u> it <u>away</u>. Don't leave a mess!
5. <u>Face up to</u> your mistakes. Apologize, ask for forgiveness, and <u>move on</u>.
6. If you should happen to <u>run into</u> an old boyfriend or girlfriend, be polite and keep the conversation short.
7. Don't be serious all the time. Do silly things together–<u>dress up</u> in crazy costumes for a party, for example.
8. Don't <u>count on</u> your spouse being available for all social events. Do some things by yourself.

Intransitive two-word verbs	Transitive two-word verbs		Three-word verbs
	Separable	Inseparable	

E Complete these conversations with the correct form of the phrasal verb in parentheses and a pronoun object.

1. A: I thought you still smoked.
   B: No, I _____ (give up) last month.

2. A: You'll never believe who I saw yesterday . . . Peter!
   B: Really? Where did you _____ (run into)?

3. A: I've finished my essay at last!
   B: I'm sorry, but you'll have to _____ (do over). You made too many mistakes.

4. A: I can't finish this homework assignment. It's too difficult.
   B: I think I know the answers. Do you want to _____ (go over) together?

5. A: Joanne has a new car and a summer home.
   B: Why do you care? You shouldn't worry about _____ (keep up with)!

6. A: Are you and your husband taking the kids to Disneyland?
   B: Yes. They _____ (talk into) going. I don't really want to go, but the kids will have fun.

> **Real English**
> Some transitive verbs, such as *do over* and *talk into*, are always separated by an object.

F Pair work. Do you know anyone who is in a happy relationship (e.g., you, a friend, your parents)?
Why is it a good relationship? Explain your ideas to a partner. Try to use phrasal verbs from B, C, and D in your answer.

4 SPEAKING

What do you mean by . . . ?

A Pair work. Read each question and the responses that follow. Which of the three answers is most likely to generate further discussion? What strategy does the respondent use in each case to keep the conversation going?

1. Q: Do you come from a big family?
   - Yes, I do.
   - Yes, I do. There are four of us.
   - Yes, I do. There are four of us, and that's because my parents both came from big families. They wanted lots of kids.

2. Q: Can money buy happiness?
   - I don't think so.
   - I don't think so, but it might.
   - It depends. I don't think it can buy long-lasting happiness, but in the short term it can make life easier.

3. Q: Do you feel happier after exercising?
   - I don't know.
   - I don't know since I don't really exercise a lot.
   - I don't know since I don't really exercise a lot, but I have a friend who says it helps her to feel calmer.

B Pair work. Another strategy to keep a conversation going is to ask follow-up questions. Interview a partner using the questions below. Use the expressions in the box to keep the conversation going.

1. Who is the happiest person in your family?
2. Are you naturally an optimist or a pessimist?
3. Do you enjoy doing things with your family?

C Pair work. Choose one of the questions below and keep a conversation about it going for three minutes by giving informative answers, expanding answers to *yes / no* questions, and asking follow-up questions. Then switch roles and choose another question.

- Which hobby or interest of yours brings you the most happiness?
- What is your happiest memory from childhood?
- If you're feeling down, what do you do to cheer yourself up?

Keeping a conversation going
Expanding answers to *yes / no* questions *Yes, I do, and that's because . . .* *Sometimes that's true, but on the other hand . . .* *No, I'm not, except for . . .* *Yes, I am, and also . . .* **Asking follow-up questions** *What do you mean by . . . ?* *Something I was wondering about is . . .* *Can you tell me a little more about . . . ?* *Why do you say that . . . ?*

Most human beings are constantly searching for happiness, but that's not what many of us are reading about. One popular online bookseller lists around 4,500 books about happiness, but almost 88,000 books about sadness!

Source: *www.amazon.com*

UNIT

8 Happy Days

Lesson B | Look on the bright side!

1 GET READY TO READ

When do you feel your best?

Do you think that things like the weather, time of day, or day of the week can have an effect on a person's mood? Explain.

A Read these statements, paying attention to the words and phrases in blue.

Spring, Summer, Winter, or Fall...
When do you feel your best?

Summer—definitely! Warm days and evenings, shorter nights. Actually, I tend to feel my best in the late afternoon anyway and like sleeping in till noon—which I can do in the summer when school's out.

I'm trying to **turn over a new leaf**, though, and get started earlier in the day. I graduate from college next spring and need to start going on job interviews. I'm not sure how I'm going to do it, though—job hunting and then doing the 9 to 5 thing. I'm **miserable** in the mornings—especially in the winter when the days here are **bleak**!

Kentaro, 23 – Toronto

I guess I'd say that October is the time of year when I feel my best. The worst of the summer heat has passed, and as a result, I feel less **lethargic** and have more energy.

I also normally schedule my vacation to **coincide** with my boyfriend's time off in October, and we go somewhere together. By the end of the month, I return to work feeling rested and **rejuvenated**.

In terms of when I'm at my worst, well, I guess that'd be in August when the temperatures here soar. The hot weather makes me tired and **grouchy**!

Elin, 25 – Stockholm

B Answer each question by circling the correct person's name. What information in A helped you make your choices?

Which person . . .

1. is trying to make a change in his or her life?	Kentaro	Elin
2. has very little energy when the weather is hot?	Kentaro	Elin
3. feels terrible in the morning?	Kentaro	Elin
4. is usually in a bad mood in warm weather?	Kentaro	Elin
5. feels reenergized after a holiday?	Kentaro	Elin

C Pair work. When do you feel your best? Your worst? Complete the chart and discuss your answers with a partner. What could your partner do to feel better when feeling his or her worst?

	I feel my best . . .	I feel my worst . . .
time of day	after the class	before go to sleep
day of the week	Thursday	Monday
season of the year	spring	automn to winter

Identify cause and effect

Certain words and phrases signal a cause or an effect.
- *Because* and *since* answer the question *Why?* and give reasons for something. *So, therefore, as a result,* and *consequently* describe an effect or consequence.
- In some texts, these words and phrases are not used. You must infer the causes and effects from the text.

A Pair work. Read the title and subtitle of the article on page 97. Why do you think that January 24 has been called the worst day of the year in Britain? Make a list of some of your ideas and discuss them with a partner.

B The diagram is describing a chain of cause and effect. Study it for a moment. Then read the article through line 33 and complete the chart.

January 24: The worst day of the year in Britain

3 main causes
1. New Year's celebrations are over.
2. _____
3. _____

People feel depressed.

Many people are at their lowest on January 24.

People are likely to
4. _____
during this time in order to feel better.

People now feel more positive and will probably . . .
5. _____
6. _____
7. _____

C Pair work. Discuss your answers in B, using words and phrases that signal a cause or effect.

January 24th is the worst day of the year in Britain because New Year's celebrations are over, and as a result, people feel depressed . . .

D Read the second half of the article on page 97 (from lines 34–52) and answer the questions.

1. What is SAD and why are people who live near the equator less likely to suffer from it?

   _____

2. Dr. Cohen mentions three possible causes for depression. What are they?

   _____

3. Who hopes to benefit from Dr. Arnall's study? What do you think they plan to do with the results of the study?

   _____

E Match each synonym below with one of the phrasal verbs in bold in the reading.

1. coming in large numbers _____
2. removed _____
3. pay money that you owe _____
4. gradually become understood _____
5. making you feel tired by gradually lessening your energy _____

F Pair work. Imagine that you work for a travel agency in London where it's currently the second week in January. With a partner, create a winter-travel brochure that takes the ideas discussed in the reading into account. Then share your brochure with the class.

World Pass NEWS

Jan. 24 called worst day of the year
British psychologist calculates 'most depressing day'
Updated: 1:51 a.m. ET Jan. 24

By Jennifer Carlile
Reporter

LONDON - Is the midwinter weather **wearing** you **down**? Are you sinking in debt after the holidays? Angry with yourself for *already* breaking your New Year's resolutions? Wish you could crawl back under the covers and not have to face another day of rain, sleet, snow, and paperwork? Probably. After all, it's Jan. 24, the "most depressing day of the year," according to a U.K. psychologist.

Dr. Cliff Arnall's calculations show that misery peaks Monday. Arnall, who specializes in seasonal disorders at the University of Cardiff, Wales, created a formula that takes into account numerous feelings to devise people's lowest point. The model is:

$$\frac{[W + (D-d)] \times TQ}{M \times NA}$$

The equation is broken down into seven variables: (W) weather, (D) debt, (d) monthly salary, (T) time since Christmas, (Q) time since failed quit attempt, (M) low motivational levels, and (NA) the need to take action.

'Reality starts to kick in'
Arnall found that, while days technically get longer after Dec. 21, cyclonic weather systems take hold in January, bringing low, dark clouds to Britain. Meanwhile, the majority of people break their healthy resolutions six to seven days into the new year, and even the hangers-on have fallen off the wagon, **torn off** the nicotine patches, and eaten the fridge empty by the third week. Any residual dregs of holiday cheer and family fun have kicked the bucket by Jan. 24.

"Following the initial thrill of New Year's celebrations and changing over a new leaf, reality starts to **sink in**," Arnall said. "The realization coincides with the dark clouds **rolling in** and the obligation to **pay off** Christmas credit card bills."

The formula was devised to help a travel company "analyze when people book holidays and holiday trends," said Alex Kennedy, spokesperson for Porter Novelli, a London-based PR agency. It seems that people are most likely to buy a ticket to paradise when they feel like hell. "People feel bleak when they have nothing planned, but once they book a holiday they have a goal, they work toward having time off and a relaxing period," Kennedy said. "When you imagine yourself on the beach it makes you feel positive. You will save money, go to the gym and come back to the optimism you had at the end of the year," she said.

In U.K., up to a third get SAD
Research shows an escape to the sun can have real health benefits. Up to a third of the population, in Britain at least, suffers from Seasonal Affective Disorder, or SAD, also known as winter depression, according to MIND, a leading mental health charity in England and Wales. Furthermore, nine out of 10 people report sleeping and eating more during the darker months.

While most cases of the winter blues are not severe, 2 percent to 5 percent of those with SAD cannot function without continuous treatment. However, it's extremely rare to find anyone with the disorder within 30 degrees of the equator, where days are long and the sky is bright year-round, according to MIND.

Although their findings appear to support a key factor in Arnall's research for Porter Novelli and its client, Sky Travel, the charity warned against overemphasizing the psychologist's claims. "These types of formulae, if anything, probably serve to oversimplify the complexities of real-life experience," a spokesperson said on customary condition of anonymity.

Others in the medical field were less skeptical. "I'm sure it's right," said Dr. Alan Cohen, spokesperson for the Royal College of General Practitioners, referring to Arnall's equation. However, "it is postulated that there are a number of different causes of depression," he said. "It may be something about one's personality, genes or external events. For those who suffer from external events, [Jan. 24] would be the most depressing day," Cohen said.

While travel companies hope to turn gloom into gold this date, for those unable to book a last-minute tropical getaway, Arnall might want to consider a formula for the "happiest day of the year."

Real English
fall off the wagon = start drinking alcohol again after giving it up
kick the bucket = die

Real English
feel like hell = (informal) feel terrible

A Read this task and then the letter that follows. Did Claudio complete the task as directed?

> TASK: You have received a letter from a friend who is going to visit you in July. Write a reply describing the activities you are planning. Give your friend some advice about what clothes to bring, ask about any special food requirements, and request flight details.

May 9

Dear Daniel,

It was so nice to hear from you. I'm really happy that you can come to Brazil in July. We are going to have a great time!

When you arrive, I want to show you around Belo Horizonte and to introduce you to my friends. There are lots of nice places where we can go out for a coffee or to dance. I'd also like to take you to some colonial towns close by, so I will ask my parents if we can borrow the car on the weekends. My Dad says he might be able to take us to Río for a few days at the end of your stay. I hope we can go there, as it's such a fun place.

Bring a camera and something to wear if we go out clubbing. Don't forget to bring clothes for the beach in case we go to Río. In July the weather here can get cold at night, so bring a jacket. What kind of food do you like? My Mom is already thinking about what we are going to eat. Brazilian food is great! You will love it.

Last but not least, can you let me know your flight details? I expect you will have to fly into São Paulo and take a plane from there to my city. I'm so excited about your visit! Write back when you get the chance.

Your friend,
Claudio

B Pair work. **Discuss these questions.**

1. How can you remember to include all the points required when you write the answer to a task?
2. What is the difference between a personal letter and a formal letter?

C Study the task and write a personal letter.

> TASK: Write a letter to a friend from another country inviting her/him to visit you. Suggest the best time to visit and explain why. Mention activities you might do together in your town or city and other places you could visit. Encourage your friend to take some classes in the native language of your country before the visit.

D Pair work. **Exchange letters with a partner and make suggestions for improvements.**

4 COMMUNICATION

Activity 1: Tips for a happier life

A Pair work. Read the tips below and underline any phrasal verbs you notice. Discuss the meaning of each with your partner. Then write two more "happiness tips" on another sheet of paper.

> *Want to live a happier, more fulfilled life? There are simple things that you can do so that you, and those around you, are more content.*
>
> Tip 1   *Remember to say "thank you"!* It's a small thing, but people often respond well to thanks and will treat you better if you show appreciation for something they've done for you. So, tell your mom you appreciate the dinner she made. Thank the person who bagged your groceries at the store. You'll be surprised how good these two little words can make you feel, too.
>
> Tip 2   *Treat yourself to something special once in a while.* Dress up and go out with friends to a trendy club or restaurant. Relax in a sauna. Sign up for a class. Buy tickets to a game and cheer on the home team. Whatever you decide to do, it'll give you something to look forward to.
>
> Tip 3   *Learn to let go of your anger.* Had a fight with a friend? Someone try to cut you off in traffic? Count to ten and simmer down. Learn to let it go. Holding a grudge will only make you feel worse, not happier, in the long run. If you're angry with yourself, remember that we all make mistakes. Learn from them and then move on.

B Group work. Explain your two happiness tips to three other pairs. Take notes on the tips they've come up with.

C Group work. Review the list of happiness tips you've collected, including the three in A. Which suggestions do you like the best? Why? Do you already practice any of these?

Activity 2: Look on the bright side!

A Pair work. Read the dialog and then discuss the questions below with your partner.

Evan: Hey, Robbie. What's going on?
Robbie: Oh, hi, Evan. Not much.
Evan: Are you all right?
Robbie: Not really. I was passed over for that promotion at work. They gave the assistant manager's job to someone else.
Evan: No way! You thought for sure you were going to get that position.

Robbie: Yeah, well, it didn't happen. I guess the other person had more experience.
Evan: Listen, Robbie . . . I'm sorry you didn't get the job, but <u>don't take it so hard</u>. <u>Look on the bright side</u>. There'll be other opportunities and if you'd gotten the job, it would've been a lot more work. You would've had almost no free time.
Robbie: Yeah, I guess you're right . . .

1. Why is Robbie feeling down?
2. What does Evan say to try to cheer him up?
3. What do you think the underlined expressions mean?

B Pair work. Choose one of these situations and role-play a dialog in which one person explains why he or she is down and the other person tries to cheer him or her up.

1. You're feeling down because your girlfriend/boyfriend/spouse of three years has just broken up with you.
2. A friend who was going to travel with you has suddenly backed out and you now have to travel by yourself.
3. You tried out for your school's soccer/basketball/cheerleading team, and were turned down.

C Group work. Perform your role plays for the group. What do you think of the suggestions people came up with?

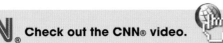 **CNN** ®   **Check out the CNN®️ video.**   **Practice your English online at** <u>elt.heinle.com/worldpass</u>

Unit 8: Happy Days

A Study the word combinations in the box and use them to complete the sentences below, making all necessary changes.

> **Word combinations with _mood_**
>
> in a bad mood   a somber mood
> in a good mood   a festive mood
> in a foul mood   mood swings
> put someone in a good mood   in the mood (for something)

1. Let's go to Tokyo Garden for lunch. I'm _____ sushi.
2. My brother was really _____ after he received his exam score—he went in his room, slammed the door, and wouldn't talk to anybody for the rest of the day.
3. Talking on the phone with my friend Maria always _____. She's so funny!
4. It's hard for me to put up with my girlfriend's _____. One day she's cheerful and talkative, and the next day she seems really depressed.
5. The holiday decorations all around the school created _____.
6. The president spoke on national television in _____ following the devastating earthquake.
7. I'm sorry I yelled at you yesterday. I was _____ because my car broke down on the way to work.
8. I heard Dr. Kim whistling as he walked down the hall this morning. He was _____ today!

B Match these words with their opposites, using your dictionary as needed.

1. grouchy ____   a. dissatisfied
2. lethargic ____   b. quit
3. rejuvenated ____   c. aged
4. content (adj) ____   d. sensible
5. absurd ____   e. indirect
6. keep on ____   f. cheerful
7. linear ____   g. energetic

C List these terms in the correct order from best to worst. Then circle the one that describes your mood today.

> miserable   overjoyed   content   OK   down   delighted   sad   happy

☺ 1. _____ 2. _____ 3. _____ 4. _____

5. _____ 6. _____ 7. _____ 8. _____ ☹

> **There's an old saying . . .** _The more, the merrier._
>
> If more people participate, a situation is better or more enjoyable. We use this saying to include other people in an activity.
>
> > "My brother is visiting me this week. Can I bring him along to the class party?"
> > "Why not! _The more, the merrier._"

D Review these words from the reading "Jan. 24 called worst day of the year" on page 97 and match them with their meaning.

1. coincide ____
2. peak (v) ____
3. residual ____
4. obligation ____
5. bleak ____
6. disorder (n) ____
7. oversimplify ____
8. skeptical ____

a. hopeless or sad
b. occur at the same time
c. describe in a way that leaves out important aspects
d. disbelieving
e. left over after something is finished
f. mental or physical illness
g. duty or responsibility
h. reach the highest level

E Use the words from D to complete the sentences, making any necessary changes.

1. People who suffer from an eating _____ may consume such a bad diet that they seriously damage their health.
2. Many rainforest animals face a _____ future, as their habitat is being destroyed at an ever-increasing pace.
3. The increase in vacation bookings every year _____ with the worst weather—they both occur in late January.
4. Companies have an _____ to treat all workers equally.
5. Even after treatment, the _____ benefits of the drug continue for some time.
6. The nation's enthusiasm for soccer _____ when the national team played in the World Cup tournament for the first time.
7. Some scientists are _____ about the idea of seasonal disorders. They don't really think that the weather can have such strong effects on people's moods.
8. Saying that overweight people should just eat less _____ the difficulty of losing weight.

In Other Words

Happy is the most general term: *I'm happy about the weather today / my new job / the baseball scores.*
If you are cheerful, you are acting in a happy way: *Kate is always cheerful in the morning—but not me!*
If you are pleased, you are happy about something that has happened: *I was pleased to see that my teacher liked my essay.*
If you are content, you are satisfied with a general situation: *Joanna is content to stay home with her new baby.*
If you are ecstatic, you are extremely happy about something very important: *Marcus is ecstatic because his girlfriend finally agreed to marry him—after five years!*

Sad is the most general term: *I was sad because everyone forgot my birthday / the weather was gloomy / my vacation was over / I only got 73% on the test.*
If you are heartbroken, you are emotionally hurt: *Dana is heartbroken because her boyfriend left her / because her cat died.*
If you are homesick, you feel sad because you miss your home: *I felt terribly homesick during my first year of study abroad.*
If you are depressed, you feel very sad and hopeless for a long time and may need to see a doctor for treatment: *Silvio became depressed after losing his job and didn't leave his house for weeks.*

 **enjoy**

Enjoy is a transitive verb followed by a noun or a gerund. It cannot be used alone or with an infinitive.
   I enjoy chess / playing chess.
It can also be used with a reflexive pronoun.
   After graduation, I'm going to take a few weeks to relax and enjoy myself.

Looking Good!

Lesson A | Fashion sense

1 VOCABULARY FOCUS

What does your look say about you?

 Do you feel you have a good fashion sense? How would you describe the way you dress?

A Nicole and Dario were interviewed about their fashion sense. Read what they said and notice the expressions in blue. Then answer this question.

Who would probably say this? Circle your answer.
1. "I don't care what other people think of me." (Nicole / Dario)
2. "I dress differently, depending on the situation." (Nicole / Dario)

I never **pair** reds **with** greens—I don't think those two colors **go together**. Basically, I **go for** anything that I think **flatters** my figure. Just like anyone else, I like to look good.

During the day, I want to **project a** more conservative **image**, so I'll typically put on a knee-length skirt and a blazer. I want my look to say that I'm confident and smart—that one day I'll be **running** this office!

When I get home, I **change out of** my work clothes **into** something more casual. At night I'm usually going for a fun and **easygoing** kind of **vibe**.

I want my look to say that I'm an original—that I **stand out** in a crowd.

Nicole, 24—administrative assistant

I'm most comfortable wearing jeans, a T-shirt, and my flip flops. My mother says that I **come across as** lazy and unintelligent because of the clothes I wear. She says they're not **distinctive** enough—they don't reflect my personality.

I don't have an **instinct** for fashion, so if I need something nice I have my older sister **pick it out**. If I need to **coordinate** an outfit for a special occasion, she does that, too. She's often annoyed at me because I have this terrible habit: when I **get undressed**, I tend to throw my clothes on the floor.

My look says that I'm a **laid-back** kind of guy who isn't too worried about fashion.

Dario, 20—student

> **Real English**
> *vibe* = (informal)
> feeling or emotional
> atmosphere

B Pair work. **With a partner, use the words or expressions in the box to answer the questions.**

change out of . . . into . . .	flatters	instinct	~~project a/an . . . image~~
come across as . . .	get undressed	laid-back	run (an office)
coordinate	~~go for (something)~~	pair . . . with . . .	stand out
distinctive	go together	~~pick out (something)~~	vibe
easygoing			

1. Which two expressions mean "choose" or "decide to do"? <u>pick out (something)</u> <u>go for (something)</u>
2. Which two expressions are concerned with how people view you? <u>project a/an image</u> _____
3. Which two expressions mention taking off your clothes? _____ _____
4. Which two words mean "feeling" or "sense"? (Which one of them is a slang expression?)
   _____ _____
5. Which two expressions are about being unique? _____ _____
6. Which three expressions have to do with matching clothes together?
   _____ _____ _____
7. Which two expressions mean "relaxed"? _____ _____
8. Which word means "compliments"? _____
9. Which word means "manage"? _____

Real English
boy/girl-next-door image
= wholesome and naïve

C Pair work. **Take this quiz. Then share your answers with a partner.**

1. How do you typically come across?
   a. laid-back   c. stylish
   b. well put together d. other: _____

2. At work or school, I wish I could
   change out of _____ into _____.

3. What's the easiest way to stand out in crowd?
   a. wear something stylish   c. be charming
   b. have a special talent   d. other: _____

4. My best friend tries to project a _____ image.
   a. boy/girl-next-door   c. other: _____
   b. bad-boy/girl

▶▶ Vocabulary Builder ▲

A. There are different ways to describe colors and patterns of clothes in English. Study this list.

Color words				Pattern words	
lime-green	off-white	jet-black	sky-blue	solid	striped
reddish-orange	bluish-green	light blue	pale green	checked	paisley
shocking pink	dark brown			polka-dotted	

B. Pair work. Use color and pattern words to describe your favorite pieces of clothing to your partner.

2 LISTENING
Concerned about appearances

A Pair work. **Combine the words on the right to create three jobs where people are concerned about appearances. Use your dictionary as necessary. What do you know about these jobs?**

couture	plastic	sketch
surgeon	designer	artist

B Listen to Andrew and Kendra. **What are their jobs?** (CD Tracks 26 & 27)

Andrew: _____   Kendra: _____

C Listen again and write *A* if it fits Andrew's job and *K* if it fits Kendra's. For some items you will write both *A* and *K*. (CD Track 28)

1. You have to try and be perfect. <u>A, K</u>
2. I work for wealthy people. _____
3. When I first meet my clients, they are upset. _____
4. I can work for up to a month on one thing. _____
5. I hear shocking things in this job. _____
6. There is some time pressure. _____
7. You have to study to do my job. _____
8. I use psychology in my job. _____

D Look back at the information in B and C and on a separate piece of paper organize it into notes about each person and his or her job. Then listen again and add any other important information to your notes. (CD Track 29)

Person: _____

Job: _____

Job Description: _____

_____

▶**Ask & Answer**
Whose job would you rather have? Why?

E Pair work. Compare your notes with a partner and answer these questions.

1. What exactly does each person do?
2. What are the good and bad points of each job?

3 LANGUAGE FOCUS
Subject and object relative clauses

A Complete the information in the box with the words below.

combination   describe   object   pronouns   things   whom

- Relative clauses _____ or give more information about people, places, and _____.
- A sentence with a relative clause can be viewed as a _____ of two sentences:
    She wants to project a new image. She wants to look professional and sophisticated.
    She wants to project a new image <u>that is professional and sophisticated</u>.
- There are subject relative clauses and _____ relative clauses.
    Subject: Andrew, <u>who runs his own studio</u>, designs haute couture.
    Object: Kendra sketches pictures of people <u>that eyewitnesses have described</u>.
- In relative clauses, the relative _____ *who*, _____, and *that* refer to people, while *which* and *that* refer to things or places.
    I'm friendly with my neighbor <u>who/that</u> lives across the street.
    My older sister, <u>whom</u> I haven't seen in months, is a couture model.
    He'll only wear clothes <u>that</u> he thinks flatter him.
    The new makeup, <u>which</u> she bought last week, makes her look younger.

B Read the article about dressing for success on page 105 and then complete these steps.

1. Underline the nine relative clauses in the article.
2. Circle the relative pronouns in those clauses. Indicate which word or words each relative clause is about.
3. Which clauses are subject relative clauses? Which are object relative clauses? Write *S* for *subject* and *O* for *object*.

FASHION WITH A PURPOSE

It's hard enough to ace an interview even in the best of circumstances. But when you can't afford to buy proper clothing for the interview, it becomes next to impossible.

That's where *Dress for Success* comes in. The organization, which is not for profit, helps low-income women prepare for job interviews. A client that is referred to *Dress for Success* is given two suits for free. After she finds a job, she can join a support group that will help her to network and get advice about the workplace.

Viola, a client, had this to say: "Volunteers helped me to pick out a suit that I loved and then I was coached for my interview. Later, the interviewer told me that I came across as very capable and confident."

The founder of *Dress for Success* is Nancy Lublin. It all started with a $5,000 inheritance that Nancy received from her great-grandfather. Nancy, who had an instinct for business, hired three nuns that knew a lot about charity work. From these humble beginnings, *Dress for Success* has grown into the organization it is today. It is a program that clients can now find in more than seventy cities in four countries. The organization has been featured on many TV networks, including CNN. Because of her hard work with *Dress for Success*, Nancy is a woman whom many admire.

> **Real English**
> Use *whose* in relative clauses to refer to people's possessions.

C Read the information about defining and nondefining relative clauses and then look at the article in B again. Which clauses are defining? Which are nondefining?

Use a **defining relative clause** to define or identify which member of a group you are talking about: *My brother <u>who lives in Paris</u> is a designer.* (I have more than one brother. The one who lives in Paris is a designer.)	Use a **nondefining relative clause** to give extra information that is not necessary to identify the noun. Use commas to separate the clause from the rest of the sentence: *My brother, who lives in Paris, is a designer.* (I have only one brother. He lives in Paris.)

D Use the relative pronoun in parentheses to combine the two sentences into one.

1. Sheryl is a client of *Dress for Success*. She is very pleased with her suits. (who) _____

2. There are two new volunteers at *Dress for Success*. I haven't met them yet. (whom) _____

3. The clients receive interview suits. The suits are donated by other women. (which) _____

4. *Dress for Success* is a great organization. Everyone respects it. (that) _____

5. He changed out of his work clothes into his jeans. He bought the jeans in Hong Kong. (that) _____

6. The clothes are so distinctive. They can't be worn just anywhere. (that) _____

E Pair work. Look at the underlined parts of each sentence and circle the letter of the incorrect or unnecessary part. Discuss your answers with a partner.

1. <u>She's</u> my neighbor <u>whose</u> dogs <u>barks</u> <u>all the time</u>.
     A   B   C   D
2. Danny is the only one of my <u>friends</u> <u>who</u> <u>live</u> <u>in Hollywood</u>.
                                   A B C   D
3. The girl <u>which</u> became <u>a famous model</u> <u>is</u> <u>from</u> my hometown.
            A   B   C D
4. He designed an expensive dress <u>that</u> <u>she</u> bought <u>it</u> <u>for</u> $20,000.
                               A B   C D
5. The movie star <u>who's</u> <u>look</u> I love <u>the most</u> is <u>Audrey Hepburn</u>.
              A   B   C   D

F Pair work. You are going to design an ad for a charity organization that gives free fashion advice to teenagers. Write the ad for this organization. Include relative clauses in your ad.

4 SPEAKING
Now I'll explain . . .

A Look at the survey and rank your choices from 1 (most important) to 9 (least important).

What do men look for most in a woman?	What do women look for most in a man?
Someone who . . . __ is well groomed __ is physically fit __ has a nice smile / friendly face __ has a good job __ has a sense of humor __ is a good cook __ is sophisticated __ is attractive __ other: _____	Someone who . . . __ is well groomed __ is physically fit __ has a nice smile / friendly face __ has a good job __ has a sense of humor __ is a good cook __ is sophisticated __ is attractive __ other: _____

B Pair work. Get together with a partner and compare your answers in A. Explain the reasons for your choices.

C Group work. Get together with another pair and show your results from A. You are going to give a presentation that summarizes the results of the survey from your group of four. Work together to plan and practice a presentation in four parts:

1. an introduction
2. the results from your group of the survey question "What do men look for most in a woman?"
3. the results from your group of the survey question "What do women look for most in a man?"
4. a conclusion

Planning a presentation of a survey

- The presentation can be structured in a way similar to a written essay, with an introduction, a body, and a conclusion.
- The introduction presents your topic and introduces your listeners to important findings that the survey brought out.
- The middle part of the presentation gives the findings with examples and explanations.
- The conclusion summarizes what you have learned from the survey and leaves your audience with something to think about.

D Group work. Take turns giving your presentation to another group. Each team member should present one section. Try to use expressions from the box.

Presentation expressions

Explaining your results	Transitions in a presentation
What this means is . . .	*We've talked about . . . Next, we'll tell you about . . .*
This shows that . . .	*We've discussed . . . Now I'll explain . . .*
The significance of this is . . .	*We have seen . . . Now, let's look at . . .*

E Class work. With the class, talk about interesting or surprising results of the survey questions. What did you learn about your classmates? What follow-up questions would you like to ask?

Looking Good!

Lesson B | Cosmetic procedures

1 GET READY TO READ

Would you have it done?

 How important do you think "looks" are? Why do you feel this way?

A Match the words in the columns to create a list of cosmetic procedures.

have / get: _____
_____
_____
_____
_____

liposuction	surgery
a hair	injections
botox	whitened
a nose	transplant
your teeth	job

B Pair work. **Look at the procedures in A and discuss the questions with a partner.**

1. What are these procedures? Explain them.
2. Who do you think would have them done? Complete the chart below with the procedures in A and the types of people who would have them done. Include as many different types of people as you can think of.

Procedure	liposuction surgery				
Who would have it done?	someone who's very overweight				

▶ **Ask & Answer**

What do you think of the cosmetic procedures in A? How do they compare, for example, with doing things like wearing makeup, shaving, or coloring your hair?

2 READING
Makeover Matters

A Pair work. Look at the woman in the pictures and read the speech bubble. Discuss with your partner: What does the underlined expression mean? What "work" do you think Samantha has had done?

Samantha looks different to me. I think she's had some work done.

B In the article "Makeover Matters" on page 109, four people talk about things that they've done to enhance their appearance. Read the article once quickly and complete the information about each person.

Li Mei	Daniela	Josh	Evan
age: cosmetic procedure:	age: cosmetic procedure:	age: cosmetic procedure:	age: cosmetic procedure:

C Read the article again and answer the questions by writing the correct person's name.

Which person . . .
1. believes that good looks are essential in getting a good job? _____
2. feels more self-assured and has a better life now? _____
3. had surgery after his or her marriage ended? _____
4. thinks that men are trying to imitate people in the media? _____

D Read the article on page 109 again and write the answers to these questions on a separate piece of paper.

1. In which countries has the number of cosmetic procedures being done increased steadily since 2000?
2. In which country is it estimated that one in every ten adults has had some work done?
3. What is one of the most common cosmetic procedures done in some Asian countries?
4. How many American men interviewed believe that one's appearance is important?
5. Which treatments traditionally considered "for women only" are more men now having done?
6. Which *nonsurgical* procedure for both men and women men ranks number one worldwide?
7. What are the most common surgical procedures being requested by men worldwide?

E Pair work. These statements are from the reading. Do you agree or disagree with each? Why? Discuss your ideas with a partner.

1. "Having work done is like taking what you have and making it better—like upgrading to a newer cell phone or computer."
2. "You always hear 'It's what's on the inside that counts,' but the reality is that appearance does matter. Employers are influenced by a pretty face or a handsome smile.
3. "I think a lot of people compare themselves to what they see on TV."

> ### ▶ Ask & Answer
> Think about the four people in the reading. What do you think of each person's decision to enhance his or her appearance? Do you think they did the right thing? Why or why not?

Makeover Matters

There was a time when having wrinkles removed, a nose reshaped, or a smile fixed was considered an expensive indulgence—a luxury reserved for the wealthy or the desperately vain. Today, however, attitudes are changing. Ads for botox and teeth-whitening products are commonly featured in many magazines. Reality TV
5 shows, such as *Extreme Makeover*, follow everyday people as they have various cosmetic procedures done in order to become more attractive.

In countries such as Brazil, China, and the U.S., the number of people having cosmetic procedures done has risen steadily since 2000. A recent *Time* magazine article suggests that in Korea, one in ten adults has undergone some cosmetic procedure. Today, it appears that "having work done"—whether it means erasing age lines or brightening your smile—is something more people of all ages are comfortable doing.
10

Never too young

Li Mei Wang, 20, is a first-year university student majoring in Journalism and Media Studies at the University of Hong Kong. Daniela Souza, 24, is trying to break into news reporting for a Brazilian TV network. Even though they're from opposite sides of the globe, it turns out that Li Mei and Daniela have quite a bit in common: they're both interested in working in the media and are stylish dressers and engaging conversationalists. They've both
15 had some work done, too.

Four months ago, Li Mei had surgery on her upper eyelids to create wider, more almond-shaped eyes. This procedure, known as "blepharoplasty," is one of the most common cosmetic procedures performed in some Asian countries.

"Before I had the work done, people said to me 'You're too young to be doing this,'" explains Li Mei. "But
20 fixing my eyes wasn't about trying to look youthful … obviously. It was about taking what I had and making it better—like upgrading to a new cell phone or computer." Li Mei laughs. "You know, a year ago, I was a shy, average-looking girl living an everyday life. But I wanted more than that … I feel like the surgery has not only made me more attractive, it's also helped me to feel better about myself. People say that now I come across as being more self-confident. I'm doing better in school, and guys notice me all the time now, too. It wasn't like that
25 before."

Daniela, who had her nose reshaped to make it narrower and slightly longer, nods her head in agreement. "For me, having my nose fixed was all about getting ahead," she explains. "You always hear 'It's what's on the inside that counts,' but the reality is that appearance does matter. Employers are influenced by a pretty face or a handsome smile. Being good-looking gives you the competitive edge. And in today's world, that's
30 important—especially in my line of work."

It's a Man's World too

Thirty-year-old Josh Donahue, a managing editor for a men's health magazine in Australia, is headed for a dental appointment where he is having his teeth whitened. "To me, visiting the dentist for a routine whitening is like having my hair cut every few months or so," says Donahue. "It's important to stay fit and to look good."
35 Like Donahue, more men today are paying closer attention to their appearance than ever before. According to AskMen.com, nine out of ten American men interviewed in a recent survey believe that looking good is important—especially in the workplace—and say that they purchase and use grooming products regularly. And they're not only buying shaving cream and hair gel. Sales for products such as facial moisturizers and skin toners have steadily increased over the last five years.
40 In an effort to look good, men from Buenos Aires to Beijing are also indulging in treatments that were traditionally considered "for women only," such as manicures, facials, and laser-hair removal. Men worldwide are also turning to surgery to enhance their appearance. Though most cosmetic procedures are still performed on women, the number of men having work done is on the rise.

And what are the most common procedures being requested by men worldwide? According to the
45 International Society of Aesthetic Plastic Surgery, the number one nonsurgical procedure is botox (this ranks first for women internationally, too). For men, some of the most common surgical procedures include eyelid surgery (to remove bags under the eyes or to create wider eyes), liposuction, nose jobs, and hair transplants.

So why are men showing more interest in their appearance? "I think a lot of people compare themselves to what they see on TV," says Josh Donahue. "You know, the actors and athletes with the great clothes and the
50 perfect bodies. You see that and you want it, too. And you know … having work done doesn't cost a fortune like it used to, so I think a lot of guys are starting to think, why not?"

For 45-year-old Evan Waterson, the decision to have routine botox injections and liposuction around his waist was simple. "I'd recently gotten divorced and was interested in dating again," he explains. "I wanted to project a fresh and energetic image, but I'd sort of let myself go while I was married." Waterson pauses. "I had the
55 work done so that I could look and feel my best … and at any age, I think that's important."

A Look at these pairs of events and label the cause (C) and the effect (E). Then combine them using the expression in parentheses and adding other necessary words.

1. people gain weight _E_ people don't get enough exercise _C_ (As a consequence,)
   People don't get enough exercise. As a consequence, they gain weight.

2. emotional problems in children ___ divorce ___ (can cause)
   _____

3. cancer and other diseases ___ heavy smoking ___ (are caused by)
   _____

4. changing weather patterns ___ global warming ___ (is due to)
   _____

5. he wanted to look cool ___ he shaved his head ____ (because)
   _____

6. many serious health problems ___ extreme dieting ___ (can result in)
   _____

7. there were more than twenty traffic accidents yesterday ___ the severe snowstorm ___ (as a result of)
   _____

B Pair work. Read the information and then discuss the questions below with a partner.
Try to use some of the expressions in the box.

> *Studies have shown that many people around the world have a poor body image. A study in the U.S., for example, found that 81 percent of 10-year-old girls are afraid of gaining weight. Men in France thought they needed to add 13 more kilos of muscle to be attractive. Forty-eight percent of Japanese women think they are fat.*

Expressions showing cause and effect	
can cause	because
is caused by	one of the results of
is due to	can result in
As a consequence,	as a result of

1. What do you think are the causes of people around the world having a poor body image?
2. What do you think some of the effects are?

C Write an essay about body image and its effects. Use expressions from the box. Follow this outline.

Paragraph 1: What has caused people to be concerned about their body image? Give examples.
Paragraph 2: What are the positive effects of this?
Paragraph 3: What are the negative effects of this?
Paragraph 4: Give your personal opinion: Are the overall effects good or bad?

D Pair work. Exchange papers with a partner and make suggestions for improvement.

A Class work. Read the Quick Poll question and think about how you'd answer it. Then take a class vote. Which response got the most votes and why?

Quick Poll

If you met someone who had a tattoo, what would your first impression be?

    a. that he or she was a bit of a bad boy/girl
    b. that he or she was an interesting, unconventional person
    c. other impressions _____
    d. I wouldn't really have an opinion one way or the other.

B Design a Quick Poll question about beauty, appearance, or fashion with three to four possible responses. Choose a topic from the box or think of your own.

> Topics to ask questions about:
> the best places to shop for cool clothes   things that make a person attractive
> beauty pageants   the latest fashions in hair and clothes
> the media and standards of beauty   changing your appearance

C Class work. Ask your classmates your Quick Poll question. Keep track of the number of votes you get for each response. Also, ask people to give you a simple explanation for the response they chose.

> *Who do you think is the most attractive celebrity right now?*

D Pair work. Get together with a partner and explain the results of your Quick Poll. Which response got the most votes? What are some of the reasons people gave for the response they chose?

> *The question I asked was: Do you think beauty pageants are a good idea? Answer B got the most votes. People who chose answer B said . . .*

World Link

Are Venezuelan women the most beautiful in the world? In the past 50 years, Venezuela has produced more international beauty pageant winners than any other country. In fact, formal training academies for beauty delegates have been established to offer aspiring beauties strict diet and exercise regimens, lessons in speech and dance, and just in case— plastic surgery and cosmetic dentistry!

Source: *The Brooklyn Rail*

CNN Check out the CNN® video.   **Practice your English online at** elt.heinle.com/worldpass

Unit 9: Looking Good!

A Study the word combinations in the box and use them to complete the sentences, making all necessary changes.

> **Word combinations with *appearance***
>
> a youthful appearance   worry about your appearance
> an outward appearance   judge people by their appearance
> change your appearance   despite appearances
> neglect your appearance   similar in appearance

1. Daniel may look calm, but that's just _____. I know he's actually very worried about his wife's health.
2. When Yasu shaved his head, it completely _____. I didn't recognize him when I saw him at the party!
3. Mr. Clark lives in a small house and drives a ten-year-old car. _____, he is actually one of the wealthiest people in this country.
4. My mother always told me that I shouldn't _____. The way they look says nothing about their character.
5. She has such _____. I can't believe that she's really 70 years old!
6. You mustn't _____ if you expect to do well at a job interview.
7. My sister and I are very _____, but our personalities are completely different—I'm pretty sociable, and she's really shy.
8. Gina constantly _____, even though people tell her she's pretty.

B English has many groups of words that express the same concept with different degrees of formality. Complete the chart by writing the words in the correct column.

> smart   offspring   relaxed   vibe   duds   brainy   expensive
> place   residence   sensation   leisurely children apparel   pricey

Formal	Neutral	Informal
1.		kids
2.	clothes	
3. unaffordable		
4.	feeling	
5. intelligent		
6.	house	
7.		laid-back

> ### I didn't know that!
> Two of the world's most popular fashions are named for European cities. The blue cloth that we call *denim* was first made in Nîmes, France. It was called *serge de Nîmes*, which was shortened to *de Nîmes*, and then to *denim*. *Jeans* were originally made in the city of Genoa, which was called *Gene* in the sixteenth century. The pants were named after the city.

C Complete the sentences with one or more particles to form the correct phrasal verb. Pay attention to the meaning.

1. I hate wearing a school uniform! I change _____ it the minute I get home in the afternoon.
2. My boyfriend doesn't like shopping. I always have to go with him to the mall to pick _____ all of his clothes for him.
3. Tracy sometimes comes _____ as unfriendly to people who don't know her, but in reality, she's just very quiet.
4. If you dye your hair green, you'll definitely stand _____ in a crowd!
5. I don't like to buy very trendy clothes. I usually go _____ classic styles that I can wear for a long time.
6. When I go to the gym, I change _____ a T-shirt and shorts to exercise.

D Review these words from the reading "Makeover Matters" on page 109 and use them to complete the sentences, making all necessary changes.

project (v)	be headed for	routine (adj)	grooming	conversationalist
enhance	desperately	undergo	indulge in	

1. To be a successful talk-show host, you must be an excellent _____. You must feel comfortable talking with all sorts of people.
2. After a hard week at work, I like to _____ a good movie and dinner in a restaurant on Friday night.
3. Before surgery, patients must _____ a number of medical tests to assess their health.
4. For men, _____ includes things like shaving and hair care.
5. When she started her business, Beth went out and bought a lot of expensive suits and jewelry to try to _____ an image of success.
6. I'm sorry I couldn't stop to talk with you yesterday. I _____ a job interview.
7. The girl's parents are _____ looking for a cure for their daughter's illness.
8. If the new movie is a success, it will _____ the director's growing reputation as an innovator in science fiction.
9. The bank robber was caught during a _____ investigation of a traffic accident.

In Other Words

Beautiful is normally applied to women, girls, and children: *My granddaughter is a beautiful little girl with big dark eyes.* Beautiful can also be used with things: *You have a beautiful voice!*

Handsome is normally applied to men: *Dave is as handsome as a movie star.* Handsome is also used to describe a woman who is attractive in a dignified or impressive way: *My grandmother was a handsome and gracious lady.*

Cute is used to describe children: *What a cute baby!* Cute is also used informally to talk about adults: *Who's that cute guy in the corner?*

Good-looking and attractive are milder terms that can be used to describe both men and women: *You don't have to be beautiful to be an actress, but you should be attractive.*

Gorgeous means extremely beautiful: *Sara isn't just beautiful–I think she's gorgeous!*

If something is ugly, it's unpleasant to look at: *That's the ugliest dog I've ever seen!* Ugly can also be used in a symbolic way: *Anger is a very ugly emotion.*

Unattractive is a milder, less emotional term: *In my opinion, the new fashions this year are rather unattractive.*

Hideous means extremely ugly: *They painted their house orange. It's hideous!*

impression

The word *impression* refers to the effect that something has on the observer–not the cause of that effect. So we can say:

Our new teacher made a good impression on me.

After meeting her boyfriend, I have a good impression of him.

We can't say:

~~You shouldn't judge people by their impression.~~

~~Kathy has a good impression, so everybody likes her immediately.~~

Review: Units 7–9

1 LANGUAGE CHECK

Circle the correct answer.

1. My grandfather was a kind and generous man who ___ by everyone who knew him.
   - a. loved
   - b. was love
   - c. was loved

2. Jeff had a terrible fight with his girlfriend, but they made ___ later when he apologized.
   - a. up
   - b. up it
   - c. it over

3. Pilar, ____ I met in elementary school, is my oldest friend.
   - a. that
   - b. which
   - c. whom

4. My father blew ___ at me when I asked him for more money.
   - a. down
   - b. through
   - c. up

5. At present, an investigation of the murder ___ by the city police.
   - a. is made
   - b. is being made
   - c. is making

6. I need new clothes ___ will make my image more professional.
   - a. that
   - b. whom
   - c. who's

7. Today, coffee ___ in a number of countries in Asia, Africa, and Latin America.
   - a. was produced
   - b. has produced
   - c. is produced

8. Passengers ____ to check in for their flight at least one hour before departure.
   - a. require
   - b. are required
   - c. are requiring

9. I saw Aliza yesterday. I ran ___ at the library.
   - a. into her
   - b. her into
   - c. in to her

10. Yuko is from Sapporo, ___ is in the north of Japan.
    - a. which
    - b. that
    - c. who

11. That's the author ___ book we studied in class last year.
    - a. who
    - b. whose
    - c. which

12. Many buildings were damaged by the hurricane, and a month later, they ___.
    - a. are still being repaired
    - b. are still repairing
    - c. are still repaired

13. I don't understand the directions to your house. Could you ___ again?
    - a. go over
    - b. go them over
    - c. go over them

2 VOCABULARY CHECK

Match the sentence parts to make statements that illustrate the meaning of the words in blue.

1. If you lose track of something, ___.
2. If you are conscientious, ___.
3. If you are inundated with work, ___.
4. If something stands out, ___.
5. If you chronicle an event, ___.
6. If an idea is absurd, ___.
7. If you enhance your memory, ___.
8. If a movie is mindless, ___.
9. If something is linear, ___.
10. If you coordinate two things, ___.
11. If you are a skeptic, ___.
12. If something is distinctive, ___.
13. If you are easygoing, ___.

a. you are very serious about your responsibilities
b. you don't believe new ideas
c. you keep a written record of it
d. you notice it easily
e. you use them well together
f. it doesn't make you think
g. you have far too many things to do
h. you like things to be relaxed and casual
i. it's not sensible or logical
j. you don't remember it
k. it's not like anything else
l. it is straight or direct
m. you improve it

3 NOW YOU'RE TALKING!

Situation 2

> You're at a party, and someone you've just met asks you about what you like to do in your free time. You try to keep the conversation going as long as you can.

> Your friend says, "The best way to master a language is by memorizing as many new words as possible every day." Do you agree or disagree? Discuss this topic for at least three minutes.

Situation 3

> You watch a fashion show on TV with a friend and discuss your opinions about some of the extreme fashions that are popular now.

A Pair work. Look at the pictures and imagine what the people in each situation might say. Then briefly review the language notes from Units 7–9 on pages 157–158.

B Pair work. Role-play situations 1, 2, and 3 with your partner. Notice how well you and your partner do the role play. Ask your partner's opinion about your performance.

C Now rate your speaking. Use + for good, ✓ for OK, and − for things you need to improve. Then add two goals for the improvement of your speaking.

How did you do?	1	2	3
I was able to express my ideas.			
I spoke easily and fluently, without hesitation.			
I spoke at a good rate of speed—not too fast or too slow.			
I used new vocabulary from the units.			
I used at least three expressions from the units.			
I practiced the grammar from the units.			
Goals for improvement: 1. _____ 2. _____			

To Buy or Not to Buy . . .

Lesson A | What's your shopping culture?

1 VOCABULARY FOCUS

Status symbols

 Why do you think some people like to wear clothing with the logo or designer's name visible?

A Pair work. **Read the paragraph below and complete the last sentence in your own words.
Then discuss with a partner why you believe that the things you mentioned are status symbols.**

A *status symbol* is something that a person owns to show that he or she is rich or important in society. Status symbols change with the times. In twelfth-century Europe, for example, books were the status symbols of the day, because they were very rare and few people knew how to read. Today's status symbols are . . .

B Pair work. **Now read three people's opinions about today's status symbols, paying attention to the words and phrases in blue. How do their answers compare to yours in A? Do you agree with their opinions? Discuss with a partner.**

Saul, 30

Eun Hwa, 21

Tony, 20

A big one is the car. Take my brother, for example. He drives a Jaguar XKR convertible. I think he paid somewhere in the neighborhood of $120,000 for it. It sends a certain message: that he can afford the best and won't settle for less. It's awfully flashy—he gets attention wherever he goes. I like to tease him and say, "You know, you may have money, but you can't buy class."

Gadgets, for sure! Having the coolest cell phone, ring tones, mp3 player, PDA, whatever—anything that differentiates you from the next person. You don't want any cheap knockoff either . . . you've got to have a brand name. I don't know what all the fuss is about, really. They're just objects, after all.

Whatever they're showing in music videos is what's in vogue. You see guys on TV snatching up cars and jewelry as fast as they can. They're all getting big homes and customizing them with the ultimate in luxury—state-of-the-art sound systems and Olympic-sized swimming pools. Of course, you can't be that extravagant with money in real life. People like you and me have to pay the bills and stuff like that.

C Choose the definition that is closest in meaning to each word or phrase from B.

1. somewhere in the neighborhood of	approximately	exactly
2. settle for	reject	accept
3. flashy	dull and cheap	showy and expensive
4. class	style and good taste	luxury goods
5. differentiate	make the same	set apart
6. knockoff	expensive original	cheap imitation
7. fuss	lack of concern	trouble, excitement

8.	in vogue	trendy, in fashion	dated, old-fashioned
9.	snatch up	buy quickly	sell quickly
10.	customizing	changing to suit your taste	keeping the same
11.	the ultimate	the most common	the greatest or best
12.	extravagant	lavish, magnificent	frugal, meager

Vocabulary Builder ▲

A. **Pair work. Look at the verbs in the box and study the parts of each word. Then, with a partner, write a simple definition for each verb on a separate piece of paper.**

customize: (custom + -ize) = *make something exactly the way someone wants it*

civilize	immunize	prioritize	trivialize
generalize	monopolize	stabilize	victimize
equalize	personalize	sterilize	visualize

The verb suffix *-ize* (written *-ise* in British English) means to make something in a certain way (i.e. equal → equalize).

B. **Group work. Get together with another pair and share six of your definitions with them. Ask them to guess the words you are defining.**

2 LISTENING
Shopping habits

A **You are going to hear two women and a man responding to a question. Look at the questions in B. Which question is each person responding to? Listen and write the number of the speaker (1, 2, or 3) next to each question.** (CD Tracks 30 & 31)

B **Listen again and complete the notes. Are any of the trends mentioned happening where you live?** (CD Track 32)

Have people's shopping habits changed over the years? __2__	Which products today are most in demand? __3__	How has the main shopping district in your city changed? __1__
1. More people are shopping at _supermarkets_ and _megastore'_ rather than _local shops._	1. _____ and _____ foods	1. Fewer stores cater to the _upscale_ shopper. Now, there are more _clothing_ stores for shoppers who are in their _Teens and twenties_ ~~more expensive~~
2. Places aren't close, so more people _drive_ to stores and buy in bulk.	2. _____ foods	2. Individual places have been replaced by _flashy shopping mall_
3. More people are shopping _on-line_.	3. All kinds of _____ that are sold year round.	3. Now, there are fewer sidewalk _cafes_ and more chain _coffee_ and _fast_-food places. _shops_

▶ **Ask & *Answer***

What places are popular for shopping where you live? Has the way people shop changed over the past few years? How?

A review of definite and indefinite articles

A Pair work. These conversations were overheard at a shopping mall. Complete each sentence with *a/an*, *the*, or leave it blank if no article is required. Discuss your answers with a partner.

1. A: This is such __ beautiful sweater!
   B: It's OK. Actually, I like __ other one better.

2. A: Shopping for __ Christmas presents is exhausting.
   B: Why don't we take __ break and have __ cup of tea?

3. A: Where did you park __ car?
   B: I don't remember. Maybe it's behind __ red truck.

4. A: You can get __ best bargains at __ Macy's.
   B: I know. But __ crowds there are unbearable.

B Read the grammar notes. Were your answers in **A** correct?

In English, an indefinite article (*a/an*), definite article (*the*), or no article (Ø) may come before a noun.

The is used before nouns that have been specified or identified. We use *the* . . .

- for one-of-a-kind nouns:
  The president is speaking at 2:00 today.
- for specific nouns that both the speaker and listener are familiar with:
  Your car keys are on the desk.
- when we've already mentioned something:
  I bought a new car yesterday. You won't believe this, but the car broke down today!
- when we're talking about a class of things in general (e.g. inventions, plants and animals, groups of people):
  The laser was invented in 1960.
  We should take better care of the poor.
- for superlatives:
  It's the best shopping center in town.
- with places such as hotels and movie theaters:
  That movie is playing at the Trident Theater.
- before a noun that has been specified or identified by a prepositional phrase or a relative clause:
  The natural beauty of the Grand Canyon is breathtaking.
  The merchandise that I ordered arrived damaged.

A/An is used before singular count nouns that have not been specified or identified. We use *a/an* . . .

- when we're mentioning something for the first time or it doesn't matter which one we're talking about:
  I found a dollar on the street so I bought some candy.
  If you want a bargain, you should shop at McSweeney's.
- before certain numbers:
  It cost a million dollars.

We use no article (Ø) . . .

- for non-count and abstract nouns that have not been specified:
  (Ø) Love is all that matters.
  I majored in (Ø) philosophy in college.
- when we're talking about plural nouns in general:
  (Ø) Shopping centers are busy places.
- with city and street names:
  I live on (Ø) North Street in (Ø) Chicago.
- with business names:
  Jin Soo works for (Ø) Samsung.

Real English
However, you can say:
Is there a Starbucks nearby? (This means a Starbucks coffee shop.)
There's a Lotte Department in my city.

C Read this article and fill in *a/an*, *the*, or no article (Ø). In some cases, more than one answer is possible.

GROCERIES TO GO

Helena lives on ___ Orchard Street in ___ million-dollar condo. She has ___ high-paying job and it keeps her busy—so busy, in fact, that she has little time to go shopping.

That's where Groceries to Go comes in. It's Saturday afternoon. ___ doorbell rings. When Helena opens ___ door, she sees ___ man in ___ uniform. ___ man hands her ___ big box of groceries and ___ bill for ___ box of goods. ___ man is ___ employee of Groceries to Go. He has brought Helena her groceries.

Helena loves ___ service. "___ convenience is what I'm looking for," she says. "___ grocery store is too far away and I don't have time to shop. ___ Groceries to Go is ___ most efficient way for me to do my shopping—it's the ultimate indulgence." It's also helpful for ___ elderly and other people who can't easily leave their apartments to shop.

Every week Helena fills out ___ order form requesting what she wants. ___ order arrives three days later. As ___ preferred customer, Helena also enjoys ___ big discounts.

Recently, though, ___ mayor urged citizens not to forget ___ local supermarkets. With everyone using ___ new service, he said, ___ number of shoppers was down. Not so, says Brian Peterson, V.P. of ___ marketing with Groceries to Go. "What differentiates our service is that we cater to those who don't have ___ time to shop. Our typical client is ___ busy working professional. It's not ___ service that everyone will use."

D Pair work. Compare your answers in C with a partner. Would you ever use a service like Groceries to Go? Why or why not?

E Pair work. Read these sentences with a partner and make corrections where necessary. Some have more than one mistake. Do you agree or disagree with each statement? Explain your reasons.

1. Every teenager should have credit card.
2. The megastores drive a smaller stores out of the business.
3. I'd love to be personal shopper for celebrity.
4. Someday, everyone will do all their shopping on web at the home.
5. In future, biggest status symbol the person can have will be a free time.
6. Harrods Department Store in the London is good place for the shopping.

Grammar X-TRA

Use no article for . . .	Use *the* for . . .
country names: *Poland, Thailand, Costa Rica*	country names that include a common noun: *the Dominican Republic*
single mountains, islands, and lakes: *Mount Everest, Pitcairn Island, Hawaii,* *Lake Huron*	mountain ranges, island chains, series of lakes: *the Rocky Mountains, the British Isles,* *the Great Lakes*

Study the information above and read the information about Palm Springs below. Then write four or five sentences about your city or town and its surroundings on a separate piece of paper.

I'm from the city of Palm Springs in the United States. The closest big city is Los Angeles. Palm Springs is about a two-hour drive from the Pacific Ocean. It's in the desert, so it's very hot in the summer. Our city offers a lot of outdoor activities, including a big golf tournament in January. The San Jacinto Mountains are nearby and you can take the Palm Springs Aerial Tramway to the top of one of the mountains. We also have a desert museum in the city and . . .

On the other hand . . .

A Pair work. Imagine that you want to buy a T-shirt. On a separate piece of paper list all the different types of places in your city where you could buy one (including any unusual places you can think of). Discuss at which place would you be most likely to shop? Why?

B Pair work. Choose one of these photos and tell your partner about the situation and what the people are looking for. Use some of the expressions for "Describing a picture" from the box.

> **Describing a picture**
>
> *This was probably taken . . .*
> *What I notice is . . .*
> *One thing that strikes me is . . .*
> *He/She/It must be . . .*
> *It seems to be . . .*

C Pair work. Choose a role and do the activity. Then switch roles. Try to use some of the expressions in the box below.

Student A: Choose two shopping situations in B for your partner to compare and contrast. Then listen and time your partner.

Student B: Try to speak for two minutes. When you have finished, ask your partner which place he or she would rather shop at and why.

Comparing and contrasting similarities and differences

When you compare two things, you talk about the ways in which they are similar. When you contrast them, you discuss the ways in which they are different. In essays and oral exams, you are often asked to "compare and contrast" two pictures, things, or ideas.

Comparing (similarities)
One thing that's similar is . . .
In both of these pictures . . .
One thing that these pictures have in common is . . .

Contrasting (differences)
What's different in the other photo is . . .
On the other hand, in the second photo . . .
In contrast, in the second photo . . .

UNIT 10

To Buy or Not to Buy . . .

| Lesson B | My possessions |

1 GET READY TO READ

Buy my stuff!

 Are you familiar with any online auction sites? If so, which ones?

Pair work. Read the information in the box, paying attention to the words in blue. Then discuss the questions below with a partner.

> On websites like *eBay, MercadoLibre,* and *Auction,* you can put almost anything you own up for sale—new or used clothing, music, furniture, even real estate.
>
> How does it work? You provide a photo and simple description of the item you want to sell, along with an asking price. Others will then bid on your item, and you sell to the person who has offered the most money.

1. Have you, or someone you know, ever bought or sold anything on sites like the ones described above?
2. If you were going to auction something of yours on a website, what would you sell? How much would you ask for it? Do you think anyone would buy it? Why or why not?

2 READING

All My Life for Sale

A Pair work. Discuss these questions with a partner.

1. Do you own a lot of things? Could you fit "the bare essentials" (the things that are necessary for you to live comfortably) into a car or a couple of suitcases if you had to?
2. Think of an important item you own now or owned in the past. Is there a "story" or special memory connected to the item? Explain.

B Pair work. You're going to read about a man named John Freyer. He wrote a book called *All My Life for Sale.* The words below all describe Freyer's autobiographical story. Think about the title of the book and then using the words below, write a sentence or two describing what you think Freyer's book is about. Share your idea with a partner.

| auction | belongings | moving | online |

_____

_____

_____

C Quickly read the article on page 123 and see if your ideas in B were correct.

D Read the article on page 123 again and explain how each of the items or places listed below are related. Write your answers on a separate piece of paper.

Example: $11, $48, $41

These are the amounts that people paid for some of the items John sold.

1. Iowa City, New York City
2. Portland, Maine; Dallas; Los Angeles
3. refrigerator magnets, a *Star Wars* bedsheet, a can of soup
4. Rani in Florida, Sandy of Lynwood, Morgan from California
5. Allmylifeforsale.com, Temporama.com
6. Australia, Japan, England
7. $5,000, $200

E Complete the story summary with the correct form of the word in parentheses.

John Freyer wanted to move from Iowa City to New York City, but was having (1. difficult) _____ because he had too much stuff. Freyer decided to sell most of his (2. possess) _____ on *eBay* and keep only what he could fit in his car.

For each item that Freyer planned to sell, he wrote a short (3. describe) _____ that told a story about the object: when he got it; who gave it to him; the memories that he had about it.

Freyer started by (4. auction) _____ each item for $1. After the first items sold, he wrote to the new owners to see how his former (5. belong) _____ were being used. To his surprise, many of the people wrote back. Freyer posted their (6. correspond) _____ at a website he created: Allmylifeforsale.com. Freyer then wrote back to the new owners and asked if he could visit them. He received over one hundred (7. invite) _____ from around the world and found people to be very (8. welcome) _____.

Freyer made $5,000 by selling his things, but by the end of his travels, had only $200 left. He made the (9. decide) _____ then to stay in Iowa. Freyer says the experience has made him more (10. caution) _____ about the things he lets into his life.

F Pair work. Take turns retelling Freyer's story to a partner in your own words.

▶ **Ask & Answer**

Read the last three paragraphs again and, in your own words, explain what you think the message of Freyer's story is. Do you agree with him? Could you live with only the "bare essentials" as Freyer did? Why or why not?

World Link

Many people say that Pierre Omidyar founded *eBay* to help his fiancée sell her collection of PEZ® candy dispensers, but Omidyar really started eBay (originally AuctionWeb) simply as a way to make money using the Internet and the principles of the free market. (By the way, the PEZ® dispensers are still around and on display at eBay headquarters!)

Source: *The Perfect Store: Inside* eBay by Adam Cohen

In *All My Life for Sale*, a man learns it's not the stuff, it's the stories

By Winda Benedetti • Seattle Post-intelligencer Reporter

It is remarkable what people will pay good money for. For instance, take a look at John D. Freyer's book *All My Life for Sale* (and the associated website Allmylifeforsale.com), and you'll discover that a man from Tumwater paid $11 to buy a can of sauerkraut from the author. A woman from California paid $48 to buy his belt buckle. And a guy from Portland paid $41 for four educational dental work photographs. Yes. You read that right—$41!

In the fall of 2000, Freyer wanted to move from Iowa City, Iowa,* to New York City, New York. One problem though: His "stuff" was weighing him down—as in, he had too much of it. And so, Freyer decided he would sell his belongings, keeping only the bare essentials (no more than he could fit in the trunk of his Honda Civic).

But what started as little more than a means to make moving easier turned into a conceptual art project that would find Freyer selling some 600 items on eBay and then traveling across the country to visit his former possessions in their new homes—his salt shaker in Portland, Maine, his Elvis shirt in Dallas, his power bill in Los Angeles.

In a culture that encourages —no, *celebrates*—consumption on a massive scale, *All My Life for Sale* is a refreshing look not so much at the things we own but at the stories that attach themselves to those things . . . and the new stories that develop when you let them go.

Real English
on a massive scale = in very large amounts

With the help of some friends, Freyer photographed and cataloged his belongings (the magnets on his refrigerator, the *Star Wars* sheet off his bed, a can of Campbell's Chunky Chicken and Rice Soup® from his kitchen cabinet) and began putting them up for sale on eBay. But in doing so, Freyer realized that each of his possessions held a piece of his history, a memory or a tale to tell.

"I started to go through all of the items . . . from my favorite shirts to the canned food in my cabinet. As I photographed each item, I reflected on the role that it played in my life and the stories that almost every object made me remember if I spent just a little bit of time with it," Freyer writes in his book—a chronicle of his objects, their histories and the journeys they and he took during the project.

A stuffed animal reminded him of a summer spent with the friend who won it for him at Coney Island.** An orange hat—the one he wore in Sweden and Norway—reminded him of his travels. A *Planet of the Apes* record reminded him of wintry Saturday afternoons spent watching reruns of the movie.

On eBay, Freyer began auctioning each item at one dollar. The descriptions he wrote about the objects had little to do with the physicality of the objects themselves. Instead, they were short stories about the items, about the people who gave him the objects, the situation in which he received them or the memories each one dug up.

When Freyer sold his first item—the toaster—to a guy named Bill in Illinois, "I wondered if Bill even cared about its history. I started to think about the history Bill would attach to my toaster."

Freyer started sending a note to the new owners, asking them to send him an update about the items they purchased. He soon started receiving letters, e-mails and even photographs about his old possessions and their new lives. Freyer posted the correspondence at Allmylifeforsale.com, and a community began to develop around the site.

Rani, in Florida, wrote to say she had used Freyer's waffle iron to try out some new low-carb waffle recipes. Sandy, of Lynnwood, bought several ears of corn from Freyer and sent photos showing squirrels enjoying them for lunch. Morgan, from California, bought Freyer's answering machine tape for $15.50 and said she hoped to use some samples from it in her music.

Over time Freyer became more interested in the people he was selling his things to than in the selling itself. "I realized there was more to it than a simple transaction," he said in an interview. And so Freyer decided to send a message to all the new owners of his possessions telling them he'd like to come for a visit.

One of the most surprising things about the book is the way people reacted to this stranger's request. Freyer says people were remarkably welcoming. He received more than 100 invitations from all over the world—Australia, Japan, England among them. He hit the road in August of 2001 and began chronicling his adventures at the website temporama.com.

Real English
hit the road = start traveling

"There were times when I sat and watched family home videos. It was almost like I was an out-of-town guest or a cousin," he says. "We live in a culture of fear. You're told, especially with the Internet, to be afraid because there are terrible people on the Internet. And there are some terrible people, but the majority of the people on the Internet are the same people who are in your supermarket."

Freyer returned to Iowa last November. Although he made about $5,000 on the sales, by the time he ended his travels he had only $200. With his possessions gone, he made a surprising decision—to stay in Iowa rather than move to New York. "After living out of the trunk of my car, location no longer seemed as relevant. I wanted a place to be grounded. I wanted to stop starting over," he writes in his book.

Freyer, who is currently a Bodine Fellow in the School of Art and Art History at the University of Iowa, not only wrote but also designed his book. "If you spend time and go through it, I hope you get a sense that we're much larger than the things that we own," he says.

As for himself, Freyer says the project has changed the way he consumes—made him more careful about the objects he lets into his life. "The things I do let back into my life, I feel like I'm less attached to them. The reason we hold on to things is the history that we attach to them. But if you can hold on to that history, that's almost enough."

---

*Iowa City, Iowa: Iowa is a state in the northern Midwest section of the U.S. and is 1,468 kilometers (912 miles) from New York.
**Coney Island: An amusement park located in Brooklyn, New York
Source: SEATTLE POST-INTELLIGENCER
http://seattlepi.nwsource.com/books/96144_lifeosale19.shtml

Writing a formal letter to a newspaper

A Pair work. **Discuss with a partner: What is the best way to express the ideas below using less casual language? Write your answers on a separate piece of paper.**

1. John Freyer's idea was really cool.
2. Anybody can see that it's a stupid plan.
3. The writer got the facts wrong.
4. People have too much stuff that they don't really need.
5. I think he's totally wrong.

B Pair work. **Read the letter below and answer the questions with a partner.**

1. What is the purpose of this letter?
2. How is the format of this letter different from the one on page 98? Find four differences.
3. Is this letter formal or informal? How do you know?
4. What is the purpose of each paragraph in the letter?

118 Grove Street
Metropolis City, PA 02210
September 26, 2005

The Metropolis Daily Mirror
P.O. Box 659
Metropolis City, PA 02203

Dear Editor:

    I would like to respond to the article about **All My Life for Sale**, which appeared in the Daily Mirror yesterday. I am shocked that the author admires John D. Freyer's "art project."

    If Freyer was troubled about having too many possessions, he should have just given them away. In today's world, there are millions of poor people who could really use his old clothes or the groceries from his kitchen. He could have given valuable help to somebody.

    The buyers who paid ridiculous amounts of money for his possessions are even worse. It's unbelievable that someone wasted $11 for a can of sauerkraut or $48 for a used belt buckle. This shows that people today care only about mindless consumption.

    I strongly believe that this kind of project should not be encouraged. Freyer is obviously not interested in art—he is only trying to become famous.

Sincerely yours,

Paula Martin

Paula Martin

C Imagine that the article on page 123 was reprinted in a newspaper you read. Write a formal letter expressing your personal reaction to the article. Give at least two reasons for your opinion and explain each one clearly.

Greetings and closings for a formal letter	
Greetings	**Closings**
Dear Mr. / Ms. / Dr. / Prof. _____:	*Sincerely yours,*
Dear Sir / Madam:	*Yours truly,*
	Yours sincerely,
	Yours faithfully, (British English only)

D Pair work. **Exchange letters. Give your partner suggestions to make his or her letter more effective.**

A Think back to the article you read about John Freyer on page 123 and then read the information below.

When John Freyer sold his things on *eBay*, he photographed and wrote a description for each. "The descriptions he wrote about the objects had little to do with the physicality of the objects themselves. Instead, they were short stories about the items, about the people who gave him the objects, the situation in which he received them, or the memories each one dug up."

B Imagine that you're going to auction something of your own. Choose an item that you have with you. It can be an article of clothing, your cell phone, a piece of jewelry, a book, etc. Think about the questions below. Then write a short personal description of the item on a separate piece of paper. Try to make it as interesting as possible.

1. When did you get the item?
2. Who gave it to you?
3. What memories does the item bring back for you?
4. What stories do you have about the item?

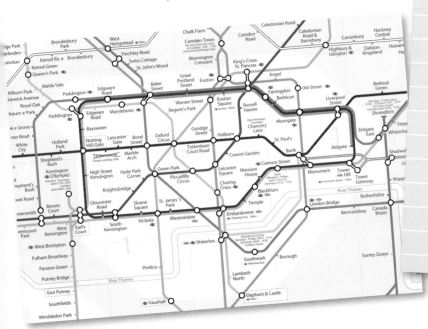

This is a subway map that I've carried with me in my wallet since I arrived in London. I live with a host family and my host mother gave it to me my first week with them. I still remember that chilly January morning. I missed my family back home so much! Even though I know my way around now, I still keep the map in my wallet. It always reminds me of those first few months here, and how much I've learned.

C Class work. Put your item and the description on display on your desk. Go around and look at the others and read the descriptions. Take notes and ask the owners questions.

D Group work. Get into a group of three to four people. Go over the notes you took and discuss the questions.

1. Which three items that you saw did you think were described most interestingly? Explain your answers.
2. Of those three, which was your favorite? Why?

E Group work. Write the name of the item your group liked the most on a small piece of paper (e.g., Maria's antique ring). Give it to your teacher. He or she will count up the votes and announce the most popular item to the class.

 Check out the CNN® video. **Practice your English online at** elt.heinle.com/worldpass

Unit 10: To Buy or Not To Buy

A What happened to the price? Did it go up, down, or stay the same (or nearly the same)? Mark each sentence with ↑, ↓, or →. More than one symbol may be used.

1. The rise in housing prices is affecting many families. ___
2. Come to Buymore Supermarket, where we've slashed prices on everything you need! ___
3. Lemon Computer announced a price cut on their most popular models. ___
4. The price of gasoline soared last week. ___
5. Farmers have experienced a drop in price for many of their crops. ___
6. The government has instituted a price freeze for basic foods like rice and cooking oil. ___
7. Prices for fish fluctuate only slightly through the year. ___
8. The price of that company's stock has fallen dramatically. ___
9. The price of fruit shot up after the bad harvest. ___

B Study the phrases in the box and then use them to complete the sentences, making all necessary changes.

Word combinations with *price*	
agree on a price	full price
a price war	the price is negotiable
a fixed price	competitive prices
afford the price	at any price
half price	

1. He wants to sell his car for $5,000, but _____. I think he's willing to accept less money for it.
2. The two big department stores are having _____. They're competing to have the lowest prices.
3. That leather jacket was supposed to be $300, but I got it on sale for _____. I think $150 was a great price for it!
4. The university bookstore sells books at _____ that are as good as at other places. I often shop there.
5. Our government wants development _____. They don't consider the effects on our country's environment.
6. My parents wanted to buy that house, but they couldn't _____ with the owner, so finally they gave up.
7. In shops in our country, you normally pay _____. You don't bargain with the shopkeeper.
8. My mother loves to shop at the summer sales. She says that she never pays _____ for anything she buys.
9. In the end, I didn't buy the motorcycle. It was very expensive and I couldn't _____.

There's an old saying . . . *The best things in life are free.*

This means that things like love, happiness, and friendship are more important than our possessions. We use this to tell someone not to be concerned about not having a lot of money.

"I'm sorry but I don't have any money this week to go out on a date."
"Well, *the best things in life are free.* Why don't we just go for a nice walk on the beach?"

C Match the descriptions to the names of places or events where things are sold. Circle the ones that are common in your city.

1. auction ___
2. benefit sale ___
3. flea market ___
4. wholesaler ___
5. boutique ___
6. Mom-and-Pop store ___
7. convenience store ___
8. thrift store ___

a. a small and expensive shop
b. a business that sells things to stores
c. an outdoor sale of antiques and old clothes
d. a small grocery store that is open very early and late
e. a store that sells used clothes and household items
f. a sale of merchandise to the highest bidder
g. an event to raise money for a charitable organization
h. a neighborhood business run by a family

D Review these words from the reading "All My Life For Sale" on page 123 and use them to complete the sentences, making all necessary changes.

catalog (v)	reflect on	chronicle (n)	update (n)
transaction	request (n)	relevant former	

1. My mother is a _____ nurse, so she was always prepared for any emergency when we were growing up.
2. I'm planning to _____ all of my CDs and list them by different types of music.
3. When Julio asked me to apologize to his girlfriend for him, I thought that was a very strange _____.
4. To win an argument about politics, you need to use facts and ideas that are _____ to the topic.
5. My brother sends me an e-mail with a weekly _____ about our father's health.
6. After you get money from an ATM, it prints a receipt to give you a record of the _____.
7. During my last year in high school, I spent a lot of time _____ my future.
8. My grandfather wrote a _____ of his experiences during the war.

In Other Words

Possessions is used in the plural to talk about things that you own: *All of the family's possessions were destroyed in the fire.*
Belongings has a similar meaning but is most often used to talk about things you carry with you: *Be sure to take all your belongings with you when exiting the train.*
Stuff (noncount) is a common informal word for possessions: *I have so much stuff that it took me a week to move it into my new apartment.*
Property is a formal or legal term: *This book is the property of the Metropolis Public Library.*

If something is expensive, its price is high: *The Richmont Inn is the most expensive hotel in town.*
If something is valuable, it would be worth a lot of money if it were sold: *The thieves stole three valuable paintings from the museum.*
If something is costly, it involves wasting a lot of money: *Redecorating the office turned out to be a very costly process.*
If something is a rip-off (slang), it's so expensive that it's like stealing: *Tickets to that movie cost $30— what a rip-off!*

Watch out!

popular and common
If something is *popular*, many people like it.
If there is no particular favorable attitude toward something but its use is widespread, use *common*.

Small cars are very popular in my country, and their sales are increasing.
Traffic accidents are very common in big cities.
~~Traffic accidents are very popular in big cities.~~

1 VOCABULARY FOCUS

A Master of Mandalas

Look at the photos in A. Have you ever seen anything like the items pictured? Why do you think people make them?

A You are going to read an interview from an art magazine. The questions listed below are missing from the interview. Read Javier's responses and then write the questions in the appropriate places.

- As an artist, have you always made mandalas?
- Do you like what you do?
- Do you make money doing this?
- What does the word "mandala" mean?

- How long does it take to make one of these elaborate creations?
- Making the mandala is a joint process. Who gets to keep it when you're finished?
- Who works on the mandala with you?

THE ARTIST SPEAKS: A Master of Mandalas

Real English

make room for = open up a space or opportunity for (something else)

Question 1: _____

Javier: No, I started out working in cast-iron doing sculptures. I made these big oval-shaped things. I also worked in stainless steel. They were hard, gigantic pieces of art. Then one day, one of my art installations had to be destroyed to make room for a shopping center. It got me to thinking about how everything changes—you know, the ebb and flow of things. That's what led me to these beautiful circular pieces of art called "mandalas."

Q2: _____

J: *Mandala* is an ancient Sanskrit word for *circle*. A mandala can have many spiritual meanings. Traditionally, mandalas are made to remind us of some important principle of life. I make my mandalas out of sand with the help of others—it's a collaborative process.

Q3: _____

J: About a month. It's a painstakingly slow process . . . but very rewarding.

Q4: _____

J: Anyone who wants to, basically. First, I am asked to come to a community. Then, we recruit local people to help with the mandala. It feels great with everyone working so diligently on such an intricate piece. It brings everyone together.

Q5: _____

J: Not really. Like I said, I'm sponsored by someone who asks me to come. They cover the cost of putting the mandala together and they pay for my food and lodging. Everyone else who works on it is a volunteer.

Q6: _____

J: No one. Before we begin, we make a mutual decision to dismantle it together. We gather all the sand into one jar and then pour it back into the sea. It's sad to take it apart after all that hard work, but it teaches us an important lesson—that nothing lasts forever. Everything always fluctuates. When the mandala is gone, I move on to my next project and the people return home.

Q7: _____

J: I love it! For the period of a few weeks, working on the mandala together can create the impression of everyone living and working together in harmony toward the same goal. It's a beautiful feeling.

B Pair work. **Categorize the words in blue from** A **under the appropriate heading. Use your dictionary to help you. Can you think of any other words for these categories?**

the sensation made by someone / something	change; go up and down	get rid of something
create the impression of		
types of material	pay for someonc clse	sizes and kinds of shapes
doing (something) together; cooperative	having detailed parts	

C Pair work. **Discuss these questions.**

1. What do you think of these aspects of Javier's art?
   - Someone else covers the costs so he can create mandalas.
   - The mandalas are dismantled once they're finished.
2. Is there any value in what Javier does? If so, what is it?

2 LISTENING
Conversations in an art gallery

>> **Vocabulary Builder** ▲

What is the difference in meaning, if any, between these words formed with *dis-* **and** *un-*?

disable	disarm	uncover
unable	unarmed	discover
discomfort	disorganized	
uncomfortable	unorganized	

A **Listen to three different conversations in an art gallery. Match each conversation (1, 2, or 3) to the piece of art being discussed.** (CD Tracks 33 & 34)

Artist's feeling or message:
_____
_____

Man ☐ likes it ☐ dislikes it
_____

Woman ☐ likes it ☐ dislikes it
_____

Artist's feeling or message:
_____
_____

Man ☐ likes it ☐ dislikes it
_____

Woman ☐ likes it ☐ dislikes it
_____

Artist's feeling or message:
_____
_____

Man ☐ likes it ☐ dislikes it
_____

Woman ☐ likes it ☐ dislikes it
_____

B **Listen again to the people's conversations and, in a word or phrase, write what the feeling or message is that they think each artist is trying to convey.** (CD Track 35)

C **Do the speakers like the art? Listen again and check the appropriate box. On the lines below the boxes, write the key words from the listening that support your answers.** (CD Track 36)

> **Ask & Answer**
> Which piece of art do you prefer? Why?

3 LANGUAGE FOCUS

Using fronted structures for emphasis

A One way to emphasize information is to put it at the front of a sentence. Read what these two visitors to an art museum said. What do you notice, if anything, about the word order of the sentences in Column B?

Column A	Column B (more emphasis)
1. I've never seen such a beautiful painting.	1. Never have I seen such a beautiful painting.
2. This sculpture is even more beautiful (than the last one).	2. Even more beautiful (than the last one) is this sculpture.
3. Three paintings by Picasso are hanging in this museum.	3. Hanging in this museum are three paintings by Picasso.
4. The Louvre Pyramid is situated in the museum's main courtyard.	4. Situated in the museum's main courtyard is the Louvre Pyramid.
5. The artist painted this picture with great care.	5. With great care, the artist painted this picture.
6. I came here today in order to learn more about art.	6. In order to learn more about art, I came here today.

Subject-object inversion (change in word order) occurs with some, but not all, fronted structures.

B Read these sentences with fronted structures. Underline the structure and then rewrite the sentence in its conventional form, by using the S-V-O (subject, verb, object) word order.

1. So popular were his paintings that they quickly sold out.

   <u>His paintings were so popular that they quickly sold out.</u>

2. Hidden from view are some spectacular cave drawings.

   _____

3. Under no circumstances will I visit a crowded museum.

   _____

4. Because he wants to study art, he's moving to Europe.

   _____

5. Working in her studio was the famous artist herself.

   _____

6. If the museum is closing, we should leave now.

   _____

7. Never have I been so mesmerized by a piece of art!

   _____

8. Adored by many art critics are the paintings by Picasso.

   _____

C Pair work. Compare your answers in B with a partner. In which of the sentences did the word order change in the fronted structures?

D Many fronted structures use the negative. Read these sentences and rewrite each one using the negative fronted structure in parentheses.

1. I didn't think they would finish the sand mandala in a month. (never)

   _____

2. I wouldn't want to be an artist. (not for anything)

   _____

3. The sand mandala isn't a permanent work of art. (in no way)

   _____

4. I didn't think I would find a new job so easily. (never in my wildest dreams)

   _____

5. She didn't cry after her mother died. (not once)

   _____

E Complete these sentences with your own ideas on a separate piece of paper. Then compare your answers with a partner.

1. Never have I laughed so hard as when . . .
2. Not once since last year have I . . .
3. So boring was my _____ class that . . .
4. Studying hard for my last test, . . .
5. Under no circumstances will I . . .
6. Even more difficult than learning English is . . .
7. Near my home . . .
8. Adored by many fans is . . .
9. Often during the day I . . .
10. In order to improve my English, . . .
11. In no way will you learn English by . . .
12. Taught in every school in my country . . .

Grammar X-TRA Cleft sentences with *wh-* words

Read the information in the box. Then rewrite the sentences below as cleft sentences. Use the words in parentheses.

Write *wh-* cleft sentences with a question word + subject and insert the verb *be*:

She wants to buy a sweater.   *What she wants to buy is a sweater.*
                                    A sweater is what she wants to buy.

1. He started out by painting graffitti on walls. (how)
   How he started out was by painting graffiti on walls.

2. Keith Haring was a true pioneer in art. (what)

   _____

3. He painted to raise people's awareness about social issues. (why)

   _____

4. He lived and died in New York City. (where)

   _____

5. He made many art pieces that carried a social message. (what)

   _____

I find that hard to believe.

A Pair work. How important or necessary are places such as art museums and zoos in big cities? Should all cities try to make such places available for their citizens? Discuss with a partner.

B Read these opinions and their four supporting arguments below. Match the opinions and supporting arguments by writing the correct letter.

> **Supporting arguments**
>
> To support their opinion, speakers use arguments (facts, explanations, or consequences) to convince their listeners that it is correct. If you want to challenge an argument, you must explain why it's incorrect, illogical, or not likely to happen.

Should our city support a project for an art museum or a zoo?

"Zoos are terrible places for animals. Our city certainly doesn't need one. _____"

Daniel Sandoval, photographer

"Children get bored during summer vacation. A zoo would certainly benefit them. _____"

Natalie Bennett, nurse

"Art is something our country is famous for, so an art museum would be a magnificent tourist attraction. _____"

Elliott McCann, retired executive

"I don't think art is a priority here. Local people won't get much out of an art museum. _____"

Leslie Hong, computer programmer

a. *Every major city supports art, so we need to spend money on this, too.*

b. *Not only are zoos bad for animals, they give the wrong message about how we should cohabit the planet.*

c. *Ordinary people here are just not interested in art.*

d. *A zoo could get young people interested in animal conservation. Our country really needs to work on that.*

C Pair work. Imagine that there are funds available in your city to support only one project, either an art museum or a zoo. You and your partner are going to choose one of the projects. Think of supporting arguments for the project you favor.

D Group work. Join with a pair who supports the other project and discuss which project is best for your city. Challenge each other's arguments and introduce counterarguments. Try to use expressions from the box.

> **Arguments and counterarguments**
>
> **Challenging an argument**
> *That's inaccurate.*
> *That's not logical.*
> *I find that hard to believe.*
> *That doesn't make sense.*
>
> **Introducing a counterargument**
> *In fact, . . .*
> *It hardly seems likely that . . . because . . .*
> *In reality, . . .*
> *The truth of the matter is . . .*

The Impact of Art

Lesson B | Hidden stories

1 GET READY TO READ

If these walls could talk . . .

Discuss this question with a partner: Is there a place in your city that has special memories for you, such as a place where you played as a child or hung out with friends?

A Read this excerpt from the reading on page 135. What do you think the underlined expression means? Look around the room where you are now. If the walls could talk, what would they say?

Stories don't just live in our books and imaginations, they belong to the buildings and homes where they take place. Stories can haunt these places like ghosts, can bring a city's architecture to life. <u>If walls could talk</u>, they'd have a lot to say . . .

B Read what these New Yorkers have to say about their city.

Your City . . . Your Stories • Is there a place in your city that has special memories for you?

Kathy

< There's a little gelato place down on East 9th Street. I used to go there as a kid with my uncle in the summer. We'd buy ice cream and sit outside watching the people go by. What made it so fun? It's hard to articulate, really, but I do know that I can't pass by that place without thinking of my uncle and the conversations we had.

Charles

> Oh, yeah . . . the Black Cat Club. It was an intimate little jazz spot up on 137th Street. There was great music and a rich mix of people in the crowd—and while we all were having fun inside, the police would be outside doling out tickets for noise and double-parked cars. It was an amazing scene.

Olga

< No, there isn't really. I mean, it's exciting . . . New York is a real microcosm with people from every corner of the world coming here to live and work. That's true, but it's also noisy and expensive. And in my neighborhood, the infrastructure is crumbling—it's falling apart. I'm reconciled to the fact that I have to stay here for now, but I plan to move to the suburbs next year.

C Pair work. With a partner, find these words and expressions in B.

1. Find a word or expression that means *express clearly*: _____
2. Find a word or expression that means *handing out*: _____
3. Find a word or expression that means *cozy*: _____
4. Find a word or expression that means *variety*: _____
5. Find a word or expression that means *accepting*: _____
6. Find a word or expression that means *miniature model*: _____
7. Find a word or expression that means *basic facilities and services*: _____

A Pair work. **Look at the title and the subtitle of the article on page 135. What do you think the article is going to be about? Discuss your ideas with a partner.**

TALES OF TORONTO
An innovative project uses cell phones to tell the hidden stories of the city

B **Read the article. Then choose the two answers that complete each sentence.**

1. Shawn, Gabe, and James met ___.
   a. in Toronto   b. in the winter   c. in 2002

2. Pedestrians with cell phones ___.
   a. call a number   b. listen to a story   c. record a message

3. The project takes place in ___.
   a. the suburbs   b. the city   c. Kensington

4. The organizers chose cell phones for this project because they're ___.
   a. easy to use   b. more intimate   c. inexpensive

5. In the future, the project is scheduled to happen in ___.
   a. Saskatchewan   b. Vancouver   c. Montreal

C **What do these words refer to in the reading? Write your answers.**

1. *they* (line 5) _____
2. *itself* (line 12) _____
3. *it* (line 16) _____
4. *there* (line 21) _____
5. *they* (line 27) _____
6. *they* (line 27) _____
7. *it* (line 34) _____

D Pair work. **Take turns. Read these questions and use the words in blue to answer them.**

1. How exactly does the installation work?
   collect / archive / cell phone / pedestrian / phone number / sign

2. Why do you think it's called a "democratic approach" to oral history?
   breakdown / official version / offer / alternative version

3. Why was the project launched in Kensington?
   vibrant / stores and restaurants / microcosm / infrastructure / immigrants

4. What do the artists hope the installation will do?
   get reacquainted / walking / feel the story

▶ **Ask & *Answer***

What sites would you put on an audio tour of your city? Why?

World Link

No tour of Toronto would be complete without a visit to—the shoe museum? Yes! The Bata Shoe Museum is home to over 10,000 shoes, ranging from sandals worn in ancient Egypt to red high heels worn by Marilyn Monroe. The museum's collections also include beautifully decorated moccasins made by North American Indians, warm reindeer-skin boots from Lapland, and special wedding shoes made of silver and gold from India.

Source: *www.batashoemuseum.ca*

TALES OF TORONTO

An innovative project uses cell phones to tell the hidden stories of the city

by Anna Bowness, from *Broken Pencil*

Is there a park you can't pass without
thinking of the dog you loved and lost? Is the city
map covered with stories of your life? Stories don't
just live in our books and imaginations, they belong
5   to the buildings and homes where *they* take place.
Stories can haunt these places like ghosts, can bring a
city's architecture to life. If walls could talk, they'd have a
lot to say; a project called [murmur]* has given them a voice.

Shawn Micallef, Gabe Sawhney, and James Roussel are [murmur]. They
10 met at the Habitat New Media Lab at the Canadian Film Centre in Toronto in the
summer of 2002 and started [murmur] as a way of letting Toronto's oral history
articulate *itself*. They collect real stories from real people and archive them for
anyone to hear. Pedestrians with cell phones can call the phone number listed
on a sign posted outside a place that has a story and hear the story that took
15 place where they're standing, while they're standing there. And hear it told in
the voice of the person who lived *it*. This democratic approach "breaks down
the hegemonic 'official' history of Toronto . . . and offers countless alternative
histories," says Micallef. The pilot project for [murmur] focuses on Toronto's
vibrant, multiethnic Kensington Market, where craft stores and ethnic restaurants
20 crowd together in a rich mix. "We decided to launch the project in Kensington
because it's a microcosm of Toronto: Layers of the city are visible *there*, from the
Victorian infrastructure to the brand-new immigrant population. People are really
attached to it," explains Micallef.

Why cell phones and why pedestrians?
25 While the boys of [murmur] admit that
cell phones may come across as a rather
elitist interface, *they* insist that *they* are the
easiest to use, the most appropriate, and the
most intimate way to dole out stories. The
30 stories are told to pedestrians because one
of the aims of this project is to get people
reacquainted with their cities, at street level.
"The city moves at the speed of walking,"
says Micallef. "Hearing a story in the space where *it* happened lets you feel the
35 story and reconcile it with what you see and feel around you."

Installations in Montreal and Vancouver were planned for the fall, but the
idea would work as well in rural Saskatchewan (find out what's really inside the
grain silo), in the wilds of Newfoundland (that antique store used to be Grandpa
Percy's), or even a suburb (one of those cookie-cutter garage doors has got to
40 have a scandal behind it). To hear, tell, or learn about [murmur] and its archive
of urban mythologies, visit www.murmurtoronto.ca

Source: *Broken Pencil* magazine

* *[murmur]* = the name given to this project. The word *murmur* means to say something in a soft, quiet voice.

A Pair work. **Look at the advertisement below and at the application form in B. Discuss with your partner what type of information is requested. Then talk about and organize your ideas for writing a cover letter to accompany the application.**

> **Cover letter:** A cover letter accompanies a job application or a résumé (sometimes called a CV). It tells what job you are applying for and highlights experiences that make you qualified for the job.

Arts Ambassadors International

Would you like to serve as an Arts Ambassador for your country? Spend two months touring Europe and/or North America, attending festivals and presenting the arts and culture of your country. A stipend and all travel expenses are paid. People of all ages and backgrounds are encouraged to apply! Download the application at **www.ArtsAmbassadors.org**. Cover letter required.

B **Complete the application with information about yourself. Then write the cover letter on a separate sheet of paper.**

> **Tips for writing a good cover letter**
>
> - Identify key accomplishments and transferable skills.
> - Use action verbs. (i.e. *worked, implemented,* etc.)
> - Conclude with a request for an interview.

Arts Ambassadors International

Name _____
          Last   First   Middle

Mailing address _____

City _____ **Zip code** _____ **Country** _____

Phone _____ **E-mail address** _____

Gender _____ **Date of birth** _____ **Citizenship** _____ **Marital status** _____

Name of parent or guardian (if under 18) _____

List any health conditions that could affect your participation in AAI activities

_____

List all educational institutions attended, beginning with most recent

Institution	City	Dates	Degree / major

List all jobs held, beginning with most recent

Employer	Position	Dates	Responsibilities

List your hobbies, interests, and activities.

_____

Cover Letter: In 200 words explain why you think you would make a good Arts Ambassador. Refer to your educational background, work experience, and interests.

I certify that all information in this application is accurate and complete to the best of my knowledge.

Signature _____ **Date** _____

Signature of parent or guardian (if under 18)

_____

> . . . Last summer I worked as a tour guide for City Tours. I first had to learn all about the history and architecture of my city. The experience I gained working with the public would be very valuable . . .

A school audio tour

A Pair work. **Read the text below and then answer the questions with your partner.**

> In the article on page 135, you read about a group of people who are creating personal walking tours in the city of Toronto. These tours enable the city's residents to tell stories and share memories about a place.

- Look at the example below. If the walls of your school could talk, what personal stories do you think they'd tell?
- Is there a personal story you could tell about your classroom?

My Classroom	
the room's official history / information	personal stories associated with the room
<ul><li>located on the second floor of a building that was built in 1998</li><li>was originally used as office space</li><li>was converted to a classroom in 2002 when the school bought the first and second floors</li><li>seats up to fifty people</li><li>has two whiteboards; Internet access is available</li></ul>	*I've had two English classes in this room. The first was last fall. It was a big class, but we had a lot of fun and learned a lot.* *—Miguel* *I remember my first day in this classroom. I didn't know anybody. I was sitting next to Kenji near the front—in that seat. I was so nervous at first that I could barely speak.* *—Junko* **Your story:**

B Group work. **Get into a group of three people. You are going to create a personal audio tour of four to five different locations in your school. Follow the directions below.**

1. Which locations are you going to include on the tour? Choose from the ideas below or think of your own.
   - the school reception area
   - a student hangout near the school
   - the cafeteria or student café
   - the library
   - different classrooms
   - the teachers' lounge

2. What personal stories are you going to tell about each place? For each stop on the tour, you should tell a 30-second to one-minute story. You can tell stories that . . .
   - happened to you or someone you know.
   - are real or made up. They can be serious or silly.
   - are about something routine (e.g., losing money in the cafeteria vending machine), or memorable (e.g., meeting your girlfriend for the first time).

C Group work. **Get together with another group and take them on your school audio tour. Use the phrases in the box below to guide the tour. Allow people on the tour to ask you questions. Then switch roles.**

> *The first stop on our tour is . . .*
> *Now you are standing in front of . . .*
> *Let's move on to the next site on the tour. To get there, turn left and proceed . . .*
> *For our last stop on the tour, we're visiting . . .*

> *The first stop on our tour is the school reception desk. Our classmate Dan signed up for her first class ever at this desk. On that day . . .*

 Check out the CNN® video. **Practice your English online at** elt.heinle.com/worldpass

Unit 11: The Impact of Art

A Classify these forms of art in the correct category.

theater	sculpture	dance	painting	photography
architecture	play	ceramics	poetry	short story
music	novel	opera	biography	

Fine Arts	Performing Arts	Literature

B Complete each sentence with a word from **A**.

1. I really enjoy going to the _____. The costumes, the orchestra, the singing—it makes me forget the real world!
2. The mayor dedicated the new _____ that stands in Memorial Park.
3. I just read a new _____ of Mother Teresa that tells about her life with the poor in Calcutta.
4. In my _____ course, we're learning to make bowls and vases by hand.
5. I read a great _____ on the subway this morning. It was only five pages long.
6. If you want to study _____, you need to be in very good physical condition.
7. There's a _____ exhibition at the Arts Center that has a lot of wonderful black-and-white landscape pictures.
8. I like to read _____ that rhymes out loud.
9. I really dislike a lot of the modern _____ in this city. Steel and glass buildings look so cold and inhuman.
10. I just started reading a new _____ by my favorite author. The first chapter was a little confusing, but there are some great characters.
11. The drama club is going to put on a _____ by William Shakespeare.
12. My mother took lessons in oil _____ and now she's done portraits of everyone in our family.
13. My younger brother is very interested in _____ and hopes to be a stage actor when he's older.
14. The traditional _____ of my country uses a lot of drums and flutes.

I didn't know that!

Museum is a Latin word meaning "place inhabited by the Muses." The Muses were nine Greek goddesses of history, arts and sciences, song and poetry. Their names were Clio (history), Erato (love poetry), Calliope (war poetry), Euterpe (music), Melpomene (tragedy), Thalia (comedy), Terpsichore (dance), Polyhymnia (religious music), and Urania (astronomy).

C Circle the word in each line that doesn't fit with the others.

1. relaxing   unsettling   disturbing   uncomfortable
2. impressive   incredible   ordinary   captivating
3. eyesore   ugly   unattractive   appealing
4. joint   solo   collaborative   mutual
5. intricate   complex   complicated   simple
6. combine   dismantle   take apart   undo
7. original   reproduction   copy   duplicate
8. be reconciled to   accept   refuse   put up with

D Review these words from the reading "Tales of Toronto" on page 135 and use them to complete the sentences, making all necessary changes.

archive (v)	haunt (v)	pedestrian	elitist
vibrant	murmur (v)	multiethnic	infrastructure

1. Singapore is a truly _____ nation. Its citizens are Chinese, Malays, Indians, and Europeans.
2. Speeding traffic on Ramsey Road presents a real hazard to _____ who are crossing the street to the post office.
3. Critics say that the government's system of university entrance exams is _____, because students who can afford private tutors usually get better scores.
4. In her speech, the president promised to invest more money in the country's _____, especially roads and bridges.
5. Sarah designed a project to collect and _____ old people's memories of their childhood, so we can include them in our town's history.
6. It is said that the ghost of a woman who drowned _____ that bridge.
7. The sick child cried and _____ in her sleep, but no one could understand what she said.
8. Seattle is a _____ city with great nightlife and a thriving arts scene.

In Other Words

In an art museum, works of art are displayed to the public: *The National Museum has a fantastic collection of sculpture.*
An art gallery is a business that displays and sells the works of one or more artists at a time: *I love to look at photographs in galleries, but the prices are too high for me to buy anything.*
An exhibition is a temporary show of art: *The Museum of Modern Art will have an exhibition of twentieth-century Mexican paintings next month.*
A studio is the place where a painter or sculptor works: *Jeffrey paints in a studio on the top floor of an old factory building.*

The theme of a work of art is its central idea: *The theme of that painting is the conflict between mothers and daughters.*
The message of a work of art is the idea that its creator is trying to teach or convey: *The message of the mandalas is that nothing in this world lasts forever.*
The subject of a work of art is the people or things that it is about: *The subject of the photograph is a tiger in the zoo.*

Watch out!

see and look at
If you *see* something, you notice it passively with your eyes. You are not making an effort.
    I didn't see you come into the room.
If you *look at* something, you move your eyes towards it and make an effort to see it.
    He looked at my drawing and said it was very good.
Don't use *see* when talking about a deliberate action.
    Don't look at me when I'm changing my clothes!
    ~~Don't see me when I'm changing my clothes!~~

1 VOCABULARY FOCUS

What does the future hold?

 When someone talks about "the future," what images and ideas come to mind?

A Pair work. Read questions 1–4 in the article "Looking to the Future" below. Don't read the answers yet. Tell your partner how you would answer each question.

B Read the questions and the responses, paying attention to the words in blue. Then match the words in blue with the word or phrase below that has a similar meaning.

1. changeable, flexible _____
2. located in a physical facility _____
3. weaken _____
4. help or make happen _____
5. advances or innovations _____
6. analysis or examination _____

7. live or be together _____
8. cause _____
9. drops sharply _____
10. unaffected, resilient _____
11. a large outbreak of an illness at one time _____
12. the wage earner in a family _____

LOOKING TO THE FUTURE
What do you think the future holds in these four areas?

Career & Employment
1. What will our work lives be like in the future?
   a. Fewer people will be employed "for life" by a single company. One's career path will be more fluid, with a person changing jobs frequently.
   b. Globalization will undermine traditional life, and there will be fewer jobs and more competition.
   c. Traditional ways and new ways of doing business will coexist harmoniously.

Education & Learning
2. What trends in education do you think will be common in the future?
   a. Online learning and virtual study groups will replace the traditional brick-and-mortar school.
   b. More people worldwide will be learning Spanish and Chinese so that they can be competitive in the workplace.
   c. Rather than being dependent on the teacher for all the answers, students will be encouraged to facilitate class discussions and to learn from their peers.

Family & Relationships
3. What will the family of the future be like?
   a. The primary breadwinner and key decision maker in many families will be a woman.
   b. More families will be multicultural as the Internet and global travel make it possible for people to meet and marry someone from another country.
   c. As the birthrate in many places plummets and there is less family support, elderly people will form communities to care for each other.

Health & Medical Technology
4. What will some of the key developments in health and medicine be?
   a. Breakthroughs in research will lead to cures for cancer, Alzheimer's, and other deadly diseases. The result: more people living to be 100 or older.
   b. Parents will use genetic profiling to select the gender and physical characteristics of their child.
   c. A new type of infectious disease that is resistant to antibiotics will emerge. It will trigger a worldwide epidemic before it can be stopped.

C Pair work. Read the questions in B again and circle the answers you agree with.
Then share your ideas with a partner. Explain your reasons.

⟫⟫ Vocabulary Builder ▲▲

Read the definitions of these words. Then choose the best answer to complete each
sentence. Can you explain your choices?

Increase or become larger	Decrease or become smaller
swell = increase as numbers are added; become larger than usual **escalate** = become larger in intensity **flourish** = to grow and do well or be successful (over time)	**plummet** = decrease or fall quickly **dwindle** = gradually become smaller **shrink** = become smaller

1. In less than an hour, the temperature plummeted / dwindled / shrank from 22° C to 4° C.
2. Plants cannot swell / escalate / flourish in a room without sunlight.
3. I can't believe I plummeted / dwindled / shrank my favorite sweater in the wash.
4. Their argument swelled / escalated / flourished and soon they were throwing things at each other.
5. As the years passed, the dictator's power plummeted / dwindled / shrank and protests became more common.
6. The crowd at the popular concert swelled / escalated / flourished to over 50,000.

2 LISTENING
A new spin on familiar products

A Pair work. You're going to listen to someone describing three recent
inventions. Look at the name of each one in the chart. What do you
think these inventions do? Discuss your ideas with a partner.

B Look over the notes in the chart describing how each invention works.
Then listen and complete them. (CD Tracks 37 & 38)

Invention	How it works
1. A washing machine called "Your Turn"	The machine's _____ button is programmed to _____ a person's _____ so that the same person isn't always _____.
2. The Sky Car	It works like a _____, but drivers will also be able to _____ from just about any location and travel up to _____ miles per hour.
3. Vivienne, The Virtual Girlfriend	Vivienne is similar to a _____ in a _____ game, only she's more _____. You access her on your _____. She's able to talk with you about _____ and can also _____.

C Pair work. Listen again. What are the disadvantages associated with each invention? Write the number of each invention
next to one or more disadvantages. What information in the listening helped you make your choices? Tell a partner.
(CD Track 39)

1. very expensive _____
2. will require a special permit _____
3. difficult to reprogram _____
4. can only be used with certain phones _____
5. not available for the consumer market yet _____

D Pair work. Using your notes from B and C, discuss these questions with a partner.

1. What are the pros and cons of each invention?
2. Can you think of any other good or bad points associated with each invention?

> **Ask & Answer**
>
> If money weren't a concern, would you buy any of the three inventions? Why or why not?

3 LANGUAGE FOCUS

Talking about the future

A Pair work. These structures can all be used to talk about the future. With your partner, look at the numbered verbs in the article and indicate which type of future structure is being used.

simple present	future continuous	future with *be going to*
present continuous	future perfect	future with *be about to*
future with *will*	future perfect continuous	

SPACE TOURISM

Imagine this. I'm in a hurry— (1) I'm leaving for the moon tonight. The shuttle (2) takes off at 8 P.M. and I haven't even packed my bags yet. Does that sound like a crazy scenario? Well, maybe it's not!

"People (3) will be taking vacations in space sooner rather than later," states scientist Pamela Shaw. "It (4) will definitely happen. By the time the twenty-second century rolls around, I predict we (5) will have been vacationing in space for decades."

Space tourism is what they're calling it—ordinary people, like you and me, buying tickets to travel to outer space. Hopefully, we (6) will be able to travel back safely as well!

The general public is excited about the idea. Take journalist Peter Marcus, for example: "As soon as space travel becomes a possibility, (7) I'm going to sign up for it. Who wouldn't want to travel to space?"

Of course, space tourism (8) isn't about to become a money-making business anytime soon. There are many problems that must be solved first, such as expense. Also, where (9) will the space tourists stay once they're up in space? (10) Will we be building space hotels to accommodate them?

By the time our grandchildren are our age, traveling to space (11) will have become routine. For us, though, it's still very exciting to think about!

B Circle the best answer to complete each sentence.

1. The writer uses I'm leaving (present continuous) for a future plan that has already been made / a prediction.
2. The writer uses takes off (simple present) for a sudden decision / a fixed schedule.
3. The writer uses will be taking (future continuous) for an event that is expected / not expected to happen in the future.
4. The writer uses will happen (future with *will*) to make a plan for / a prediction about the future.
5. The writer uses will have been vacationing (future perfect continuous) to emphasize the length / end of an action in the future.
6. The writer uses am going to sign up (future with *be going to*) to talk about an intention / a prediction for a future event.
7. The writer uses isn't about to become (future with *be about to*) because the event will / will not happen soon.
8. The writer uses will have become (future perfect) for an event that will be / will not be completed at a specific time in the future.

Pair work. **Follow the steps below.**

- Read the first sentence in each pair of sentences. Then complete the second sentence so that it has a similar meaning to the first sentence. Include the verb in parentheses in your answer.
- You may need to change the form of the verb. Also, there may be more than one appropriate answer.
- Compare your answers with a partner.

1. Look at those dark clouds; it's about to rain.
   Look at those dark clouds; _____. (rain)
2. In three days, our final exams are going to be over.
   By this time next week, we _____ our final exams. (finish)
3. I plan to visit my aunt this weekend.
   _____. (visit)
4. According to this schedule, the train is leaving at 6 A.M. tomorrow.
   According to this schedule, _____ at 6 A.M. tomorrow. (leave)
5. Next Friday, we're going to be on a beach in Hawaii.
   By this time next week, _____ on a beach in Hawaii. (relax)

D Group work. **Imagine yourself ten or twenty years from now. Get into groups of three or four and make statements using the future continuous, future perfect, and future perfect continuous.**

Ten years from now, I will still be living in my hometown. I will have gotten married and . . .

Twenty years from now, I will have successfully raised two children and they will be attending college . . .

Grammar X-TRA ▷ Final review of tenses

You've learned about a lot of different tenses in the *World Pass* series.
Read the pairs of sentences below and follow these steps.

- Identify the tenses being contrasted in each pair.
- Check whether the meaning of the two sentences is the same or different.
- If the meaning is different, explain how.

1a. I live on Mercer Street.
1b. I'm living on Mercer Street. ☐ Same ☐ Different _____

2a. We will find a cure for cancer.
2b. We're going to find a cure for cancer. ☐ Same ☐ Different _____

3a. I worked there for five years.
3b. I've worked there for five years. ☐ Same ☐ Different _____

4a. Not many scientists have studied space travel.
4b. Not many scientists have been studying space travel. ☐ Same ☐ Different _____

5a. I've painted a portrait.
5b. I've been painting a portrait. ☐ Same ☐ Different _____

6a. We were eating dinner when the phone rang.
6b. We had eaten dinner when the phone rang. ☐ Same ☐ Different _____

7a. It's going to start raining at any moment.
7b. It's about to rain. ☐ Same ☐ Different _____

8a. She's loud.
8b. She's being loud. ☐ Same ☐ Different _____

This has the advantage of . . .

A Group work. Which kinds of innovations do you hope we will see in the next ten years? Get together in a small group and list as many as you can—serious or not.

> a vaccination against AIDS
> an automatic dog-walking machine
>
> solar-powered computers
> sidewalks made from recycled plastic

B You are going to give a two- to three-minute presentation to persuade your audience that the world needs one of the innovations you listed in **A**. Choose one and list three benefits.

Innovation: _____

Benefits:

1. _____

2. _____

3. _____

C Plan your presentation and make notes in outline form. The presentation should include these sections:

- **Introduction:** Describe the innovation.
- **Body:** Talk about three benefits this innovation would have. Support each with facts, examples, explanations, and specific details.
- **Conclusion:** Why would this innovation be useful for the world?

> *Plastic sidewalks*
>
> • Introduction
> Problems today
> 1. sidewalks have holes—hard for kids and elderly people to walk on
> 2. too much plastic is thrown away
> Plastic sidewalks
> 1. could be made in a factory
> 2. could use recycled plastic (bottles, etc.)
> • Body
> Benefit 1. Better to walk on

Describing benefits and supporting points

One / Another / The most important benefit would be . . .
This has the advantage of . . .
If we do this . . .
One result would be . . .

Giving support to main points

Let me give you an example of this.
For instance, / For example,
You might not realize it but . . .
This is important because . . .

D Pair work. Take turns giving your presentation to a partner. Try to use some of the expressions in the boxes. Don't READ your presentation—use your notes and refer to them only if you forget something. For the listener: Don't forget to give your partner comments and suggestions for improvement.

E Give your presentation in front of the class. Remember to speak slightly more loudly than normal and to look at different members of your audience while speaking.

F Which speakers made the most persuasive arguments for the innovation they chose? Which of these innovations do you think we will actually see in the future?

UNIT 12 Our Changing World

| **Lesson B** | Are we up to the challenge? |

1 GET READY TO READ
Facing the facts

 In your opinion, what are some of the most serious challenges facing the world today?

A Pair work. **Read the short excerpt below and then, with your partner, discuss the questions.**

1. The words in blue are all related to the topic of the environment. What do you think these words mean?
2. Can you think of other words or phrases that have to do with the environment?
3. How would you answer the question asked at the end of the excerpt?

Saving the Tropical Rainforests

Several regions are losing their biodiversity as a variety of plant and animal habitats are destroyed to make way for human dwelling. The loss of these plant and animal species presents us with an important ecological challenge: What can we do to stop the destruction and to safeguard one of the world's most important natural resources?

B Check (✓) the three environmental challenges that you think are the most serious. **You may add another if you wish.**

- [ ] deforestation, particularly of the world's rainforests
- [ ] global warming / climate change
- [ ] increasing scarcity of resources, such as fresh water
- [ ] population (too high in some places; too low in others)
- [ ] disease
- [ ] pollution
- [ ] poverty
- [ ] war
- [ ] other: _____

C Pair work. **Compare your answers with a partner and explain your choices.**

D Class work. **Share your answers with the class. Which of the challenges in B was mentioned most often?**

A Look at the words and phrases in bold in the first paragraph of the article on page 147.
What do they mean? Use your dictionary if you need help. Then circle an answer in the following sentence.

The words and phrases are mostly calm and positive / negative and dramatic in tone.

B Pair work. Read the title of the article and the first paragraph only.
Then discuss with your partner how the author feels about the future of the Earth.

C Read the remainder of the article. Then match the remaining bolded words from the reading with the correct definitions.
There is an extra definition that you will not use.

1. destabilize ___   3. fluctuations ___   5. staggering ___
2. affluence ___   4. reverberations ___   6. unprecedented ___

a. wealth, prosperity	c. returned, unused	e. incredible, amazing	g. repeated effects
b. unmatched, first-time	d. weaken, undermine	f. changes, variations	

D What are the concerns that the author expresses about each of these topics? Read the article again, and then using the key words and phrases provided, write a summary of each problem in your own words.

1. CLIMATE: greenhouse gases / 20 million years / storms and droughts / stress / ecosystems
   _____

2. POVERTY: divide between rich and poor / 4 billion people / $3 a day / shut out / the good life
   _____

3. POPULATION: 2 billion / 6 billion / 8 billion / Los Angeles / the poorer countries / shantytowns
   _____

4. RESOURCES: 2020s / fresh water / scarce / 40 percent / non-local food /
   demand and cost / oil / skyrocketing / affect / global economy
   _____

5. EXTINCTION: human activities / rapid extinction / plant and animal species / 20 percent / 30 years /
   100 years / 50 percent
   _____

E Group work. Get into a group of three or four people and choose one of the trends, such as an unstable climate or increased poverty, described in the article. Discuss the questions below.

1. What are the specific problems associated with the trend that you chose?
2. What are some of the things that might be causing these problems?
3. What are three suggestions you can think of that might help to solve these problems?

F Group work. Present your ideas to another group.

> Our group recognizes that poverty is a worldwide problem. However, we have some good ideas that might help to solve it . . .

The Gathering World Storm and the Urgency of Our Awakening

by Duane Elgin

Although human societies have confronted major **hurdles** throughout history, the challenges of our era are unique. Never before has the human family been **on the verge** of **devastating** the Earth's biosphere and **crippling** its ecological foundations for countless generations to come. We are now encountering the leading edge of **a world storm** whose **fierce winds** will **tear loose** many institutions
5 from their traditional moorings. In turn, the awakening of a reflective consciousness at the scale of the entire species is fast becoming an evolutionary necessity if we are to avoid **an evolutionary crash** and a long detour leading to **a new dark age** for humanity. The circle has closed and there is no escape—the Earth has become a single, tightly interconnected system. To illustrate, here are five powerful, driving trends that are reinforcing one another and seem likely to produce, within the next decade or two, an
10 unyielding, global, whole-system **crisis**:

1. CLIMATE: Human activity has already begun to **destabilize** the global climate, as greenhouse gases reach levels that are higher than they have been for 20 million years. Experts predict that we will experience increasing climate **fluctuations** with more intense storms, droughts, and stress to all ecosystems. Dramatic changes in global climate patterns will require us to make equally dramatic
15 changes in the patterns of human living.

2. POVERTY: There is a **staggering** level of poverty in the world, and the divide between rich and poor is rapidly increasing. In terms of real income, it is estimated by the United Nations that the majority of people on the Earth (approximately 60 percent, or upwards of 4 billion people) live on the equivalent of $3 a day or less! Despite being effectively shut out[1] of the global economy, they still see the American
20 media's vision of "the good life," of material **affluence**, advertised each day on television.

3. POPULATION: Human population has grown from 2 billion people in 1930 to roughly 6 billion today and, although moving toward stabilization, is expected to grow to roughly 8 billion by the 2020s. In practical terms, human beings now occupy all of the land favorable for human habitation. We are continuing to add people to the Earth at a rate equal to another Los Angeles every month, with the majority living in
25 enormous urban shantytowns[2] in the poorer countries.

4. RESOURCES: Fresh water is becoming a scarce resource at a global scale. It is estimated that by the 2020s, 40 percent of the people on the Earth will not have enough water to be self-sufficient in growing their own food and so will become increasingly dependent on non-local food sources. In this same time frame, we are expected to see an end to the era of cheap world oil. Much of the world's easily
30 accessible oil has already been pumped out of the Earth, so that at the same time that the demand for oil is skyrocketing[3], the cost of supplying that oil is also increasing. The net result is that within a decade or so, world demand for oil will grow beyond what can be cheaply supplied, and we can expect the price of oil to permanently increase with **reverberations** throughout the global economy.

5. SPECIES EXTINCTION: There may be no greater measure of the integrity and resilience of the
35 biosphere than its biodiversity. Yet scientists estimate that 20 percent of all plant and animal species could be extinct in the next 30 years, and 50 percent could be extinct within the next 100 years. Human activities are causing a massive, rapid, and worldwide extinction of both plant and animal species that is **unprecedented** in human history. Indeed, the last great extinction of the current magnitude occurred with the die-off of dinosaurs and other life after an asteroid impact roughly 65 million years ago. We are
40 tearing at the very fabric of life.

We no longer have the luxury of centuries for a gradual awakening. A world storm is gathering and we are being challenged to pay attention to how we pay attention as an entire species.

[1] shut out: excluded, kept out
[2] shantytown: a slum or small town made of poorly built shacks
[3] skyrocketing: rising very fast

Source: http://www.wie.org/j24/elgin.asp

A What will the world be like 20 years from now? Make notes of your predictions for each of the areas listed below.

food	
the environment	
housing	
technology	
health	
education	
war/peace	

Organizing an academic essay

In an academic essay, you make an argument (an opinion that you want your readers to agree with) and support it with evidence (reasons why they should agree). The introduction gives general information and includes the thesis statement, which presents the argument that you are making. The body contains several support paragraphs. Each of these paragraphs covers a different area and contains facts, examples, explanations, and specific details to support your argument. The conclusion summarizes and comments on the argument of your essay. It should leave your reader with a strong impression.

B You are going to write an academic essay about life in the future. Circle your answer to form the thesis statement.

20 years from now, the world will be a better / worse place to live in.

C Plan your essay, then write it. Choose three areas from the chart in **A** that you will use to support your thesis statement.

Paragraph 1: Introduction, containing your thesis statement
Paragraph 2: Ideas from the first area to support the thesis
Paragraph 3: Ideas from the second area to support the thesis
Paragraph 4: Ideas from the third area to support the thesis
Paragraph 5: Conclusion, with recommendations for what we should do

D Pair work. Exchange papers and comment on your partner's ideas. What was the most interesting or surprising point in your partner's essay? What point would you like to hear more about?

E Class activity. Take a class vote. How many students in the class feel optimistic about the future? How many feel pessimistic? Discuss your reasons.

World Link

Believe it or not, some places are being invaded by killer plants and animals! The future of the world's ecosystems may depend on how we handle invasive species—organisms transported from one part of the world to another. In the Mediterranean Sea, an imported seaweed used in aquariums is taking over, and the cane toads brought to Australia to eat insects have now overrun parts of the continent since their poisonous skin means they have no predators.

Source: NOVA

4 COMMUNICATION

Looking at the future from the past

A Pair work. **Read the predictions below and discuss these questions with a partner.**

1. What do you think of the predictions? Were any accurate? Why do you think people made them?
2. What predictions are people making today that you're sure will turn out to be wrong?

- In 1943, the chairman of IBM predicted that there would never be a world market for computers.
- In 1967, Anthony Wiener and Herman Kahn wrote a book called *The Year 2000*. In it, they predicted that by the start of the twenty-first century, humans would be spending significant amounts of time hibernating.
- In the early 1980s, some people predicted that the rise of home video and VCRs would cause movie theaters everywhere to close.
- In the 1990s, people predicted that e-mail and computers would eliminate the need for paper and lead to a "paperless office."

> **A good guess!**
>
> In his 1898 story, author H.G. Wells envisioned a machine that would allow people to travel through time. Today, some physicists believe that, in theory, travel into the distant future is indeed possible. Others think that travel into the past may also be feasible.

B Group work. **You are going to have a debate. Get into a group of four people and look at the statement below. Then choose one of the roles.**

By 2040, many of the world's cities will have become unlivable.

Student A: You AGREE with the statement.	Student B: You DISAGREE with the statement.	Students C & D: You are the JUDGES.
• On a separate piece of paper, make a list of as many reasons as you can that will support your side of the argument. • Try to anticipate some of the points your opponent will make. • Study the rules for debate below.		Listen to the two sides debate the topic. Your role is not to agree with one side or another, but to decide which side argued better—based on the rules for debate below. Take notes as you listen to the two sides.

Rules for debate
• State each reason in your argument clearly. Use facts or other data to support your point. • Do not go over the time given to speak. • Don't introduce ideas randomly. When you offer a rebuttal, make sure that it's related to something your opponent has just said. • At the end of the debate, summarize your arguments briefly.

C Group work. **Get together with your group and begin the debate.**

1. Student A begins by stating and explaining his or her first point (1 minute).
2. Student B responds with an opposing idea (1 minute).
3. Repeat steps one and two for three or four rounds. Then each side will summarize its main points (2 minutes).
4. The Judges will compare notes, choose a winner, and explain their decision.

D Group work. **Choose one of the statements below. Then switch roles and repeat B and C.**

- In the future, we'll be working less and will have more free time to enjoy our lives.
- By the mid–twenty-first century, people will be marrying later in life or not at all.

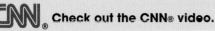 **Check out the CNN® video.** **Practice your English online at** elt.heinle.com/worldpass

Unit 12: Our Changing World

A Match these phrases with the word *future* with their meanings.

1. have a promising future ___
2. there's no future in it ___
3. the future looks bright ___
4. face an uncertain future ___
5. hopes for the future ___
6. shape the future ___
7. predict the future ___
8. in the foreseeable future ___

a. work to influence what will happen
b. say what is going to happen
c. have a good probability for success
d. in the time that you can plan ahead for
e. have a potentially difficult time ahead
f. things will be very good
g. something won't be successful
h. dreams and expectations

B Complete each sentence with one of the phrases from **A**.

1. I don't think I'm going to look for a new job _____. I'll just keep working here.
2. For graduates who can speak English and Japanese, _____. There are some excellent job opportunities available.
3. If we all work together, we can _____. We can build a better world with a cleaner environment and a sustainable economy.
4. My friend Tanya says that she can _____ with cards. She told me I'm going to win a lot of money soon!
5. My cousin decided to give up his dream of becoming a professional clown because he thinks _____.
6. In an increasingly global workplace, bilingual people _____.
7. I have great _____. I believe we'll develop the technology to solve our biggest environmental problems.
8. Many children in developing countries _____. Without an adequate education, it will be very difficult for them to find work.

There's an old saying . . . *All's well that ends well.*

This means that as long as a situation has a happy ending, it doesn't matter what happened before.
We use it to tell someone not to worry about the past. (It's also the title of a comedy by William Shakespeare.)

"I can't believe I left my wallet in the store! How could I be so stupid?"
"Well, it was still there when you went back, so *all's well that ends well.*"

C How does the speaker feel about these future predictions? Match the underlined word in each sentence with one of the explanations.

1. <u>Realistically</u>, we will have to adapt to a changing climate. ___
2. <u>Ideally</u>, countries will work together to develop alternative sources of energy.___
3. <u>Eventually</u>, petroleum production will not be enough to meet increasing demand. ___
4. <u>Hopefully</u>, developing countries will take steps to protect the environment. ___
5. <u>Basically</u>, we will need to produce much more food from the same amount of land. ___

a. This is the best thing that could happen, but it might not occur.
b. This is my simple explanation of what will happen.
c. This is bad, but we can't avoid it.
d. This is what I wish would happen.
e. This is what will happen in the end.

D Cross out the word that <u>doesn't</u> fit with these sentences.

1. I met Roberto's future _____ yesterday.   wife   neighbor   son
2. See our website for more information on all of our future _____.   concerts   gifts   programs
3. We agreed to meet again at a future _____.   date   time   place
4. Be sure to save this instruction book for future _____.   complaints   use   reference

E Review these words from the reading "The Gathering World Storm and the Urgency of Our Awakening" on page 147 and use them to complete the sentences, making all necessary changes.

hurdle	detour	staggering (adj.)	resilience	favorable
unyielding	affluence	massive	gradual	unprecedented

1. Conditions for growing coffee are very _____ in Brazil. The rich soil, ample rainfall, and warm climate provide the perfect environment.
2. Getting a good score on the entrance exam is a big _____ for many students in the process of applying to a university.
3. We were late because the road was closed for construction and we had to take a long _____ on another highway.
4. The _____ in the tourist areas of some countries contrasts with the severe poverty in other areas.
5. The _____ disappearance of the world's forests is changing our climate. It's a slow process, but it has serious negative effects.
6. Every year, people in this country throw away _____ number of bottles and cans. I was really shocked when I found out how many.
7. People showed great _____ after the hurricane. Even though their homes were destroyed, they were able to recover and rebuild quickly.
8. My father is completely _____ in his opinions. He never changes or gives in.
9. _____ earthquake struck the capital city yesterday, leaving thousands of people homeless.
10. There was an _____ response to the tragedy and thousands of people donated money and medicines.

In Other Words

Progress is the process of moving closer to a goal or accomplishment: *Scientists are making progress toward finding a cure for cancer.*
An improvement makes something better: *The city's program of road improvement has helped traffic to move faster.*
Development is an increase in size or activity: *Rapid economic development in many Asian countries has provided better living conditions for their citizens.*

A challenge is something that tests your strength and ability in a positive way: *Providing more housing will be a challenge for the new mayor.*
A problem is a difficult situation that does not have positive aspects: *Dave is having a lot of problems with his car.*
A dilemma is a difficult choice: *New parents often face the dilemma of choosing between work and family responsibilities.*

Watch out!

hope and want
We use *hope* to talk about future situations that we can't control or influence:
    I hope the mail will come soon.
    ~~I want the mail to come soon.~~
We use *want* to talk about future situations that we may be able to control or influence:
    I want my kids to do their homework as soon as they come home from school.
    ~~I hope my kids will do their homework as soon as they come home from school.~~

Review: Units 10–12

1 LANGUAGE CHECK

Fill in the spaces with the correct form of the items in parentheses.

1. I _____ on vacation early Saturday morning. (leave: future time)
2. My new math teacher is OK, but actually, I think I liked _____ old one better. (*article*)
3. I can't go shopping tomorrow. I _____ a doctor's appointment after work. (have: future time)
4. I think yesterday's newspaper is still on _____ kitchen table. (*article*)
5. _____ a more beautiful view than this one. (I / never / see: emphasis)
6. Some day, people _____ to other planets on vacation. (travel: future time)
7. _____ the exhibition that it closed after only a week. (was / so / unpopular: emphasis)
8. _____ are three early paintings by Picasso. (display / in / this room: emphasis)
9. By the end of this semester, Emi _____ English for ten years. (study: future time)
10. _____ I would meet such a famous artist. (I / never / believe: emphasis)
11. _____ after he got sick. (he / complain / not once: emphasis)
12. Five years from now, I think I _____ in the same house. (still / live: future time)
13. _____ X-ray was discovered by a Polish scientist named Marie Curie. (*article*)
14. Would you like to go and get _____ cup of coffee after class today? (*article*)

2 VOCABULARY CHECK

Choose the correct answer.

1. Companies that produce brand-name fashions try to ____ their products from others.
   a. differentiate   b. customize   c. knock off
2. Online businesses are taking away customers from traditional ____ stores.
   a. co-existing   b. brick-and-mortar   c. resistant
3. After the show, a group of volunteers helped to ____ the exhibits.
   a. dismantle   b. disable   c. disorganize
4. The salesman claimed it was an expensive watch, but in reality, it was actually ____.
   a. flashy   b. the ultimate   c. a knockoff
5. Developments like the Internet and cell phones ____ communications between countries.
   a. undermine   b. facilitate   c. plummet
6. Scientists are hoping for a ____ in the search for a cure for cancer.
   a. breakthrough   b. profile   c. trigger
7. Carlos makes beautiful, ____ jewelry from many tiny pieces of wire.
   a. intricate   b. mutual   c. uncovered
8. In many countries, schoolchildren wear uniforms to ____ social differences.
   a. generalize   b. personalize   c. equalize
9. I wanted the gold bracelet, but it cost too much, so finally I had to ____ the silver one.
   a. snatch up   b. take over   c. settle for
10. The series of free concerts in the parks was ____ by the city government.
   a. covered   b. sponsored   c. fluctuated
11. Leather coats and jackets are really in ____ these days–everybody has one!
   a. vogue   b. flash   c. fuss
12. Cleaning up air and water pollution will ____ improvements in people's health in the future.
   a. incite   b. bring about   c. set off
13. Tenzin is working on a ____ video project with a group of international students.
   a. disinterested   b. collaborative   c. circular

3 NOW YOU'RE TALKING!

Situation 2

> You're at a photo exhibition with your partner, and you see these two pictures. Talk about how they're similar and how they're different.

> Your friend says, "Kids shouldn't study art in school because it's just a big waste of time and money." Challenge this argument.

Situation 3

A Pair work. Look at the pictures and imagine what the people might say in each situation. Briefly review useful language from Units 10–12 on pages 158–159.

B Pair work. Role-play situations 1, 2, and 3 with a partner. Notice how well you and your partner do the role play. Ask your partner's opinion about your performance.

C Now rate your speaking. Use + for good, ✓ for OK, and – for things you need to improve. Then add two goals for the improvement of your speaking.

> A younger relative asks you about the most important new invention you've ever seen. Explain your answer in detail, giving examples, and answer any questions.

How did you do?	1	2	3
I was able to express my ideas.			
I spoke easily and fluently, without hesitation.			
I spoke at a good rate of speed—not too fast or too slow.			
I used new vocabulary from the units.			
I used at least three expressions from the units.			
I practiced the grammar from the units.			
Goals for improvement: 1. _____ 2. _____			

Language Summaries

Unit 1 *Big Screen, Small Screen*

Lesson A

Vocabulary Focus

blockbuster	nerve-wracking
B-movie	shot on location
distracting	strike a
drawback	compromise
give away	tearjerker
guilty pleasure	wholesome
mainstream	

Additional Vocabulary

be a sucker for	indie
(something)	life-threatening
car chases	illness
chick flick	special effects
daring stunts	superhuman
failed romance	forces

Language Focus

Such and *so*

Speaking:

Managing a discussion

Sorry, I'm not sure I understand.
Why do you say that?
Can you clarify your reason?

Can I just add something here?
I have a point I'd like to make.
Sorry to interrupt, but . . .

To get back to our topic . . .
Let's hear what someone else has to say.
We only have five minutes left.

Lesson B

Vocabulary

addictive
authentic
average Joe
compelling
contestant
contrived
cutthroat
disturbing
dramatic
entertaining
heartfelt
inspiring
nerdy
scripted
shocking
staged
unrehearsed

Unit 2 *The World Awaits You*

Lesson A

Vocabulary Focus

atmosphere	hypnotic
bustling	landscape
guarantee	relatively
firsthand	relish
household names	take in

Additional Vocabulary

ageless	meaningless
childless	powerless
countless	priceless
effortless	timeless
have (something)	up for
to oneself	(something)

Language Focus

Past modals

Speaking:

Using polite language

How may I direct your call?
I'd like to speak with someone
 in Reservations, please.
Certainly.
One moment, please.
This is Cassandra.
How may I help you?
Could you please tell me the cost of a
 double room?
I'm afraid that's a little out of my
 price range.
I was wondering whether your hotel is
 located on the beach or not.
Would you mind spelling that for me?

Lesson B

Vocabulary

buy an idea
commune with nature
can-do
rooted
show-off
sorted out
surreal
wanderlust

Unit 3 *School and Beyond*

Lesson A

Vocabulary Focus

apprehensive	hectic
bond with	mishap
compulsory	rash
cope with	sign up
drop out	sleep deprivation
expectation	stick to

Additional Vocabulary

accept	except
ace (something)	it seems like a blur
advice	loose
advise	lose
affect	passed
effect	past

Language Focus

Hope and *wish*

Speaking:
Interviewing phrases

That's an interesting question.
Let me think about that a moment.
Just so that I understand, what you're
  asking is . . .

What I meant was . . .
What I'm trying to say is . . .
Let me put it another way.

What do you mean by . . . ?
When you asked . . . , did you mean . . . ?
Are you asking about . . . ?

Lesson B

Vocabulary

apply
a solid foundation
coeducational (coed)
coherent
cram school
cultivate
foster
goofing off
I couldn't agree more
so be it

Unit 4 *Contemporary Issues*

Lesson A

Vocabulary Focus

churn out	monopoly
compensate	panic
consumer	pending
crack down	rip off
emerge	take to court
greedy	unauthorized
mediocre	unethical

Additional Vocabulary

be all for (something)
(it) opened my eyes
remains to be seen
see eye to eye
see the light
see what I can do
turn a blind eye
wait and see

Language Focus

Past and present unreal conditions

Speaking:
Expressing an opinion

I strongly believe . . .
I'm convinced that . . .
Without a doubt, . . .

For instance . . .
Take, for example, . . .
To give you an idea . . .

Not only that, but . . .
Not to mention the fact that . . .
And besides, . . .

Lesson B

Vocabulary

beat (someone) up
behind my back
clash
combat
confront
dork
dreading
fitting in
get into a brawl
harass
insecure
intimidate
keep an eye on (someone)
lose your temper
lost it
opponent
pick on
threaten

Language Summaries

Lesson A

Vocabulary Focus

brush up on	passable
carry on	primary
convey	language
halting	proficient
immerse	retain
master	rusty
mother tongue	

Additional Vocabulary

AC (air-conditioning)
ASAP (as soon as possible)
ASL (American Sign Language)
ATM (automated teller machine)
PIN (personal identification number)
TBA (to be announced)
TGIF (thank G-d it's Friday)
whim

Language Focus

Reduced adverb clauses

Speaking:
Talking about charts and data

This chart explains . . .
As you can see, . . .
The key point is that . . .
It's clear that . . .
It's important to note that . . .
This ___ represents . . .
This ___ stands for . . .
This ___ shows . . .
This ___ describes . . .
This ___ compares . . .

Lesson B

Vocabulary

build rapport
converse
dismissive
dominate
perceive
upshot

Lesson A

Vocabulary Focus

apprentice	juggle
aspiration	renowned
blessing	sidetracked
bump into	storied
cause (quite)	swap
a (stir)	have something
channel	in mind
fall into	twinkle
fixture	

Additional Vocabulary

at the drop of a hat
hooked on (something)
keep it under (one's) hat
old hat
take my hat off to (someone)
wear two hats

Language Focus

Reported speech

Speaking:
Presentation phrases

Today, I'm going to talk to you about . . .
I'd like to tell you about . . .
In this presentation, I'm going to . . .

Before I finish, let me say . . .
So in conclusion . . .
To conclude, . . .

Lesson B

Vocabulary

cram into	ragged
crumple	rancid
dart	rapid-fire
desperate	sandwich between
disoriented	scarce
filthy	sibling
get out in time	stain
hang out	stampede
impassable	stranded
logistics	stuff (something)
make it	under
malnutrition	submerge
meager	sweep away

Unit 7 *Who Are You?*

Lesson A

Vocabulary Focus

absentminded	enhance
arbitrary	inundate
association	lapse
chronicle	slip (one's) mind
draw a blank	utilize

Additional Vocabulary

conceive
concentrate
contemplate
imagine
recall
regimen
remember
remind
reminisce

Language Focus
Overview of the passive form

Speaking:
Expanding on a topic

I am in complete agreement with . . .
There's no doubt that . . .
I couldn't agree more with . . .

I can't agree with . . .
I can't accept that . . .
I couldn't disagree more with . . .

I have several reasons. First, . . .
Take for example the case of . . .
Let me explain what I mean by . . .
Consider what would happen if . . .

Lesson B

Vocabulary

agreeable	know-it-all
ambitious	outgoing
amusing	peacekeeper
baby	privilege
be in (one's)	responsible
shadow	see both sides of
comfortable around	an issue
adults	self-disciplined
conscientious	set a good
creative	example
dependable	social
diplomatic	spoil
fun-loving	tag along
get on (one's) nerves	take on
keep (one's)	responsibility
grades up	

Unit 8 *Happy Days*

Lesson A

Vocabulary Focus

absurd	simultaneously
keep on	skeptic
keep up	think on your feet
linear	warm up to
lose track	win (someone)
mindless	over
misgivings	

Additional Vocabulary

absent-minded	peers
labor-saving	pleasure-seeking
light-hearted	smooth-talking
long-lasting	space out
mind-numbing	thick-skinned

Language Focus
Phrasal verbs

Speaking:
Keeping a conversation going

Yes, I do, and that's because . . .
Sometimes that's true, but on the
  other hand . . .
No, I'm not, except for . . .
Yes, I am, and also . . .

What do you mean by . . . ?
Something I was wondering about is . . .
Can you tell me a little more about . . . ?
Why do you say that . . . ?

Lesson B

Vocabulary

bleak
coincide
fall off the wagon
feel like hell
grouchy
kick the bucket
lethargic
miserable
pay off
rejuvenate
roll in
sink in
tear off
turn over a new leaf
wear (one) down

Language Summaries

Unit 9 *Looking Good!*

Lesson A

Vocabulary Focus

change out of	instinct
. . . into . . .	laid-back
come across as . . .	pair . . . with . . .
coordinate	pick (something)
distinctive	out
easygoing	project a/an . . .
flatters	image
get undressed	run (an office)
go for (something)	stand out
go together	

Additional Vocabulary

bluish-green	paisley
boy/girl-next-door	pale green
image	polka-dotted
checked	reddish-orange
dark brown	shocking pink
jet-black	sky-blue
light blue	solid
lime-green	striped
off-white	vibe

Language Focus

Subject and object relative clauses

Speaking:
Presentation expressions

What this means is . . .
This shows that . . .
The significance of this is . . .

We've talked about . . . Next, we'll tell
you about . . .
We've discussed . . . Now I'll explain . . .
We have seen . . . Now, let's look at . . .

Lesson B

Vocabulary

first impression
have/get a hair transplant
have/get a nose job
have/get botox injections
give you the edge
have/get liposuction surgery
have/get your teeth whitened
let (oneself) go

Unit 10 *To Buy or Not to Buy . . .*

Lesson A

Vocabulary Focus

class	knockoff
customizing	settle for
differentiate	snatch up
extravagant	somewhere in the
flashy	neighborhood of
fuss	the ultimate
in vogue	

Additional Vocabulary

civilize	prioritize
customize	stabilize
equalize	sterilize
generalize	trivialize
immunize	victimize
monopolize	visualize
personalize	

Language Focus

A review of definite and indefinite
articles

Speaking:
Comparing and contrasting similarities and differences

One thing that's similar is . . .
In both of these pictures . . .
One thing that these pictures have in
common is . . .

What's different in the other photo is . . .
On the other hand, in the second
photo . . .
In contrast, in the second photo . . .

Lesson B

Vocabulary

auction
belongings
bid
hit the road
moving
on a massive scale
online
put (something) up for sale
stuff

Unit 11 *The Impact of Art*

Lesson A

Vocabulary Focus

cast-iron	gigantic
circular	intricate
collaborative	joint
cover the cost	mutual
create the	oval-shaped
impression	sponsor
dismantle	stainless steel
ebb and flow	take (something)
elaborate	apart
flunctuate	

Additional Vocabulary

disable	unable
disarm	unarmed
discomfort	uncomfortable
discover	uncover
disorganized	unorganized
make room for	

Language Focus

Using fronted structures for emphasis

Speaking:
Arguments and counterarguments

That's inaccurate.
That's not logical.
I find that hard to believe.
That doesn't make sense.

In fact, . . .
It hardly seems likely that . . . because . . .
In reality, . . .
The truth of the matter is . . .

Lesson B

Vocabulary

a rich mix
articulate
can't pass by . . .
  without thinking of
dole out
infrastructure
intimate
microcosm
reconcile

Unit 12 *Our Changing World*

Lesson A

Vocabulary Focus

breadwinner	fluid
breakthrough	plummet
brick-and-mortar	profiling
coexist	resistant
epidemic	trigger
facilitate	undermine

Additional Vocabulary

dwindle
escalate
flourish
shrink
swell

Language Focus

Talking about the future

Speaking:
Describing benefits and supporting points and giving support to main points

One/Another/The most important benefit
  would be . . .
This has the advantage of . . .
If we do this . . .
One result would be . . .

Let me give you an example of this.
For instance, / For example,
You might not realize it but . . .
This is important because . . .

Lesson B

Vocabulary

affluence
an evolutionary crash
a new dark age
a world storm
biodiversity
crippling
crisis
destabilize
devastating
ecological
fierce winds
fluctuate
habitat
hurdle
on the verge
reverberation
staggering
tear loose
unprecedented

Grammar Summaries

Unit 1 *Big Screen, Small Screen*

Language Focus: *such* and *so*

Use *such* and *so* to express emphasis:
It's *such* a beautiful day!   He's *so* happy in his new job.

Use *such* before a noun:
She has *such* energy for a 90-year-old!

Use *so* before an adjective or an adverb. If the adjective is followed by a noun, use *such* instead:
It was *so* scary.   You walk *so* fast that I can't keep up!
It was *such* a scary movie that I couldn't watch it.

So can be followed by a determiner *(much, little, many, few)* and a noun:
So many Hollywood movies have predictable endings.

So can have the same meaning as *very*. However, since *very* cannot be followed by a *that* clause, use *so* in those cases:
I was *so* disappointed when I failed the exam. (= *very disappointed*)
He was *so* sleepy that he fell asleep during the movie.

Unit 2 *The World Awaits You*

Language Focus: Past modals

Use past modals (also called "perfect modals") for actions or situations that were not realized in the past or have not been realized:
I **should've saved** more money. Now I'm broke. (expresses regret)
We **would've taken** a taxi, but we couldn't find one. (shows willingness to do something)
They **could've left** a message on your cell phone. (shows possibility)
The post office **couldn't have been** open yesterday because it was a holiday. (shows impossibility)
He **must've left** already. His coat is gone. (shows a logical conclusion)

Could have and *should have* can also be used to make suggestions and give strong advice:
You **could've phoned** earlier. You knew my number. (mild judgment)
You **should've phoned** earlier. I've been worried sick about you! (stronger judgment)

Couldn't have can show the speaker's disbelief at an unexpected situation:
You **couldn't have paid** $1,000 for that plane ticket! That's too much money.

Unit 3 *School and Beyond*

Language Focus: *Hope* and *wish*

Use *hope* + simple present to describe a present or future desire or expectation. (The verb after *hope* usually takes *not* in negative sentences.) Use *hope* + *will* for future expectations only:
I *hope* I **pass** my driver's test.   I *hope* I **don't fail** my driver's test.
I *hope* she**'ll graduate** on time.

Use *hope so* and *hope not* in short answers:
Is she coming to the party?   I *hope so.* I'd love to see her. / I *hope not.* I don't like her.

Use *wish* + *would* to express annoyance or dissatisfaction:
  Please sit down. (to make a suggestion)   I *wish* you**'d** sit down. (to show annoyance)

Use *wish* + simple past / past continuous to express desire for a change in a present situation:
  I *wish* you **didn't yell** at the children so much. (wanting the person to change his/her behavior)

Use *wish* + past perfect to express regret about a past situation. Use *wish* + *could* / *would* + base form to express desire for a different situation in the future:
  I *wish* I **hadn't taken** that cruise.   I *wish* I **could get** a refund and use the money for something else.

Unit 4 *Contemporary Issues*

Language Focus: Past and present unreal conditionals

Use the present unreal conditional for present or future situations that are improbable. In the *if* clause, the verb can take the simple past, past continuous, or *could* + base form. Use *would/could/might* + verb in the result clause:
  If they **allowed** me to download music for free, I**'d do** it. (But they *don't* allow downloading, so I won't do it.)
  I **would be** too tired to enjoy school if I **took** five classes this semester.
  If I **could take** a trip anywhere in the world, I**'d visit** the North Pole.
  If she **were passing** all her classes easily, I**'d suggest** that she skip a grade. (But she's not doing so well in some
    of her classes, so I won't suggest skipping a grade.)

Use the past unreal conditional for situations in the past that could have happened but didn't. In the *if* clause, the verb is in the past perfect. Use *would have* + verb in the result clause. If you're uncertain about the result, use *might have* or *could have*:
  If downloading music for free **had been allowed**, they **wouldn't have been arrested**. (But it *wasn't* allowed and
    so they *were* arrested.)
  If I **had been traveling** in the U.K. then, **I might have been caught** in the airport workers' strike.
  I **would've called** the police if I**'d seen** anything suspicious.

Unit 5 *In Other Words*

Language Focus: Reduced adverb clauses

Adverb clauses of time and reason tell when or why something happened. Those beginning with the subordinators *after, before, since, while* and *because* can be reduced to phrases that modify the main clause in a sentence:
  After finishing his work, he drove home.
  (adverb clause)   (main clause)

Reduced time clauses can appear in different places in a sentence. Note the use of punctuation. The reduced pattern is typically "subordinator + V-*ing*" except with the passive:
  He's lost 5 kilos since he started the diet. = He's lost 5 kilos **since starting the diet.**
  While I was waiting for the bus, I read. = **While waiting for the bus,** I read.
  After he was found guilty, he was sentenced. = **After being found guilty,** he was sentenced.

Reduced clauses of reason do not include the subordinator. Clauses of reason with *because* and *since* can only be reduced if they are in the initial position:

  Since she had studied German, she offered to translate. = **Having studied German,** she offered to translate.

  Because we didn't have a map, we got lost. = **Not having a map,** we got lost. (We got lost not having a map.)

If the subjects of the main and adverb clauses are different, you cannot reduce the adverb clause:
  The phone rang while we were talking.   (The phone rang while talking.)

Unit 6 *Ordinary People, Extraordinary Lives*

Language Focus: Reported speech

Reported speech (also called *indirect speech*) is used to report what someone else has said. A clause that includes a reporting verb (e.g., *say* or *tell*) introduces a reported statement. The verb in the reported statement usually shifts to a past form. Quotation marks are not used with reported speech:

Quoted speech	Reported speech
"The meeting **is** on Friday," he said.	He said (that) the meeting **was** on Friday.

The reporting verb *say* can be followed immediately by a reported statement. Reporting verbs that behave like *say* are *announce, explain, mention,* and *report.* The reporting verb *tell* is always followed by an indirect object and then the reported statement. Reporting verbs that behave like *tell* are *advise, instruct, persuade,* and *remind.* The words in parentheses can be omitted:

"I never went to college," she said.   She *explained* (to us) (that) she **had** never **been** to college.

She *reminded* us (that) she **had** never **been** to college.

With reported commands, use an appropriate reporting verb + the infinitive:

"Stretch for five minutes before exercising."   He *said* **to stretch** five minutes before exercising.

He *advised* us **to stretch** five minutes before exercising.

Pronouns and time adverbs also shift in reported speech:

"I'll call <u>you</u> when I **arrive** in Paris later <u>today</u>," said Sabina. She said (that) she would call <u>me</u> when she **arrived** in Paris <u>yesterday</u>.

Ask and *want to know* are used to report questions. Use *if* or *whether* with *yes/no* questions. Statement-word order is used in the reported question. Question marks are not used:

Yes/No question	"Are you running in the marathon this weekend?"	He *asked* (me) *if / whether* <u>I was running</u> in the marathon (or not). He *wanted* to know *if / whether* <u>I was running</u> in the marathon (or not).
*Wh-*question	"Where do you go to school, Daniel?"	She *asked* (him) *where* <u>he went to school</u>. She *wanted* to know *where* <u>he went to school</u>.

Unit 7 *Who are you?*

Language Focus: Overview of the passive form

Use the passive to focus on the receiver, rather than the doer, of an action. The object of an active sentence becomes the subject of a passive sentence:

active: A jury of three men and nine women convicted <u>the man</u> of the crime.

passive: <u>The man</u> **was convicted** of the crime by a jury of three men and nine women.

The agent is not always used in passive sentences. It is omitted when the agent is unknown, obvious, or has been previously mentioned. Also, it can be omitted to avoid having to say it:

The door handle **has been broken**.   Last Thursday I **was fired** from my job.

The agent may be used, especially if it gives additional or surprising information:

The English class **was taught** by a mathematics professor.

Another group of passives are called stative passives. Stative passives are used to describe states or conditions. They don't take an agent, and they are often followed by prepositions:

Stative passive: The buildings **are connected** by a 20th floor walkway.

Mount Kilimanjaro **is located** in Tanzania.

Complex passives are followed by *that* clauses or infinitive clauses:

It **is believed** that you can build a better memory.

He **is reported** to be an expert on the subject of memory.

Unit 8 *Happy Days*

Language Focus: Phrasal verbs

Phrasal verbs consist of a verb and one or two particles (preposition and/or adverb). The particle extends and changes the meaning of the verb. Sometimes, it's possible to figure out the meaning of a phrasal verb by studying its parts. Most often, however, this isn't the case:

He **took off** his hat. *took off = removed*   The plane **took off** at noon.   *took off = left*

Phrasal verbs can be transitive (meaning they take an object) or intransitive (don't take an object):

Transitive: Please **fill in** the form with your name, address, and date of birth. (object = *the form*)

Intransitive: The bus **broke down** near Pusan and it took almost an hour to fix.

Most transitive phrasal verbs are separable. A noun object can follow the particle or come between the verb and particle. If the direct object is a pronoun, it must go between the verb and particle:

Could you **turn up** the TV? I can't hear what the reporter is saying.

Could you **turn** the TV **up**?

Could you **turn** it **up**?   (Could you turn up it?)

Note that when the noun object is part of a long phrase, the phrasal verb is usually not separated:

I **called up** the man in charge of the operation.   (I called the man in charge of the operation up.)

A small group of transitive phrasal verbs are always inseparable:

Can you **look after** the dog while we're away?   (Can you look the dog after while we're away?)

Transitive (with object)		Intransitive (no object)
Separable	*Inseparable*	
bottle up give up burn down hold up call in put away cheer on use up clear up win over	count on look after face up to run into go over warm up to keep up (with)	blow up make up burst out move on dress up sign up go out simmer down keep on show up look forward to storm out

Unit 9 *Looking Good!*

Language Focus: Subject and object relative clauses

A sentence with a relative clause can be viewed as a combination of two sentences. A relative clause defines or gives more information about a noun or pronoun. A relative clause usually comes directly after the noun or pronoun it describes:

subject relative clause: I like to wear the latest styles **that are worn by celebrities.**

object relative clause: I only buy clothes **that I can find on sale.**

Relative clauses begin with a relative pronoun such as *who(m)*, *that*, or *which*:

Gray's Department Store, **which is on Broadway,** has inexpensive and attractive clothes.

In speaking, use pauses to separate a nondefining relative clause from the rest of the sentence. In writing, use commas:

My sister, (pause) **who lives in Boston,** (pause) is married.
(I have only one sister. She lives in Boston.)
My sister **who lives in Boston** is married. (no commas or pauses)
(I have more than one sister. This one lives in Boston.)

Don't use an object pronoun together with an object relative pronoun in a relative clause:

This is the dog **that he rescued.**

In object relative clauses, the relative pronouns *who(m)*, *that*, or *which* (but not *whose*) can be omitted:

He designed the dress **(that) she wore to the party.**
I spoke to the actor **whose new movie is a big hit.**

In everyday conversation and writing, when a verb is followed by a preposition, put the preposition at the end of an object relative clause. In more formal writing or speaking, place the preposition at the beginning of the clause:

Everyday conversation	More formal
He's the man I was speaking <u>to</u>.	He's the man <u>to</u> whom I was speaking.
He's the man that I was speaking <u>to</u>.	
He's the man who(m) I was speaking <u>to</u>.	

Where and *when* can also introduce relative clauses. Use *where* to refer to a place and *when* or *that* to refer to a time:

That's the college **where I teach.**   I remember the night **(when/that) I met you.**

Unit 10 *To Buy or Not to Buy . . .*

Language Focus: A review of definite and indefinite articles

Use an indefinite article (*a/an*) to refer to something in general or for the first time. Indefinite articles are used with nouns that are singular and countable. The definite article (*the*) is used before a noun when a speaker is referring to something more specific that both the speaker and listener are familiar with:

A man robbed *a* bank downtown.   Which bank? And have they caught *the* man yet?
The final price comes to fifty dollars.

Singular/plural count nouns (definite)	I put *the* letters on *the* table.
Singular count nouns (indefinite)	I applied for *a* job today.
Singular count nouns (generic)	*The* iPod is popular right now. She's *an* airline pilot.
Plural nouns (generic)	Ø Friends are hard to find.
Noncount nouns (definite)	*The* violence in our cities is alarming.
Noncount nouns (generic)	What do you think causes Ø violence?
Most proper nouns	Ø Namibia is in Ø Africa.
Some proper nouns	He's from *the* United Kingdom.

* generic = relating to a whole group of similar things, rather than just one of them

The zero article (Ø) is also used in certain preposition + noun combinations as well as after some verbs of movement:

in (Ø) school   to (Ø) college   at (Ø) home   on (Ø) vacation   leave (Ø) town

Unit 11 *The Impact of Art*

Language Focus: Using fronted structures for emphasis

To emphasize certain information, move it to the front of a sentence. This can sometimes be used for dramatic effect:

I invited <u>him</u>.   *Him* I invited.

I've <u>never</u> heard such an outrageous story.   *Never* have I heard such an outrageous story!

There are different rules for inversion (reversal of word order) in fronted structures:
- *be* verbs: <u>He was so upset</u> that he started to cry. / So upset was he that he started to cry.
- *be* + auxiliary: <u>I have never been</u> late to class. / Never have I been late to class.
- simple verbs: <u>She drove so poorly</u> that they took away her driver's license. / So poorly did she drive that they took away her driver's license.

There are many negative expressions that are commonly fronted in spoken English:

Not since last year have I felt this good.

Under no circumstances can my client answer your question.

Cleft sentences with *wh-* words and *it* are another way of showing emphasis:

Cleft sentence with a *Wh-* word: *What* I need most is a new computer.

Cleft sentences with *it*: *It* is the CEO's assistant who will be attending the party.

It's "15" that I said, not "50!"

Unit 12 *Our Changing World*

Language Focus: Talking about the future

Use *will* + future for general predictions and for when something has been decided at the moment of speaking:

We **will take** a trip in outer space someday.

The white one is sold out? I'll **take** the blue one, then.

Use *be going to* for future plans or intentions or when there is proof that something is going to happen:

I've bought my ticket. I'm **going to visit** Russia in August.

There are only ten seconds left in the game—they're **going to lose.**

Use the simple present to talk about fixed schedules in the future:

The train **leaves** the station at 7 P.M. sharp.

Use the present continuous to talk about future plans that have already been made:

I'm **staying** home tonight to watch TV.

Use *be about to* for events that are on the verge of happening:

Move those papers away from that candle. They're **about to catch** fire.

Use the future continuous to emphasize an ongoing event at a specific time in the future or an event that is expected to happen in the future:

Next week at this time, we'll **be writing** to you from Italy!

Use the future perfect with expressions like *by* and *by the/this time* to talk about an event that will be completed at a specific time in the future:

By this time next year, I'll **have paid off** my loan.

Use the future perfect continuous to emphasize the continuity of an event that will be completed in the future:

By 2070, people **will have been vacationing** in space for decades.

Skills Index

Grammar

Agreeing and disagreeing formally, 82
Asking follow-up questions, 94
Cause and effect expressions, 110
Challenging arguments, 132
Closings for formal letters, 124
Comparing and contrasting, 86, 120
Definite and indefinite articles, 118–119
Describing pictures, 120
-*ed* endings, 5
Expanding answers to *yes/no* questions, 94
Expanding on a topic, 82
Explaining results in a presentation, 106
Expressing opinions, 44
Fronted structures for emphasis, 130–131
Future tense, 142–143
get passive, 81
Greetings for formal letters, 124
happens to, 43
hope and *wish*, 28–29
-*ing* endings, 5
Identifying cause or effect, 96
Interviewing phrases, 30
Introducing counterarguments, 132
Low possibility, 43
make, allow, and *let*, 29
Passives, 80–81
Past and present unreal conditionals, 42–43
Past modals, 16–18
Phrasal verbs, 92–93
Presentation phrases, 68
Reduced adverb clauses, 54–55
Reported speech, 66–67
say and *tell*, 66
should (happen to) . . . might, 43
Subject and object relative clauses, 104–105
such and *so*, 4–5
Tense, review of, 143
Text organization using contrasts, 58
Transitions in a presentation, 106
Transitive and intransitive phrasal verbs, 92–93
were to, 43
whose in relative clauses, 105
wh- questions, 67
wh- words, 131
wish, showing regret in the past, 18
see and *watch*, 13

Listening

Conversations, 27, 117, 129
Descriptions, 16, 141
Films, 3
Interviews, 3, 41, 65–66, 91, 103–104
News reports, 79–80
Sales pitches, 11
TV shows, 53

Skills

Accents, 117
Asking and answering questions, 3, 8, 15, 16, 20–21, 27, 31, 33, 39, 41, 46, 53, 58, 66, 67, 69, 70, 79, 84, 104, 107, 108, 122, 134

Reading

Announcements, 30
Articles, 9, 22, 40, 43, 46–47, 58–59, 64, 70–71, 84–85, 96–97, 104–105, 108–109, 121–123, 134–135, 142, 146–147
Biographies, 72
Blurbs, 14
Book reviews, 90
Brochures, 35
Charts, 11, 28, 42, 54, 65, 106
Conversations, 16, 18, 99, 130
Definitions, 141
Descriptions, 11, 73, 83, 86, 121
E-mail messages, 57
Essays, 34
Excerpts, 4, 145
Interviews, 20–21, 26, 44, 67, 94, 102, 128
Letters, 18, 42, 67
    Letters to newspapers, 124
    Personal letters, 98
Online postings, 2, 32–33
Opinions, 52, 132
Opposing viewpoints, 82
Paragraphs, 80, 116, 133
Polls, 111
Predictions, 41, 148–149
Presentations, 68
Profiles, 52
Quotes, 19
Reports, 60
Reviews, 4, 10
Sentences, 17, 54, 75, 81, 92
Statements, 58, 95
Stories, 17, 23, 92
Summaries, 8
Testimonials, 78, 79
Tips, 30, 93, 99
TV guide, 7

Skills

Guessing meaning from context, 70
Identifying cause and effect, 96
Inferencing, 146
Inferring author's opinion or attitude, 8
Matching questions with answers, 21
Prereading activities, 7, 19, 31, 45, 57, 69, 83, 95, 107, 145
Scanning, 32, 58
Skimming, 84
Understanding pronoun references, 134
Understanding text, 46
Using contrasts, 58

Speaking

Arguments and counterarguments, 132
Asking and answering questions, 3, 8, 15, 16, 20–21, 23, 27, 31, 33, 39, 40, 41, 46, 53, 58, 66, 67, 69, 70, 79, 84, 104, 107, 108, 122, 125, 134, 140–141
Conflict resolution, 49
Conversations, 94
Debating, 61, 149
Describing, 5, 23, 45, 67, 69, 83, 120
Discussing, 7, 11, 14, 18, 19, 23, 30, 31, 35, 41, 44, 45, 48, 49, 52, 56, 57, 65, 68, 69, 70, 72, 73, 78, 82, 83, 84, 86, 91, 96, 98, 99, 105, 107, 108, 110, 116, 121, 125, 129, 132, 133, 136, 141, 142, 145, 146
Explaining, 7, 11, 17, 35, 42, 77, 79, 93, 99, 106, 111, 122, 141, 145
Expressing opinions, 44, 82
Interviewing, 11, 30
Making a reservation, 18
Managing discussions, 6
Polite language, 18
Presentations, 68, 106, 144, 146
Reporting to class, 6, 23, 44, 145
Retelling stories, 64, 70, 122
Role playing, 5, 18, 26, 29, 30, 39, 44, 49, 61, 77, 99, 120, 149, 153
Sales pitches, 11

Topics

Are we up to the challenge?, 145–149
Conflict resolution, 45–49
Cosmetic procedures, 107–111
Fashion sense, 102–106
Feature films, 2–6
Follow your dream!, 64–68
Hidden stories, 133–137
In the city, 40–44
The kindness of strangers, 69–73
Looking to the future, 140–144
Look on the bright side!, 95–99
Memory and the mind, 78–82
My possessions, 121–125
New school, old school, 31–35
Personality plus, 83–87
On the road, 14–18
School life, 26–30
Talk to me, 57–61
There and back, 19–23
Total immersion, 52–56
TV time, 7–11
What does it say to you?, 128–132
What makes you happy?, 90–94
What's your shopping culture?, 116–120

Viewing

Charts, 56, 77
CNN® videos, 11, 23, 35, 49, 61, 73, 87, 99, 111, 125, 137, 149
Illustrations, 31, 108
Photographs, 16, 20–21, 45, 64, 69, 77, 120, 128, 129

Vocabulary

abroad, 24
accent, 63
ace (something), 26
Acronyms, 53
Actions speak louder than words, 74
All's well that ends well, 150
argument, 51
ASL (American Sign Language), 52
attractive, 113
audience, 13
average Joe, 9
be all for (something), 40
be a sucker for, 2
beautiful, 113
belongings, 127
best things in life are free, The, 126

Student Book Answer Key

Page 6, 4 Speaking, Activity B: Pair Work
Answers: 1. Oscar, 2. France, 3. British Academy of Film and Television Arts, 4. 1982

Page 7, 1 Getting Ready to Read, Activity A: Pair Work
Answer: 1. *Blind Love* is not actually a reality TV show.

Page 19, 1 Getting Ready to Read, Activity B: Pair Work
Answers: 1. largest, 2. English, 3. Soccer, 4. oil, 5. hot and spicy, 6. the musician Sade

Page 23, 4 Communication, Activity B: Pair Work
Answer: The Baileys were rescued by the crew on the Weolmi, a Korean fishing boat.

Page 57, 1 Getting Ready to Read, Activity A: Pair Work
Answer: The first e-mail, at left, was written by a woman. The second e-mail, at right, was written by a man.

Page 87, 4 Communication, Activity A: Pair Work
Answers: 1. c, 2. b, 3. a, 4. d, 5. c, 6. d, 7. d, 8. b, 9. c, 10. a

Expansion Pages Answer Key

Unit 1   Pages 12–13
A. 1. credits   2. dubbed   3. soundtrack   4. subtitled   5. on location
6. flashback   7. stunts   8. studios   9. screenplays   B. 1. g   2. h   3. c
4. f   5. b   6. a   7. e   8. d   C. 1. with   2. second   3. small
4. large   5. about   6. number   7. between   8. and (plus)   D. 1.
genuine   2. spin-off   3. episode   4. distracted   5. vie   6. producer
7. footage   8. nasty   E. 1. remote   2. networks   3. cable
4. channels   5. satellite   6. antenna   7. show   8. host

Unit 2   Pages 24–25
A. 1. missed   2. delayed   3. caught   4. called   5. canceled
6. got in   7. diverted.   B. 1. f   2. g   3. a   4. j   5. c   6. i   7. e   8. b
9. d   10. h   C. 1. stamped   2. show your   3. apply for   4. a valid
5. an expired   6. renew   7. check   D. 1. a bat   2. an ox   3. a feather
4. a beet   5. night   6. a mouse   7. a bone   8. snow   9. a bee
10. nails

Unit 3   Pages 36–37
A. 1. i   2. b   3. h   4. j   5. d   6. f   7. g   8. e   9. c   10. a
B. Positive: I aced it, I passed, I did well   Negative: Don't ask, I failed,
I flunked, I did very poorly, I bombed   Informal: Don't ask, I aced it. I
flunked, I bombed   C. 1. seminary   2. law school   3. medical school
4. art academy   5. university   6. technical college   7. dental school
8. military academy   D. 1. c   2. h   3. f   4. b   5. a   6. g   7. d   8. e
E. 1. higher education   2. primary education   3. physical education
4. Secondary education   5. pay for his education   6. adult education
7. standard of education   8. get an education

Unit 4   Pages 50–51
A. 1. peace talks   2. a symbol of peace   3. live in peace   4. a peace
treaty   5. a threat to peace   6. the peace process   7. work(s) for peace
8. a plea for peace   B. 1. revitalize   2. slum   3. unchecked
4. proposition   5. engage in   6. Overall   7. widespread   8. forefront
9. advocate   10. sustainable   C. 1. c   2. a   3. g   4. d   5. i   6. b
7. e   8. h   9. f   D. 1. I've heard that one before.   2. turned a deaf
ear   3. are up to our ears   4. heard it through the grapevine   5. lends
a sympathetic ear   6. I'm all ears.   7. grinning from ear to ear   8. it
went in one ear and out the other   9. has the ear

Unit 5   Pages 62–63
A. 1. pointless discussion   2. broaden the discussion   3. a heated
discussion   4. generate a discussion   5. under discussion
6. take part in a discussion   7. a great deal of discussion   B. 1. sign
language   2. difficult   3. lose   4. verb   5. passable   6. speech
C. 1. g   2. c   3. f   4. d   5. b   6. a   7. h   8. e   D. 1. interrupts
2. dominates   3. feedback   4. widespread   5. upshot   6. dismissive
7. perceive   8. build rapport   E. 1. already   2. illegal   3. OK
4. develop   5. occurred   6. OK   7. professor   8. safety   9. receive
10. affect   11. definite   12. twelfth   13. succeed   14. government
15. disappear   16. jewelry   17. assistant   18. unbelievable   19. OK
20. necessary

Unit 6   Pages 74–75
A. 1. d   2. b   3. f   4. g   5. h   6. a   7. e   8. c   B. 1. How's life?   2. a
new life   3. save your life   4. risk their lives   5. a matter of life and
death   6. Life's too short.   7. lost their lives   8. my social life   C. 1. e
2. g   3. c   4. a   5. f   6. b   7. d   D. 1. stranded   2. impassable
3. immaculately   4. disoriented   5. scarce   6. submerged   7. filthy
8. upheaval   E. 1. generous   2. unfriendly   3. strange   4. intelligent
5. dishonest   6. annoying

Unit 7   Pages 88–89
A. 1. h   2. g   3. d   4. a   5. e   6. c   7. f   8. b   B. 1. has a mind of
her own   2. slipped my mind   3. read my mind   4. take my mind off
5. out of your mind   6. make up your mind   7. keep in mind
8. speak your mind   C. 1. a   2. a   3. b   4. c   5. b   6. b   7. b   8. a
D. 1. conscientious   2. a peacekeeper   3. fun-loving   4. bossy
5. social   6. quiet   7. diplomatic   8. creative   9. a risk-taker
10. organized   E. 1. g   2. e   3. f   4. d   5. c   6. a   7. b

Unit 8   Pages 100–101
A. 1. in the mood for   2. in a foul mood   3. puts me in a good mood
4. mood swings   5. a festive mood   6. a somber mood   7. in a bad
mood   8. in a good mood   B. 1. f   2. g   3. c   4. a   5. d   6. b   7. e
C. 1. overjoyed   2. delighted   3. happy   4. content   5. OK   6. down
7. sad   8. miserable   D. 1. b   2. e   3. e   4. g   5. a   6. f   7. c   8. d
E. 1. disorder   2. bleak   3. coincides   4. obligation   5. residual
6. peaked   7. skeptical   8. oversimplifies

Unit 9   Pages 112–113
A. 1. an outward appearance   2. changed his appearance
3. Despite appearances   4. judge people by their appearance
5. a youthful appearance   6. neglect your appearance   7. similar in
appearance   8 worries about her appearance   B. 1. offspring, children
2. apparel, duds   3. expensive, pricey   4. sensation, vibe   5. smart,
brainy   6. residence, place   7. leisurely, relaxed   C. 1. out of   2. out
3. across   4. out   5. for   6. into   D. 1. conversationalist   2. indulge in
3. undergo   4. grooming   5. project   6. was headed for
7. desperately   8. enhance   9. routine

Unit 10   Pages 126–127
A. 1. ↑   2. ↓   3. ↓   4. ↑   5. ↓   6. →   7. →   8. ↓   9. ↑
B. 1. negotiable   2. a price war   3. half price   4. competitive prices
5. at any price   6. agree on a price   7. a fixed price   8. full price
9. afford the price   C. 1. f   2. g   3. c   4. b   5. a   6. h   7. d   8. e
D. 1. former   2. catalog   3. request   4. relevant   5. update
6. transaction   7. reflecting on   8. chronicle

Unit 11   Pages 138–139
A. Fine arts: sculpture, painting, photography, ceramics, architecture
Performing arts: theater, dance, music, opera   Literature: play, poetry,
short story, novel, biography   B. 1. opera   2. sculpture   3. biography
4. ceramics   5. short story   6. dance   7. photography   8. poetry
9. architecture   10. novel   11. play   12. painting   13. the theater
14. music   C. 1. relaxing   2. ordinary   3. appealing   4. solo
5. simple   6. combine   7. original   8. refuse   D. 1. multiethnic
2. pedestrians   3. elitist   4. infrastructure   5. archive   6. haunts
7. murmured   8. vibrant

Unit 12   Pages 150–151
A. 1. c   2. g   3. f   4. e   5. h   6. a   7. b   8. d   B. 1. in the
foreseeable future   2. the future looks bright   3. shape the future
4. predict the future   5. there's no future in it   6. have a promising
future   7. hopes for the future   8. face an uncertain future   C. 1. c
2. a   3. e   4. d   5. b   D. 1. son   2. gifts   3. place   4. complaints
E. 1. favorable   2. hurdle   3. detour   4. affluence   5. gradual
6. a staggering   7. resilience   8. unyielding   9. A massive
10. unprecedented

168   Answers